THE PEACE MOVEMENT IN ISRAEL, 1967–87

The Peace Movement in Israel, 1967–87

David Hall-Cathala

St. Martin's Press
New York

First published in the United States of America in 1990

Printed in Great Britain

ISBN 0–312–03071–1

Library of Congress Cataloging-in-Publication Data
Hall-Cathala, David, 1960–
The peace movement in Israel, 1967–87/David Hall-Cathala.
    p.   cm.
Bibliography: p.
Includes index.
ISBN 0–312–03071–1
1. Israel—Politics and government.   2. Peace—Societies, etc.
3. Jewish–Arab relations—1973–   I. Title.
DS126.5.H347   1990
956'.04—dc19   88–38366
                                                            CIP

This book is dedicated to
Leila and Jonathan
May you know peace in your time

Table of Contents

List of Tables and Figures

Acknowledgements

There are numerous people 'without whom this book would not have been written'. To begin with little could have been said about the Israeli peace movement had not dozens of peace activists in Israel given freely of their time to provide me with information about their organisations and insights into their complex society. My thanks go to all those mentioned in the list of interviews as well as to the unnamed activists with whom I had informal discussions while 'in the field'. Of all the activists interviewed, I wish to thank in particular Thoma Shick and Gideon Spiro who gave most freely of their time to share their extensive knowledge of the Israeli peace movement and Israeli society with me.

Secondly, thanks must be extended to my fellow students at St. Antony's who assisted me throughout my time in Oxford: Azar Gat, Gilat Zemach, Joel Peters and Cynthia Cohen.

My third set of thanks go to the academics who made the book a reality. I wish firstly to thank those in the Department of Sociology and Anthropology at Memorial University of Newfoundland who provided my basic grounding in the social sciences. In particular, I should single out Robert Paine, who awakened my academic interest in Israeli society. Thanks are also extended to Professor Kenneth Kirkwood (St. Antony's), the supervisor of my thesis on which this book is based.

Special thanks are due to Rosalynd Bourne and my mother for their proof-reading efforts. Likewise, very sincere thanks to Jane Williams who gave freely of her time and skills to type the manuscript, thus ensuring that dead-lines were met.

The book would obviously not have been written had it not been for my parents, who not only brought me into the world, but who always had the grace and wisdom to encourage me to explore what interested me most. Finally, it certainly would not have been completed without the loving support of my wife, Brigitte, who not only helped with field and archival work but also with proof-reading and essential editing.

List of Abbreviations

AIC	Alternative Information Centre
BSC	Birzeit Solidarity Committee
CAR	Citizens Against Racism
CAWL	Committee Against the War in Lebanon
CCIF	Committee Confronting the Iron Fist
DFPE	Democratic Front for Peace and Equality
ICIPP	Israeli Council for Israeli–Palestinian Peace
ICPME	International Centre for Peace in the Middle East
IDF	Israeli Defence Force
IFOR	International Fellowship of Reconciliation
IPJAC	Intervention Programme in Jewish–Arab Contacts
LIM	Land of Israel Movement
MK	Member of Knesset
MO	Movement Organisation
PAS	Parents Against Silence
PFLP	Popular Front for the Liberation of Palestine
PLO	Palestine Liberation Organisation
PCSN	Palestinian Centre for (the Study of) Non-Violence
RCL	Revolutionary Communist League
UN	United Nations
VLJF	Van Leer Jerusalem Foundation
WRI	War Resisters International
WZO	World Zionist Organisation

Introduction

The activities of the Israeli peace movement first came to international attention not long after the visit of President Sadat to Jerusalem, when tens of thousands of Israelis took to the streets to demonstrate their support for peace talks with Egypt and their opposition to the continued occupation of the territories captured in 1967. Between April 1978 and June 1982, the peace movement frequently opposed the settlement of the West Bank and grew to become a significant force in Israeli politics, representing an alternative vision of the future to that presented by the right-wing Likud government. Then, in 1982, following Israel's invasion of Lebanon and, in particular, the massacre of Palestinians in the Sabra and Shatilla refugee camps outside Beirut, the peace movement once again attracted international attention with massive anti-war demonstrations.

International interest in the movement rapidly waned once the media-grabbing demonstrations were over and, despite considerable academic interest in Israeli society, little of note has been published on the peace movement. The absence of academic literature on the subject – in contrast to the prolific amount being produced on such subjects as the settler movement – motivated the writing of this book.

The reader unfamiliar with Israeli society should note at the outset that, unlike in Europe or America, the peace movement in Israel is basically *not* concerned with nuclear weapons. Rather, its energy is focused almost entirely on the conflict between Jews and Arabs in Israel and the occupied territories and between Israel and its Arab neighbours. Consequently the development of the movement can only be understood within the context of this broader conflict which has dominated Israeli society from the outset.

The Israeli peace movement is made up of numerous relatively autonomous groups and organisations, with very different approaches to promoting coexistence and peace. They are united primarily in their common opposition to the continued occupation and settlement of the

West Bank and the Gaza Strip. The majority of organisations and
activists are Jewish. This is mostly because Jews form the majority in
Israel and also perhaps because it is more in the interest of the
conqueror than the vanquished to pursue peace. However, many of
these organisations have both Jewish and Arab activists and supporters
and there are also a few that were created and are managed by
Palestinians alone.

As, to the best of my knowledge, this is the first comprehensive
study of the Israeli peace movement, it is largely descriptive. I have
attempted above all to provide the reader with a clear account of:
why the movement emerged amongst the most privileged sector of
Israeli society – the Ashkenazi middle and upper classes; why it
suddenly became a *mass* movement in the later seventies– after having existed in seminal form since the pre-state era – and why it is
made up of over thirty different organisations rather than a single,
united one. Indeed, what is most fascinating about the complex
'structure' the movement assumed during its peak years (1978–85) is
that the divisions between the different organisations reflect the
profound ideological, religious and ethnic divisions that affect
Israeli society as a whole.

In providing this account of the emergence and 'structure' of
the Israeli peace movement, I have given the reader two key
theoretical leads to hold on to – lest he or she be drowned in the
confusion created by the multitude of peace organisations flooding
from the pages of the book. The first of these, presented in Chapter 1 and then applied throughout the book, is that the peace
movement emerged partly in defence of *universal* values which
appeared to be threatened by highly *particular* trends in Israeli
society. Because, in a sense, the peace movement is a 'reactionary'
movement – *reacting* to 'negative' developments in society rather
than forging new alternatives – Chapter 1 explores those forces in
Israeli society which may well be considered as the polar opposite
of the peace movement.

The second theoretical lead offered to the reader maintains that the
Israeli peace movement is an example of a specific kind of *social
movement*. Together the two theories provide a basis of reference for
the understanding of a complex and, at times, amorphous social
phenomenon.

The book is then primarily sociological. However, as in any such case study, academic disciplines cannot be isolated from each other: historical analysis is essential when tracing back ideas which emerge and re-emerge at different epochs from within apparently unrelated groups; psychological concepts have to be kept in mind when seeking to understand subtle changes in attitude, or why one individual joins the peace movement while another (of a similar background) joins the settler movement on the West Bank; likewise, the role of political parties and ideologies has, of course, to be considered.

Many of the organisations in the peace movement are involved in working in education, others in law. Naturally, it has been beyond my capacities to give due attention to all these specific areas. I have therefore concentrated primarily on the extra-parliamentary protest groups and the divisions between them, giving special attention to the important division based on ethnic differences as I have a special interest in the subject.

Research for the book was carried out over a three-year period primarily at the Middle East Centre of St. Antony's College, Oxford. Field-work was conducted in Israel between June 1985 and February 1987. During this time, numerous in-depth interviews were conducted with leading peace movement activists (a complete list of interviewees is included after the bibliography). All these interviews were open-ended, allowing for the free exploration of issues which were of specific interest to the interviewee. While in Israel, I took every opportunity to observe and participate in the activities of various peace groups and organisations: Jewish–Arab work camps and encounters, conferences and, of course, demonstrations. Besides formal (recorded) interviews, I had many informal discussions and conversations with different peace activists at these events, as well as in their homes and offices. These greatly contributed to my understanding of both the peace movement and Israeli society. I also relied on the pamphlets, hand-outs, newsletters and other publications of the different groups to supplement information gathered through interviews. Some work was done in the archives of *The Jerusalem Post*, of the English Weekly of *Al Fajr* and of the Truman Institute for the Advance of Peace (Hebrew University of Jerusalem). The archives of *The Jerusalem Post* proved to be invaluable when compiling Table 1 (the seven-year, week-by-week record of all Peace Now's activities).

In order to assist the reader I have included in the glossary the names of most groups and Hebrew mentioned in the book. Groups with short Hebrew names are generally left in the original language, while those which are long – or translate easily – are in English.

D. H-C.
MORIJA
December 1987.

1 Upsetting the Balance

Sociologists generally agree that people become involved in various forms of protest after experiencing dissatisfaction, frustration or a sense of 'relative deprivation'.[1] This observation is often backed by accounts of peasant revolts, workers' strikes, bread riots and the like. In these cases, the source of dissatisfaction is usually obvious and it comes as no surprise when frustrations become manifest in collective action. Such action ranges from sporadic acts of protest to full-fledged revolution. Although sustained protest only rarely develops into revolution, it may develop into a social movement – a sustained form of collective action aimed at rectifying perceived 'defects' in society.[2]

When a social movement forms amongst people who are clearly not 'deprived' and whose source of frustration and dissatisfaction is far from clear, the sociologist is confronted with the task of identifying and describing the source of discontent, before being able to analyse the form and nature of the movement itself. This is certainly true in the case of the Israeli peace movement which is made up *primarily* of middle-class Ashkenazim[3] who are generally regarded as the least deprived segment of Israeli society.

Evidently, the emergence of the Israeli peace movement is related to more subtle feelings of frustration and dissatisfaction than those which usually prompt the formation of social movements. Before plunging into a detailed account of this movement, some of the changes in Israeli society most responsible for creating discontent amongst the economically privileged segment of society should be explored.

UNIVERSALISM AND PARTICULARISM

In most societies (or nations) of the world there is a certain tension between values that are considered to be unique – or *particular* – to the society, and those *universal* values which are shared in common with other societies. Very often the tension between these values is

1

minimal and hardly noteworthy. However, in certain societies, the tension is striking and worthy of close examination; this is certainly the case in Israel. Key universal values such as liberty, equality and justice – that were once central in Israeli society – are rapidly losing their position as greater stress is placed on the particular values of Jewish nationalism, religiosity and devotion to Eretz Yisrael (the Land of Israel). It is argued that the Israeli peace movement emerged largely in response to this shift and in defence of universal values perceived to be under threat. It is important to note that it is not suggested that particular values are 'bad' and universal values 'good' but rather that they are not always compatible and that an over-emphasis of the one may undermine the other.

During the long period of exile, dispersion, political subjugation and isolation of the Jewish people, the importance of universal values declined. Political debate lost its immediate relevance for the nation while the hope of redemption became a mystical dream in the distant messianic future. Confined to ghettos throughout the Diaspora, the daily lives of Jews evolved around values and customs particular to their religion and tradition. Jewish involvement in the world beyond the ghetto was limited to the bare minimum both by external and internal factors. As a result, there was little tension between universal and particular elements in Jewish society for hundreds of years.[4] However, in the seventeenth century, this began to change. The failure of Sabbatai Zevi's messianic movement (1665–6) to bring redemption to East European Jewry, set the stage for secularisation and brought to an end the long period in Jewish history when particular, religious solutions were considered to be the only legitimate responses to adverse conditions.

The emancipation of Jews in Western Europe, and the growth in secularisation which accompanied the Haskalah (the Jewish Enlightenment, c.1750–1880), created mounting tension between the old particular values and the new universal values emphasised by Jews who were influenced by changes in the broader European society. Jews responded in different ways to this tension. Some hung on to the narrow, particular, solidarity of traditional, orthodox Judaism. They remained isolated from the wider society. Many of these Jews joined the mystical Hassidic movement. Other Jews sought to assimilate into their host societies. This was especially true of German Jewry who believed that the universal values advocated in Europe since the

Enlightenment would erode anti-semitism, allowing for the equal participation of Jews in European society. Eastern European Jews who were attached to universal ideals, often joined revolutionary movements whose ideologies depicted a future of equality regardless of origin. The Russian Revolution owed a great deal to such Jews.

Towards the end of the nineteenth century, a movement emerged amongst European Jews that was to be relatively successful in combining particular Jewish values with universal European values stemming from the Enlightenment and the French Revolution. Modern political Zionism was initially a predominantly secular movement, strongly influenced by both European nationalism and socialism. However, in emphasising national redemption, Zionism drew on older particular messianic themes, notably the 'redemption' and 'ingathering of the exiles' in the Land of Israel. The Zionists combined this desire, so particular to Judaism, with modern universal themes inspired partly by socialism, but also by the dominant imperialist thinking of the day. The founder of the Zionist movement, Theodor Herzl, attempted to persuade Western powers that a Jewish homeland in Palestine would be an outpost of Western civilisation which the Arabs would welcome for the prosperity it would bring. When the socialist Zionists became the dominant force in the movement, they argued that the return to the Land of Israel would enable the Jews to become a 'normal' people again. By tilling the soil and through the creation of egalitarian agricultural communities (kibbutzim), the socialist Zionists aspired to fulfil not only Biblical prophecy but also the socialist utopian vision of the future.

The relatively successful manipulation by the socialist Zionists of both universal and particular values to mobilise support, did not resolve the tension between the two. The Zionist movement, like most social movements, was not a homogeneous movement. Different factions within the movement placed varying degrees of stress on the different components of Zionist ideology. The positions ranged from the highly particular view of the orthodox Zionist parties, which held a religious interpretation of the reconstruction of Jewish civilisation in the Land of Israel, all the way to the highly universal secular view of the Hashomer Hatzair, which advocated the establishment of a secular, bi-national Jewish–Arab state.

Despite the tension that prevailed in the pre-state period, the dominant socialist bloc, led by Ben-Gurion, managed to maintain a certain balance. From the outset the leaders of the new state emphasised particular values based on Jewish religion, philosophy and history as well as the universal values of modern Western civilisation – freedom, democracy and justice for all citizens. The Israel they envisioned would grow not only to be a Jewish homeland but also a democratic 'light unto the nations' (especially to the undemocratic nations of the region). In the years following the creation of the state, a degree of balance was maintained despite the fact that the Arab minority could not be expected to identify with the symbols of the state – flag, anthem and currency – all of which relate to the particular historical and religious experience of the Jews. The Arabs, as a 'minority', were expected (once military rule was lifted) to lend their allegiance to the universal components of the state – notably democracy, citizenship and civil liberties. However, in 1967, this delicate balance was irrevocably upset. The scales began to tip dramatically in favour of particular Jewish values. It was in response to this that the peace movement began to form amongst the very people who felt most threatened by the changes which challenged the universal-particular equilibrium in general, and the legitimacy of socialist Zionist ideology and rule in particular.

RESPONSES TO THE SIX-DAY WAR

Virtually all studies of Israeli society written since 1967 recognise the Six-Day War as a major watershed in the history of Israel. The intention here is not to repeat well-known facts, but rather to recall how major particular trends were set in motion by the war and the ensuing occupation of the territories which had once formed the heartland of ancient 'Biblical' Israel.

The immediate effect of the swift and spectacular Israeli victory was a huge sense of relief and euphoria. The weeks preceding the war had been extremely tense as the mobilised nation waited, knowing well that war was about to break out. Chemists reported Holocaust survivors pleading for poison lest they should fall once again into the hands of the enemy.[5] The government began preparing mass graves, anticipating many thousands of casualties.[6] The euphoria which followed the victory was due, in part, to relief, but in the long term it was due more to the capturing of territories central to the religious-mythical past of the nation. The most significant recovery for the Israelis was the Old

City of Jerusalem. This included the ancient Jewish quarter with the Western Wall – the only surviving remnant of the ancient Jewish temple destroyed by the Romans. The captured West Bank, which had once formed the heartland of the ancient Israelites, contained numerous sites of significance, notably the Tomb of the Patriarchs in Hebron. Holy to both Muslims and Jews the site was destined to become one of conflict as well as prayer. The Golan Heights, the Gaza Strip and the Sinai were of more strategic than religious importance.

The occupation of the territories, in the eyes of many Israelis, re-established for them what is described as the 'covenantal' relationship between 'People, God and Promised Land', reawakening in them a sense of their *Jewish* (as opposed to modern *Israeli*) identity. The place of the Land of Israel in Jewish national identity has always been significant. After 1967 it apparently became all the more important. Some observers have gone so far as to suggest that an 'idolatry of the land . . . superseded the covenantal relationship between "People, God and Promised Land".'[7] The significance of the newly-occupied territories evidently cannot be overstated. Anthropologist Gwyn Rowley argues that the relationship of the Jews to the Land of Israel should be seen in 'totemic' terms and defines a totem as 'something which is regarded as the property of a particular clan and which plays a crucial part in its identity'.[8] The repossession of this lost totem awakened and confirmed, in many Israelis, particular religious-nationalist tendencies.

The occupation of the territories reopened a fierce debate, which had begun in the 1930s, over the acceptability of boundaries for the Jewish state. It is worth noting that the pre-state debate had not been over whether the Jewish claim to the whole of the Land of Israel (most commonly considered to cover at least the British Mandate of Palestine) was legitimate, but as to whether or not it was legitimate to accept a limited portion of this land to provide an immediate home for Jewish refugees from Europe. (As a matter of interest, this debate has a modern parallel amongst Palestinians who do not question *their* legitimate right to the whole of Palestine, but who now debate the possibility of accepting a portion of Palestine – that is the West Bank and the Gaza Strip – to facilitate the return of Palestinian refugees and allow a degree of sovereignty.) The Jewish debate was rendered redundant by the UN vote which partitioned Palestine and brought the Jewish state into being in a portion of Eretz Yisrael. In 1967, Israeli control over the whole *Land* of Israel reopened the debate over what the legitimate boundaries of the *State* of Israel should be.

THE LAND OF ISRAEL MOVEMENT

The government's immediate position on the occupied territories was a declared willingness to negotiate 'land for peace' – with East Jerusalem being the non-negotiable exception. Within a very short time, influential Israelis, from a wide range of political backgrounds, began to oppose the government's readiness to exchange the territories for negotiated peace treaties with the Arab states. They formed a movement known as 'The Movement for a Whole Land of Israel' (Tenuah Lemaan Eretz Yisrael Hashlema – hereafter, Land of Israel Movement, LIM). It rapidly gained the sympathy and support of those who had always stood for Israeli sovereignty over mandatory Palestine. In the words of a student of the movement, 'the Land of Israel Movement represented the revival of a traditional ideology never renounced by some groups within Israel, that had now found new relevance and unaccustomed bearers as a result of the 1967 war.'[9] Besides Revisionists (whose ideology best fitted that of the LIM), the movement attracted a number of well-known individuals from within the Labour camp as well as a large number of young National Religious Party members.

Although the majority in the LIM were not religious, part of the movement's manifesto was couched in clearly religious terms. It stated that:

> The whole of Eretz Yisrael is now in the hands of the Jewish people, and just as we are not allowed to give up the State of Israel, so we are ordered to keep what we receive there from Eretz Yisrael. We are bound to be loyal to the entirety of our country – for the sake of our people's past as well as its future, as no government in Israel is entitled to give up this entirety.[10]

Implicit in this statement is the notion that a power higher than state sovereignty prohibits withdrawal from the territories 'returned' to the Jewish people through a 'miraculous' conquest. In addition, the manifesto guaranteed security and peace as well as the opening up of 'unprecedented vistas of national and spiritual consolidation'. Clearly, the formation of the LIM reflected the new emphasis on religious-national (that is particular) ideals which were rapidly gaining force.

The LIM's prime aim was the dissemination of ideas in an attempt to swing public and governmental opinion. It was the adherents who were also Labour party members who insisted that the LIM define itself as 'an ideological movement directed to the persuasion of decision makers, rather than as a mass movement aimed at mobilising the maximum number of adherents to put direct pressure on the government'.[11] They were evidently reluctant to embarrass the government and it is noteworthy that the LIM only once acted against this policy. That was in 1968 when the movement became involved in supporting a group of religious settlers, led by Rabbi Moshe Levinger, who occupied the Park Hotel in Hebron during the Passover period. This was done in order to put pressure on the government to allow Jews to settle in the city – the second most sacred to Jews. The Labour government eventually conceded to the pressure and established the Jewish town of Kiryat Arba close to Hebron.

The fact that the LIM was basically an 'ideological' rather than an 'action' group (with the one exception noted above), contributed to its eventual decline. Activists and supporters eventually grew tired of endless discussions with few concrete results. In any event the government did not seem all that determined to give up the newly-occupied territories – thus taking the wind out of the LIM's sails. However, another reason is that it was eventually 'overtaken' by a group which shared the same basic goals but which was unambiguously religious and prepared to *act* out its convictions, regardless of the government's position: a group which upheld very particularistic, religious-nationalist views that were in keeping with the mood of much of the nation.

THE BLOCK OF THE FAITHFUL

While the LIM had justified Israel's retention of the occupied territories by equally emphasising religious-mythical and strategic-material reasons, the new group – called Gush Emunim (the Block of the Faithful) – emphasised the former above all others. The peace movement, as we shall see, began to form partly in response to the formation of the LIM. The establishment of the Gush Emunim, with its highly particular (or 'primordial') views, provided all the more incentive.

Although Gush Emunim was officially founded in 1974, in protest against the return of the territories demanded by the peace initiative of Dr Kissinger, the nucleus of the group had in fact formed much earlier around the 1968 attempt to settle Hebron. It was made up mostly of *hesder yeshivah* students (combining Talmudic studies and army service) who were directly influenced by the teaching of Rabbi Zvi Yehuda Kuk. The influence of Rabbi Kuk and his father, Abraham Isaac Hacohen Kuk, cannot be overestimated. Rabbi Kuk senior broke with the religious orthodox establishment – which had opposed Zionism as heretical and as a form of false Messianism – and paved the way for a fusion of religious and nationalist thought. He declared the return to Palestine to be a holy task which would end the danger of assimilation in the Diaspora and bring redemption to the Jewish people.[12] His son continued to emphasise the redemption of the Jews through return but also stressed that, through settling Eretz Yisrael, the Jews were 'redeeming' the Land.

The 'liberation' of the Land in 1967 was considered by Rabbi Kuk junior to be miraculous. He believed this was an act heralding the return of the Messiah. Unlike the leaders of the LIM, Kuk urged *action* – in particular the active settlement of the West Bank, a task of 'sacred' significance demanding total devotion. He considered 're-demption through the settlement of the land of such value that it required devotion to the point of martyrdom'.[13] Since the retention and settlement of the land was sacred, opposition to it – from government or the public – was intolerable. Those demanding a return of the territories would be 'cursed by God' and any such attempt would have to be resisted. This extreme view was to bring members of the peace movement who advocated territorial compromise from the outset, into violent confrontation with supporters of Gush Emunim who attacked them for their 'heretical' views.

While supporting the institutions of the State of Israel, Gush Emunim placed acts of settlement above the law. In their view: 'It is the right and duty of every Jew in Eretz Yisrael to struggle against any tendency to compromise on the issue of settlement in Judea and Samaria, even if it is proposed by the majority.'[14] In this respect, the movement was (and is) non-democratic, a fact recognised by many of the Israelis who witnessed with alarm the growth of Gush Emunim's popularity. Even more disturbing were the threats of the Gush Emunim settlers to resist – with violence if necessary – any territorial compromise negotiated with the Arabs in exchange for the formal recognition of Israel and a peace treaty. In December 1985, Rabbi Moshe Levinger announced at a Gush Emunim debate that he believed 'there would be bloodshed (between Jews) in the struggle over the future of Judea and Samaria'. A resolution was passed that warned the government against 'any fateful steps which could, God forbid, bring a division of the Land and the nation.' It stated that: 'The government has no authority to negotiate concessions in Eretz Yisrael; such negotiations and decisions lack any legal or moral authority.' The resolution ended by urging people to treat 'any government which makes territorial concessions as General de Gaulle had treated the Vichy traitor Marshal Pétain'.[15] The movement's appeal to the government not to divide the nation could only be regarded by the peace movement as a hollow appeal; in the peace movement's view, it was the Gush Emunim settlers who bore prime responsibility for the deep divisions which already marked the nation.

The threats of Gush Emunim to resist peace negotiations which might result in territorial compromise, are not taken lightly by Israelis. It is well known that the settlers have become a significant armed force on the West Bank in recent years. In his study on the role of the army in Israeli politics, Kurt Kanowitz points out that 'Gush Emunim has a private army with weapons provided by the military and enjoys governmental support for the execution of its political aims.'[16] What is significant about the movement's military strength and its disregard of the legitimacy of the authority of the state (at least over decisions concerning the occupied territories) is that it indicates a decline in the unique power of the state – in particular in its 'monopoly' over the legitimate use of force. States are sometimes defined as institutions with a monopoly on the use of 'legal violence': the police and the armed forces are usually accorded the unique 'privilege' of using violence to control the external and internal enemies of the state. This is true of both democratic and non-democratic states – the essential difference being the limit to which violence is carried before the intervention of legal constraints designed to protect the accused. By allowing the extension of military power beyond the army and police to a political group it favoured, the government effectively broke its own essential monopoly on the use of force. The justification of this was of course the 'self-defence' of the settlers against Arab attack. The *result* was quite different.

JEWISH TERRORISM

If the violent threats of Gush Emunim disturbed those Israelis who joined the peace movement, they were quite horrified by the discovery of Jewish terrorists. In a sense, terrorism may be regarded as the ultimate rejection of universal values; inhumane means are adopted to achieve extreme particular ends.

Jewish terrorists have engaged in vigilante violence in at least three categories: they have expropriated Arab land, retaliated against Arab terror and civilian resistance and sporadically attacked Israeli Defence Force (IDF) soldiers enforcing order.[17] The extent to which the violence was carried out by Gush Emunim members was revealed with the arrest and trial of twenty-seven high-ranking members who had engaged in a 'Terror against Terror' campaign. In July 1985, they were convicted of acts of terror which included: conspiracy to blow up the Temple Mount mosque, an attack on the Islamic University of Hebron, the crippling of three West Bank mayors and the attempted sabotage of five Arab-owned buses.[18] The arrest and prosecution of the Jewish terrorists may be seen as an attempt by the state to reassert its monopoly over the use of force.

Most Israelis were horrified by the revelation that extremism in Israel had reached the point of terrorism and that this terrorism was being carried out by men who claimed to be redeeming Eretz Yisrael. Not only were universal values being sacrificed on the altar of extreme Jewish particularism, but Jewish values, based on the Torah, were being distorted to justify acts of violence. This disturbed many religious Jews, whose belief in core Jewish values is beyond question, but who realised that Gush Emunim's blind devotion to such 'holy tasks' as the settlement of Eretz Yisrael had blinded members to universal, human ideals – many of which were grounded in the Biblical heritage the Jews had given to the world. A number of these religious Jews were to become involved in the formation of religious peace groups which play an important part in a predominantly secular movement. As we shall see, their importance lies in the fact that they can confront the Gush Emunim on their own ground – speaking the same 'language', debating the interpretation of crucial Biblical texts. The Gush Emunim cannot so easily reject them as heretics or 'Hellenists'.

THE DELEGITIMISATION OF LABOUR ZIONISM

It is important to note that Gush Emunim is not a marginal movement. Rather it is the 'tip of a serious cultural and social iceberg'[19] which has been developing within Israeli society, gradually up until 1967, and extremely rapidly thereafter. The movement contributed to the delegitimisation of the '*ancien* (Labour) *régime*' and helped to develop a radical new ideology (often referred to as 'New Zionism') which legitimised the accession to power of Begin's Likud.[20]

The complex process by which the Labour establishment lost its legitimacy has been the subject of many studies. Some argue that it was due primarily to the failure of Labour Zionism to convince the new immigrants who arrived from Arab countries after 1948 of the legitimacy of Labour's rule. There can be no doubt that most Mizrachim (Jews of North African and Middle Eastern origin)[21] gradually withdrew their electoral support for the Labour alignment. They blamed Labour for the immense difficulties they faced as new immigrants; they rejected Labour's socialist, universalistic leanings and came to support the more nationalistic, particular position of the Likud. This process is explored in greater depth when the question of ethnicity and the peace movement is examined.

Other analysts have seen Labour's decline as being similar to that experienced by other 'revolutionary' societies: '... a result of the problems attendant on the transformation of revolutionary groups from socio-political movements (in this case Socialist Zionism) into rulers of states and the concomitant institutionalisation of the revolutionary vision within the framework of a modern state.'[22] Recently, it has been suggested that the 'belated impact of the Holocaust' adversely affected Labour's standing, as the Revisionists began to question the role played by the established leadership of the Yishuv (the Jewish community in Palestine), suggesting that their 'methods of political manoeuvring and seeking compromises – rather than confrontation – actually fostered the uninterrupted continuation of the Holocaust.'[23] It seems clear that, by the seventies, the three basic components of Labour Zionist ideology had been depleted: *national* redemption by the return of the Jewish people to the Land of Israel had been achieved – but the majority of Jews still chose not to return; *social* redemption through the creation of an egalitarian economic order had failed – the kibbutzim had become wealthy islands of egalitarianism while Mizrachi immigrants remained impoverished in isolated 'development' towns. Finally, the idea of *individual* redemption through 'tilling of the soil' was despised by the majority of Ashkenazi and Mizrachi immigrants who preferred to settle in urban areas rather than on kibbutzim and moshavim.[24] The delegitimisation of socialist Zionism clearly resulted from the fact that the 'pioneering' values of asceticism, voluntarism, egalitarianism and communalism lost their relevance and appeal to the majority of Israelis after the creation of the state. The peace movement was to gain considerable support from Israelis who still believed in the ideals of socialist Zionism (notably from members of kibbutzim) and who were disturbed by the fact that these ideals were being rejected by the general public as well as by the ruling Labour establishment. Many of the more elderly supporters of the peace movement, who had been pioneers themselves before the foundation of the state, resented the way in which Gush Emunim members were portraying themselves as the new pioneers. This resentment is worth investigating further as it perhaps throws light on the feelings of frustration which motivated an economically privileged class to become involved in a social movement. It also helps to explain one of the ways in which the Likud party gained support and legitimacy at the cost of Labour.

THE NEW PIONEERS

The decline of Labour's ability to mobilise widespread support – as the party of the early socialist pioneers – did not spell the death of the pioneering ideal. The generation of Israeli school children who came of age after 1967 were imbued with the idea through the formal education system as well as the informal (youth movements, literature, public media). The conquest of new territories created 'new frontiers' for Israeli society – frontiers impregnated with religious-mythical meaning central to Jewish identity. A new class of 'pioneers' emerged after 1967 in response to the opening up of these primordial frontiers. They were, however, a totally different breed of pioneers – quite unlike the generation which had preceded them.

To begin with, the Gush Emunim settlers were not inspired by secular socialist ideals. They were religious-nationalists who occasionally welcomed secular (Jewish) participation in the sacred task of 'redeeming the promised land in preparation for the coming of the

Messiah'. Nevertheless, they adopted 'pioneering postures' and attitudes reminiscent of the early socialist pioneers. In effect, they
portrayed themselves as the vanguard of New Zionism, which was to
replace worn-out socialist Zionism and rejuvenate the Jewish nation
through a 'return' to its Biblical heartland. The usurping (and
perceived distorting) of the pioneer role was, as mentioned, resented by
many socialist Zionists. This was made abundantly clear by Amos Oz
(well-known writer and kibbutznik) in a speech to the Gush Emunim
settlers of Ofra on the West Bank. He described the sense of shock felt
by kibbutz movement intellectuals who discovered that, after the
Six-Day War, yeshivah students, caught in a wave of euphoria, were
blind to the moral dilemmas presented by the occupation and were
talking only of redemption and the coming of the Messiah. The
yeshivah students appeared to the kibbutz intellectuals to be 'power
drunk, bursting with messianic rhetoric, ethnocentric,"redemptionist",
apocalyptic – quite simply inhuman. And un-Jewish.'[sic][25] Then with
the formation of Gush Emunim, the kibbutzniks were horrified to
discover that these same students had taken on the 'kibbutz mantle' of
the pioneers. In the words of Oz:

> ...the appearance of Gush Emunim was also a blow to the ego of
> the youth in the kibbutzim and the Labour movement. A part of
> society that had been accustomed to being regarded as the
> standard bearer, accustomed to being looked up to by the country,
> had then been swindled – it, the firstborn – by people who were
> masquerading *their* sloppy army jackets, running round hilltops
> with submachine guns and walkie-talkies, who had adopted the
> mannerisms and the slang of the kibbutz. And although they
> represented a position far removed from our own, they managed to
> steal away from us the hearts of some of our spiritual mentors, as if
> here were the heirs of the pioneering spark that had dimmed; the
> heir apparent was ousted by the pretender to the throne. . . . You
> have brought the storm upon yourselves by electing yourselves the
> guiding elite.[26]

The sense of frustration which emerges from the words of Oz is
unmistakable: a sense of 'relative deprivation' which evidently contributed to the decision of many Labour Zionists to join the peace
movement in opposition to Gush Emunim.

BEGIN'S SUCCESS AND GUSH EMUNIM

While many Labour Zionists may have resented Gush Emunim's success in attracting broad public attention and support by becoming the 'new pioneers', what really appears to have disturbed them is the support and legitimacy given to Gush Emunim's previously illegal acts of settlement by Prime Minister Begin after his 1977 victory.

The first act of Begin, after his victory at the polls, was to visit Eilon Moreh, a Gush Emunim settlement on the West Bank over which settlers and the IDF (under orders from the Labour government of Rabin) had fought incessantly. The settlers had been ejected from the site no less than seven times. Begin promised that many more such settlements would be put up. The blessing he gave to the Gush Emunim settlement was reciprocated by the spiritual mentor of the movement – Rabbi Kuk junior. Having been charged with forming a new government, Begin went from the President's residence straight to Rabbi Kuk to receive *his* blessing and not that of the Chief Rabbis of Israel as is the custom.

Begin was not alone in his overt support for the Gush Emunim. The Likud government, as a whole, concurred with the movement's programme to settle the occupied territories. The movement had many friends and supporters in the Knesset, the Cabinet and the military, ready to fight its battles at the centre of governmental decision making. (The most vocal supporter was probably Ariel Sharon, who later engineered the invasion of Lebanon.) While supporting the movement, the government was also able to use it to encourage acts of settlement which it could not easily undertake on its own, for particular political reasons – such as during the negotiations with Egypt and the USA who both strongly opposed settlement.[27] Likud's support of Gush Emunim, and governmental adoption of the basic components of its ideology, created considerable disquiet amongst Labour Zionists and (even more so) amongst those to the left of Labour.[28]

EXTREMIST FRINGE GROUPS

Disquiet within the broad Israeli Left was due not only to the close relationship between the right-wing Likud and Gush Emunim, but also to the sudden appearance of a number of extremist fringe groups in the late seventies and early eighties. These groups, whose highly particular world view left little room for universal values, were regarded as symptomatic of a deeper malaise of intolerance affecting Israeli society.

The best known of these groups is Rabbi Meir Kahane's Kach (Thus!), which openly advocates 'transferring' Arabs out of the Land of Israel. Kach members have frequently been involved in violent clashes with members of the peace movement whose beliefs are diametrically opposed to their own. Kach was not considered to be politically relevant until the dramatic election of Kahane to the Israeli Knesset in 1984. Although Kach only won a single seat, it became evident that, within certain sections of Israeli society, Kahane's blatantly fascist ideas had wide support. In particular, Kahane's simplistic platform fired the imagination of Israel's youth. Different polls indicate that up to 15 per cent of school children, given the opportunity, would vote for Kahane.[29] Support is also much in evidence in religious orthodox groups and amongst low-education and low-income groups – primarily Mizrachim. It is interesting to note that there has been a decline in the 'grass-roots' activity of major political parties in low-income and religious orthodox areas.[30]

Support for Kahane grew extremely rapidly. In 1980 a foreign journalist described how he found it 'comforting to hear Israeli friends dismiss the Rabbi from Brooklyn [Kahane] as an unsavoury bigot whose ranting appalled the vast majority of people.'[31] Yet four years later Kahane had been elected to the Knesset and was being described by the Prime Minister as the 'greatest danger to Israeli democracy'.[32] In fact, to be accurate, Peres described 'Kahanism' as the danger, for it had become evident that the danger did not lie in the man himself but rather in the forces behind his election. The man simply represented a marked shift away from universal values; an upsurge in racist thinking and open intolerance. In the words of a leading Labour dove: 'Kahane is articulating what the other right-wingers so far dare not say out loud.'[33] The success of Kahane's 1984 entrance into the Knesset provoked, as we shall see, a considerable response from the peace movement and extensive general debate on 'how to deal with Kahane'.

Extremism knows no ends. As inconceivable as it may seem, certain members of Kach believed that the group was not going far enough in putting its ideas into practice. They formed a small splinter group (called El Nakam) which strove to actively 'encourage' Arabs to leave Eretz Yisrael. They were behind the 1984 attack on an Arab bus in which six Palestinians were wounded.

The ranks of the fringe groups have been swelled by a large number of Jewish fundamentalists, many of whom were previously secular in outlook. Since 1967 there has been a marked increase in the number of Hozerim Betshuva (literally 'those who return in repentance' – but also translated as 'born-again Jews'). They have swelled the ranks of both the ultra-orthodox yeshivot and the religious-nationalist groups – notably Gush Emunim. They have also supported fundamentalist fringe groups such as the Ne'emanei Har Habayit (The Faithful of Temple Mount) whose ultimate goal is the rebuilding of the Jewish Temple on Temple Mount, which has belonged to Muslims since the seventh century.[34] There have been frequent attempts by fundamentalists to enter and pray on Temple Mount (which remains under Muslim religious authority) as well as plots to blow up the mosque and shrine located there.

The growth of extremist fringe groups may have disturbed secular Israelis but what affected them more directly was the growing power of the religious parliamentary parties which entered into coalition with the Likud in 1977. The religious parties, due to proportional representation and the delicate balance of power in the Knesset which necessitates coalitions, have always been influential. Under Likud they became all the more powerful, managing to introduce a string of bills curtailing such things as abortions, autopsies, archaeological digs and the 'desecration of the Sabbath' (one result of which was the grounding of El Al flights on Saturdays). Marriage and divorce have always been controlled by the religious establishment – a fact not much appreciated by secular Israelis. The new laws, which further infringed on the citizen's private life, created renewed resentment increasing the sense of dissatisfaction and frustration.

THE IMPACT OF BEGIN'S VICTORY

All the developments in Israeli society which have been discussed so far contributed to the conditions of disquiet, discontent and frustration upon which the peace movement was built. But, what really laid the foundations of an *extra-parliamentary* social movement was the dramatic loss of power of the Labour coalition – which had ruled the State of Israel since its foundation – to a party led by a man whom Labour Zionists (and the Israeli left as a whole) thoroughly mistrusted.

To fully appreciate the impact that Begin's victory had on the broad

Israeli Left, we need to recall the long history of animosity between Labour and the Revisionist Zionists whom Begin represented. The history of this stormy relationship reaches back as far as Vladimir Jabotinsky's resignation from the executive of the World Zionist Organisation (WZO) in 1923 and the establishment of the United Revisionist Party in 1925.[35] Within a few years of this split, the new revisionist youth movement – Betar – became the chief rival of the well-established, left-wing Hashomer Hatzair from Poland. The movement spread, under Jabotinsky's dynamic leadership, to Europe, overseas and of course to Palestine.[36]

The competition between the two main Zionist movements was intense. This was partly due to the political climate of Eastern Europe and the fact that competition and ideological debate took place within a 'stateless vacuum', where no point of resolution could be reached. But the conflict was intense primarily because the two movements developed all-encompassing world views, which conflicted, and which presented the opposing movement in the most negative way possible. One writer notes:

> Labour had a universal social democratic ideology which empha-sized pioneering settlement of the land, and egalitarianism. Labour's leaders perceived the militaristic, militant nationalism of the Revisionists as fascist. Revisionism was strongly influenced by Polish nationalism and stressed 'blood and iron', the values of martial heroism. The Revisionists were convinced that Labour's universalism was assimilationist and feared its links with com-munism. The policies of the two regarding the partition of Palestine, attitudes toward the Arabs, and relations with the British Man-datory regime were contradictory.[37]

The framework of the competition was somewhat changed when Jabotinsky decided to lead the Revisionists out of the WZO and established, in 1935, the New Zionist Organisation. The results of this decision were far-reaching. Labour, under Ben-Gurion, benefited by gaining a more dominant position in the WZO and thus gained further access to its vital resources. But of greater lasting importance, Ben-Gurion 'successfully insinuated that the Revisionists (by leaving) had placed themselves beyond the bounds of mainstream, if not legitimate, Zionist politics'.[38]

Labour's distrust of the Revisionists increased when the military auxiliaries of the two camps came precariously close to clashing during the last phase of the British mandatory rule. The basic disagreement was over Labour's policy of restraint towards the British during the Second World War. When the Revisionist leaders, Begin and Stern, refused to bring their two dissident militias under the discipline of the elected institutions of the Yishuv, Labour sent out the élite Palmach units of the Haganah to impose control by tracking down the dissidents, abducting and interrogating them, or by informing the British of their hide-outs. In some cases, they actually turned captured dissidents over to the British themselves.

The conflict between the military wings of the two movements reached something of a climax with the arrival of the *Altalena* (a ship bought by the Revisionists to bring arms and ammunitions to Israel in June 1948, shortly after the creation of the new state). Begin defied Ben-Gurion's orders to turn over the arms and began unloading the ship with his Irgun soldiers. Ben-Gurion sent in the Palmach. The battle over the ship resulted in fifteen dead and dozens wounded, leaving a wake of bitter memories that was to rock the relationship between the two for years to come.

After the dissolution of Irgun, Begin turned his attention to the formation of a new party – the Tnuat Ha Herut (Freedom Movement). This caused immediate concern amongst leading liberal Jews. The party was described, in a letter sent to *The New York Times* (signed by Hannah Arendt, Albert Einstein and others), as 'closely akin in its organisation, methods, political philosophy and social appeal to the Nazi and Fascist parties'. The letter noted that the party had preached a mixture of 'ultra-nationalism, religious mysticism and racial superiority'.[39]

In the early years of the state, Begin's Herut party was generally regarded as being 'Zionism's lunatic fringe'. This idea was reinforced when conflict once again broke out into the open. On 7 January 1952, Begin addressed a mass rally held to protest against receiving reparations from Germany. In a highly emotional speech, he rejected the idea of German reparations and accused Ben-Gurion of arming the police with tear gas made in Germany, 'the same gas that suffocated our parents'. Declaring his willingness to suffer concentration camps and torture rather than receive German money, Begin marched off to the Knesset with the crowds following him. The mob broke through the police barricades and stoned the Knesset building, bringing the sounds of their angry cries and police tear gas into the Knesset Chambers. Ben-Gurion was forced to call in the army to restore order; over 200 were hurt and over 400 arrested.[40] The incident confirmed many people's view of Begin as a maniac, and clearly contributed to Ben-Gurion's success in portraying Begin and his followers as irresponsible extremists. As late as 1963, Ben-Gurion expressed his fear that, if ever Begin came to power, he would 'replace the army and command with his ruffians and rule the way Hitler ruled Germany, using brute force to suppress the Labour movement.'[41]

While the fears of Ben-Gurion and others may not have had any rational basis, they remained a constant factor in the subconscious mind of the broad Israeli Left. So much so that, despite Begin's increased moderation – and his participation in the National Unity Government of 1967–70 – his victory in 1977 provoked a wave of alarm amongst many of those who were soon to join the peace movement.

Finding themselves out of the corridors of power and led by a man they distrusted, Labour Zionists were increasingly ready for extra-parliamentary activity. One of the reasons for this is that many of them had become disillusioned with their own party which had been rocked by the wave of protest that came in the wake of the 1973 war, as well as by a series of corruption scandals involving high-ranking party members. A large number of discontented members and voters supported a new party which entered the elections for the first time in 1977. The new party – Dash (the Democratic Movement for Change) – totally failed to live up to the expectations of the discontented Labour Zionists who supported it. The reasons for this are discussed in Chapter 2, as well as the reasons for the sudden development of the peace movement as a *social movement* after 1977 and not 1967. What is to be noted here is that the failure of Dash, as a parliamentary party, opened the way forward for an extra-parliamentary movement to deal with the fears and frustrations raised by the emergence of extreme particular trends in Israeli society.[42]

The intention of this chapter has not been to examine the significant political events which gave impetus to the formation of the peace movement – such as the visit of President Sadat to Jerusalem. Rather, an attempt has been made to describe the broader shift from universal to particular values, marked by the appearance of religious-nationalist groups as well as by the victory of the right-wing Likud, which created the necessary sense of dissatisfaction amongst an otherwise privileged sector of society and gave rise to a social movement.

2 The Peace Movement Emerges

WHAT IS MEANT BY A SOCIAL MOVEMENT

In the late 1970s the Israeli peace movement emerged as a veritable social movement. This is the essence of this chapter. What, however, is meant by a 'social movement'? Sociologists have produced volumes in attempts to deal with this question. Without entering into any polemics, a number of characteristics may be spelled out. Firstly, true social movements cannot be fabricated. They are spontaneous expressions of widespread discontent. For this reason they tend, in the early stages, to be amorphous. What 'structure' they possess is likely to change at any given moment. Social movements are usually 'carried' by many unknown and obscure people who work in different areas and ways. If a movement endures, it is likely to acquire a certain form, albeit a fluid one: an enduring division of labour, as well as leadership and established social rules and values.

What is most interesting is that social movements manifest themselves through a whole range of 'movement organisations' (MOs). These form the basic infrastructure of the social movement. They are the only focal institutions of a fluid mass of activists, sympathisers, supporters and financial backers who make up any social movement. They represent the views of particular sections of the movement and present these views to the public – usually through media-attracting events such as demonstrations. The divisions between the MOs within a single movement are profound. Even though there may be common goals, co-operation between the MOs is usually very limited. They will, however, join together at times to demonstrate or to pool resources for certain projects. Yet, typically, MOs maintain their own distinct organisational identities. The more unattainable short-term goals are, the more likely it is for the movement to split into an ever increasing

21

number of MOs. These are usually based on ideological, ethnic, class, religious and tactical differences. In the case of the Israeli peace movement, these differences reveal divisions which affect the whole society.

The success of MOs in a social movement depends on a number of factors which include: an ability to mobilise a 'significant' percentage of the population, and to come to represent its views; the power to command positive media attention and to provoke some kind of governmental response; and the ability to survive the doldrums of apathy, exhaustion and inactivity without becoming 'becalmed' or radically altering course. The success of the social movement as a whole depends, to a great extent, on how much 'in tune' it is with what, in German, is called *Zeitgeist* (spirit of the time). If a social movement's ideology is in accord with the *Zeitgeist* of the day, its chances of producing social change are considerably better.

A final characteristic to be kept in mind is that not all MOs in a social movement may be involved in the same kind of action. Some are engaged in what is described as 'restorative collective action'. This involves attempts to move an increasingly fragmented society back to a time of shared beliefs and values – real or imagined. The relative harmony of the past is idealised and compared with the apparent disorder of the present which threatens to tear society apart. The Israeli peace movement, as a whole, is involved in restorative collective action; it seeks to restore the balance between the universal and particular values which is believed to have been lost in the wave of religious-nationalist euphoria that swept the nation after the 1967 war. Activists tend to idealise the pre-1967 era, before Israel became an occupying power; before religious-nationalists became the new pioneers; before neighbouring states were invaded to achieve absurd geo-political ends; and before an outspoken racist was elected to the Knesset. They appeal to universal values embedded in socialist Zionism in a struggle to reform their society, purge it of 'social defects' and restore lost values.

A small number of radical MOs in the peace movement tend more towards revolution than reform. They call for a total upheaval in Israeli society which would strip the state of all its Jewish characteristics and bring about the creation of a multi-ethnic, socialist state with no division between Palestinians and Jews. Reform, they believe, will never result in peace as long as Israel remains a Jewish state with a large Palestinian population under its control. The radical MOs, which form a small but vocal part of the peace movement, tend to be more exclusive than the reform MOs. Their membership is small and generally only open to those who share their ideological beliefs. The reform movements, whose ideology is not clearly defined but which appeal, as mentioned, to a balance of universal and particular values in Zionism, are more inclusive. They accept a wide range of members with varying 'reformist' ideologies. The only limit is that members (or supporters) stay within the accepted bounds of Zionist ideology – that the dismantling of the State of Israel, as a *Jewish* state, may not be advocated as a way to resolve the conflict. Bearing these factors in mind, let us consider the development of the Israeli peace movement as a social movement.[1]

ROOTS AND HISTORICAL DEVELOPMENT

Despite the seemingly spontaneous manner in which social movements form, they are not ahistorical. They have historic antecedents and they usually draw on a well-established universe of ideas. The Israeli peace movement is no exception. Although the focus of this book is on the years 1967–87 (marking the twentieth anniversary of the occupation), some historical background will help to make the reader aware of its importance and also underline the fact that certain salient ideas, which are debated today, are by no means new.

Ideas relating to ways of achieving peace with the Arabs have been fiercely debated by Jews since the outset of the Zionist movement. It should be recalled that, from the beginning, Zionism never had the unanimous support of Jews. In the decades preceding the Second World War, Zionism was opposed, for various reasons, by many Eastern European Jews. Many of these belonged to a Jewish socialist organisation known as the Bund. The Bund, with its universal, socialist outlook, was strongly opposed to Zionism. In its view, Zionism was utopian and 'socialist' Zionism all the more so. In heated debates Bundists argued that the socialist Zionists' collaboration with the religious orthodox Jews and the Jewish bourgeoisie would lead inevitably to the creation of a capitalist state where domination by clerical forces would be the order of the day. The Bund's slogan was 'Nationhood without Statehood'; they believed the Jews were a dispersed people and, as such, they should secure national rights in the lands of their residence. They opposed the Zionists' claim that the Jews were strangers everywhere but in Palestine and insisted that the establishment of a Jewish state would perpetuate the conflict between Jews and Arabs.[2] The Bund, as an organisation, came to an end with the extermination of Polish Jewry but their key ideas lived on – even after the creation of the State of Israel disproved their belief that Zionism was purely utopian.

The Bund is mentioned primarily because, as we shall see, there are those in the peace movement today who argue along basic Bund lines: that collaboration with the Jewish bourgeoisie and the religious parties has indeed led to the creation of a capitalist state, where the religious establishment dominates or controls many spheres of life of a secular (or at least non-orthodox) majority. They argue that the creation of a Jewish state, and the perpetuation of Zionism beyond the creation of the state, is the underlying cause for the conflict between Arab and Jew. The bottom line of their argument is quite simply that Zionism is incompatible with peace.

Within the main body of the Zionist movement itself, debates took place at a very early stage about how to establish peaceful relations with the Arabs – illustrating that the well-known slogan about Palestine being 'a land without a people for a people without a land', was nothing more than propaganda. The Zionist leadership was well aware that a large Arab population lived in Palestine. Their initial response, seen with hindsight, was naïve and hopelessly optimistic. They wishfully believed that the Arabs would welcome the spread of European civilisation brought by the Jews and that millions of Jewish immigrants could be settled in the country without the displacement of Arabs. The growth of Arab nationalism and anti-Zionist attacks, which took place as early as 1905, laid bare the naïve thinking of the early Zionists and set in motion a serious debate about improving Jewish–Arab relations which continues, in many ways, to this day.

Yitzhak Epstein, an early Zionist pioneer, was one of the first to demand that the Zionist movement realise that the very success of its enterprise was dependent on the establishment of positive Jewish–Arab relations. In an address to the Seventh Zionist Congress, Epstein pointed out that the purchasing of cultivated land, from wealthy Arab landlords, was leading to the mass displacement of the Arab tenants (fellahin) who worked the land. This, he said, was sowing seeds of bitterness which would ultimately be reaped as violent conflict between

Arab and Jew. He placed great emphasis on the rights of the Arabs to continue to live and work the land, and claimed that the Jews had come to Palestine to take that which had not been taken by others, to settle in all places where others had not yet settled, to find in the land what others had not found, and 'to reveal the wealth hidden in the layers of its earth for our own benefit and for the happiness of all its inhabitants.'[3]

As a Zionist, Epstein never questioned the 'right' of the Jews to settle in Palestine; yet, he believed that the act of settlement had to be based on universal moral principles, so that the rights of the Arabs would not be infringed. For this reason, he opposed the purchasing of cultivated lands which would result in the unjust expropriation of land worked by Arab fellahin. In his opposition to injustice, he stated:

> We will be sinning gravely against our people and its future if we recklessly cast aside our finest weapon: the justice of our actions and the purity of our way . . . It is not in vain that our young people aspire to realise, through the rebuilding of our land, the social ideals that excite mankind today. But if this is the case, we must refrain from ugly deeds and their like; in other words, from every unseemly project, from every suspect step and from every practice containing even a tinge of exploitation.

Epstein put forward a number of practical suggestions for improving Jewish–Arab relations – including the opening up of Jewish institutions (hospitals, libraries, savings co-operatives) to the Arabs. He proposed that Jewish schools 'avoid narrow-minded, covetous nationalism that sees only itself' and, as if to give strength to his argument, he concluded with the words of the prophet Ezekiel calling on the tribes of Israel to treat strangers amongst them as 'homeborn among the children of Israel', entitled to inheritance.[4]

Epstein's full lecture, aside from perfectly illustrating a balanced mixture of universal and particular values, reflects the basic ideas of those Zionists who have advocated Jewish–Arab understanding and *rapprochement* since the early days of the Zionist movement: that the Jews have the right to settle and develop the Land of Israel *but* that this settlement should not undermine the rights of the Palestinian Arabs to part of the land *and* that the Arabs should not be the exploited losers but rather the beneficiaries of Zionist development.

Another early Zionist whose thinking has influenced members of
the peace movement, is Ahad Ha'Am. He played a role in obtaining
the Balfour Declaration in which the British government pledged itself,
in 1917, to establish in Palestine 'a national home for the Jewish
people'. He was, however, one of the few Zionists who stressed the
parallel obligation that nothing should be done to prejudice the civil
and religious rights of the existing non-Jewish communities in
Palestine. Ahad Ha'Am, who described himself as a 'cultural Zionist',
wanted the political aims of Zionism limited in consideration of the
rights of Palestinian Arabs. He called on the Zionist movement to
recognise that Palestine was the national home of two peoples. He died
in 1927 having had considerable cultural impact on Zionism (through
his writing), but little political impact on the Zionist movement, the
mainstream of which 'insisted on reading the Balfour Declaration as a
promise not to create a Jewish national home in Palestine but to turn
all Palestine into a Jewish state'.[5]

Ahad Ha'Am's political ideas were upheld after his death by Judah
Magnes, the American-born Zionist who became the first chancellor of
the Hebrew University of Jerusalem. As a pacifist, he dedicated himself
to improving Jewish–Arab relations, believing Palestine to be the
rightful home of the two peoples.[6] Magnes was supported in this belief
by a number of fairly influential Zionists who shared his basic ideas.
One of these was Haim Kalwariski who helped establish many of the
earliest and most famous pre-First World War settlements in the
Galilee. He has been described as the 'father of the movement of
rapprochement and co-operation between Jews and Arabs,' for the role
he played in initiating meetings between Zionist leaders and Arab
nationalists in the face of the rising Arab and Jewish nationalism.

Kalwariski also became well-known for his involvement in what
may be described as Palestine's first peace group, Brit Shalom
(Covenant of Peace). Brit Shalom – founded in 1925 – was made up of
leading intellectuals, amongst whom were Arthur Ruppin, Hans
Khon, and Gershon Scholem (Magnes supported the group although
he did not join). The group never numbered more than one hundred
but, because of the prominent position of its members and their ability
to articulate their views, it attracted considerable attention. Brit
Shalom only lasted until 1933, but it was succeeded by three similar
organisations: Kedma Mizrachi (Forward to the East), the League for
Arab–Jewish Rapprochement, and Ihud (Union). Kalwariski played a

leading role in these groups which also had the prominent support of Magnes and the philosopher Martin Buber.[7]

Like later groups, the pre-State peace groups were dominated by Ashkenazi intellectuals. These early groups shared, in common with the left-wing party Mapam, a belief in bi-nationalism, based on an understanding of Palestine as the home of two peoples with equal rights. They were prepared to limit Jewish immigration to a level of parity with the Arabs. The government of a united bi-national state (which would eventually unite with neighbouring countries to form a 'Semitic Confederation'), would be based on parity. Jews and Arabs would be appointed in equal numbers to an Executive Council and a Constituent Assembly.[8]

In keeping with Epstein's thinking, bi-nationalist Zionists believed that (in the words of Buber): 'Independence of one's own must not be gained at the expense of another's independence. Jewish settlement must oust no Arab peasant.'[9] They argued that the only alternative to bi-nationalism would be the partition of Palestine and that this would lead to war with the Arabs. Unfortunately events were soon to prove them right. The bi-nationalists were never able to mobilise significant support. They were, in fact, exceedingly unpopular and were bitterly attacked. They were accused of being 'devoid of Jewish feeling. . . deep down assimilationist [with] the mentality of the diaspora'.[10] As the historian Walter Laqueur points out, these accusations were grossly unfair. 'Their Zionism was as deeply rooted as that of their opponents. But they feared that, without an agreement, there would be perpetual strife between Jews and Arabs which would lead to a deterioration in Zionism and ultimately perhaps to its ruin.'[11] The basic problem appears to have been that, although the bi-nationalists' analysis was accurate and their sentiments sincere, they could not provide practical political proposals which would be equally acceptable to Jewish and Arab nationalists. Their proposals were rejected by their fellow Zionists, who were not prepared to make concessions on such vital demands as unrestricted Jewish immigration to Palestine – or to question the right of the Jews to a *Jewish* state. The Arabs saw no reasons to make concessions, of any kind, which would endanger their majority position in Palestine. The only influential Arab who was prepared to enter into serious negotiations with the bi-nationalists was Fauzi Darwish el-Husseini, a cousin of the Mufti of Jerusalem. The price he paid for this was assassination.[12] In short, the bi-nationalists

were left 'to make peace with themselves' – a reproach frequently
levelled at the contemporary peace movement.

The lack of support from the Arab side is not altogether surprising.
As Zionists, the bi-nationalists were entangled in a complex web of
contradictions. It is ironic that members of Brit Shalom and others,
who most wanted close relations with Arabs, often contributed to a
sharpening of the conflict by their positions in the Zionist movement.
Ruppin, for example, who was a founder of Brit Shalom, was
responsible for purchasing Arab land. So was Kalwariski, whose land
purchases in the Tiberias district provoked open Arab resistance. The
pacifist, A.D. Gordon, who advocated the redemption of the Jewish
people through manual labour – and consequently a boycott of Arab
labour – raised Arab anger over Jewish separatism and the displacement of Arab workers. This irony has not been missed by those who
see Zionism, in any form, as being incompatible with peace. Even
today, Arabs in Israel and the territories regard the contemporary
peace movement with scepticism, precisely because they recognise the
contradictions that Zionist members of the peace movement still face.
On the one hand, they wish to achieve peace with the Arabs, while on
the other they are loyal to the Zionist state which the Arabs see as
being responsible for their misfortunes and oppression.

Bi-nationalism failed largely because Arab and Jewish nationalists
would not respond to proposals which necessitated compromise on
both sides. It also failed because of the highly polarised situation –
exacerbated by each outbreak of violence – which emerged in mandatory Palestine. By 1931 (the year of the first pan-Arab congress against
Zionist colonisation), the Zionists and the 'Mufti racialists' had
adopted radically opposed positions. Author Maxim Ghilan describes
the early 1930s as: 'the era in which an independent and bi- or
multi-national Palestine was stillborn'.[13] The division of Palestine by a
United Nations' vote brought the war predicted by the bi-
nationalists – it also brought an end to the bi-nationalist peace groups.

The creation of the State of Israel may have sounded the
death-knell of bi-nationalist aspirations, but it did not end the
activities of Zionists and anti-Zionists struggling for justice and
Jewish–Arab *rapprochement*. The main issue, in the years between the
creation of the state and the 1967 war, was the rights of the
Palestinians who became refugees outside Israel, or who were subject
to military rule within the borders of the new state. The problem was

seen largely as a 'refugee problem', rather than as a national problem resulting from a clash between *two* national movements – one of which had gained the upper hand – in a fight for *one* territory. Although these years were not without activity for Israeli peace groups, as the Israeli peace publication *New Outlook* makes evident, they fall beyond the scope of this book. The pre-1967 groups remained small; they mobilised few Israelis and never commanded much attention from the press. In short they never took on any of the attributes of a social movement as described earlier. The acquisition of territories in 1967 re-opened the debate, not about the rights of Palestinian 'refugees', but about the very character which the Land of Israel should assume.

THE INITIAL RESPONSE TO THE OCCUPATION

Although the *de facto* reunification of what was Palestine opened up the theoretical possibility of creating a bi-national state, there were few who advocated bi-nationalism as a solution to the conflict. In fact, the majority of those who *did* support bi-nationalism were the supporters of the Land of Israel Movement. However, their aim to maintain the unity of Eretz Yisrael could only result in a distorted bi-nationalism – where one national group would dominate the other. The unacceptability of a *true* bi-national solution (based on parity) led most Israeli doves to move from opposing the division of Palestine (their pre-1948 position) to the complete opposite – support for the division of the land between the two peoples.

The apparent willingness of the government to make territorial concessions in exchange for peace retarded the development of the peace movement. As time passed, however, a variety of issues arose which cast a shadow of doubt over governmental intentions *vis-à-vis* peace with the Arabs. These included: the Jewish settlement of Hebron (see Chapter 1); the military crackdown on Palestinian resistance in the Gaza Strip; the displacement of bedouin by Jewish settlements in northern Sinai; the destruction of the houses of Palestinian families believed to be co-operating with 'terrorists'; the continued refusal to allow the former Palestinian residents of the villages of Ikrit and Bir'am (on the Lebanese border) to return to their homes; the refusal of the government to sanction a meeting between Nahum Goldman, President of the World Jewish Congress, and President Nasser of Egypt.[14] These successive events had a cumulative effect on the broad

Israeli Left, increasing their scepticism about the government's willingness to resolve the ongoing conflict through territorial compromise and peaceful negotiations.

The peace movement was to draw on different sectors of the Israeli Left. Mapam, which had advocated bi-nationalism until 1948, was particularly prominent in its support for peace organisations. The party had been seriously divided before the elections of 1969 when it had to decide whether or not to join the Labour alignment. More than a third of the party's central committee voted against joining and some members actually broke away to form an extra-parliamentary group called Brit Hasmol (Federation of the Left). This constituted one of the groupings in the post-1967 peace movement that began to form in response to the lack of government initiative. Dissatisfaction, amongst those who remained in Mapam, was apparently highest amongst the youth of the Mapam-affiliated Kibbutz Hartzi Federation. Many of these young people became involved in Siach (The Israeli New Left) which was one of the largest and most active groups in the growing peace movement.[15]

The post-1967 peace movement, as with the pre-1948 groups, drew considerable support from the academics of Israel's major universities. Significantly, a number of religious academics and members of the National Religious Party (Mafdal) voiced their support for the movement. Although, from a religious point of view, there was no question of Jewish *title* to an undivided Land of Israel, the religious 'doves' believed that, in the interest of saving lives and preserving peace, the occupied territories should not be retained. They hence supported the overall demands of the nascent peace movement for territorial concession. For reasons which will be considered later, the religious doves eventually came to form their own unique 'movement organisations'.

In addition to the groups mentioned above, the post-1967 peace movement, which slowly began to emerge in the late 1960s, had the support of a number of non-Zionist and anti-Zionist groups. These included Maki (the Israeli Communist Party) and Matzpen (the Israeli Socialist Organisation). The movement was also supported by a number of well-known journalists, writers and students who were motivated more by concepts of justice, civil and national rights – and by the fear that the occupation would undermine Jewish democracy – than by revolutionary ideologies.

Considering the wide range of diverse groups, it is not surprising that the movement failed to achieve the degree of unity reached by its polar opposite – the Land of Israel Movement. The diverse groups shared a common view of the conflict. They saw it as being one between two national movements – Jewish and Palestinian; they believed that concessions had to be made by the two opposing sides and that the land common to them had to be divided to accommodate their respective national aspirations. The groups all believed that the continued occupation of the territories would undermine Israel's democracy and 'be an affront to all basic morals, whether Jewish, socialist, humanitarian, or liberal'.[16] Consequently, they were unanimous that the government should make a 'grand gesture' to convince the Arabs of Israel's peaceful intentions. They considered that the war had provided Israel with the unique opportunity of demonstrating to the Arabs that their view of Zionism (as inherently expansionist and aggressive) was wrong; that Israel, on the contrary, desired peace and was prepared to prove it by forfeiting territories won in a war that was forced upon her. At this point the consensus ended.

THE LACK OF UNITY

There was no consensus on exactly what Israel's grand territorial gesture towards the Arabs should include. Notions of justice and morality served as no guide to exactly *what* territories should be included, or *how* they should be returned or, indeed, to *whom*. Some believed that all the territories should be returned; most felt that Jerusalem should be kept, others proposed the retention of certain 'strategic' areas for 'security' reasons. Few were prepared to accept the unilateral return of territories to the Arab states which had governed them between 1948 and 1967.

The proposal to create a Palestinian state on the West Bank and the Gaza Strip generated considerable interest within the ranks of the different peace groups. It appeared to some that it would be possible for Israel to unilaterally establish such a state for the Palestinians, thus eliminating the need to negotiate complex peace treaties with the Arab states which had, in any case, openly expressed their refusal to negotiate with Israel. The immense difficulties involved in the proposal soon became evident. Setting aside such questions as the acceptability of a Palestinian state to the Israeli public, it was obvious that, if the state was brought into being through Israel's unilateral initiative, it would appear to be a puppet state – unrecognised by the Arabs and the world. Numerous alternative proposals were put forward, but none gained the unanimous support of the peace groups.

The divisions between the peace groups were not simply due to disputes over the extent of territories to be returned; the groups were also divided by their totally different world views. The anti-Zionist Left, in the tradition of the Bund, believed that Zionism itself was at the heart of the conflict. Some continued to maintain that Jewish–Arab unity could be achieved through a common class struggle and advocated a 'democratic secular state'. The anti-Zionists, of whatever persuasion, were not considered legitimate partners by the Zionist doves. In an extremely divided society, a general commitment to Zionism had become one of the few factors uniting Israelis. The anti-Zionists were hence considered to be beyond the pale of popular acceptance and legitimacy. The Zionists were themselves ideologically divided along party lines as well as being divided between secular and religious groups. The nascent peace movement, which began to emerge after the Six-Day War, failed to develop. It never assumed the characteristics of a social movement mentioned above. Not only was it unable to obtain any reasonable degree of unity but, more significantly, it also failed to mobilise any significant amount of public support. This was only partly because of differing world views and proposals for the resolution of the conflict; it was primarily because the majority of Labour Zionists (the largest single 'reserve' of peace movement supporters) still believed that the Labour-led government was sincerely exploring all avenues in an attempt to find a peaceful solution. This view was reinforced by the government's acceptance of a United States-backed proposal for a cease-fire on the Suez Canal which came in 1970, through the efforts of US Ambassador Jarring. Those members of the peace groups who remained convinced of governmental inflexibility (which they believed was due to the government's desire to maintain the territories) failed to persuade the majority of Labour Zionists to support the peace movement.

Social movements, as noted, emerge during periods of dissatisfaction and discontent. The failure of the peace movement to grow into a full-fledged social movement immediately after the Six-Day War was perhaps due, above all, to the fact that the general mood of the nation was not one of dissatisfaction and discontent. On the contrary, as the well-known Israeli sociologist S.N. Eisenstadt points out: 'The first years after the Six-Day War were often perceived . . . within Israel and beyond it, as the apogee of the implementation of the Zionist vision, as a period in which the feeling "we never had it so good" was very widespread.'[17] The time of extra-parliamentary protest stemming from widespread discontent was yet to come.

THE AFTERMATH OF THE YOM KIPPUR WAR

The widespread sense of security, satisfaction and accomplishment which built up after the Six-Day War, crumbled rapidly in the wake of the 1973 Yom Kippur War. The war came as a severe shock. A judicial inquiry established after the war accused the high military echelons of being unprepared. The occupation of the territories captured in 1967 had provided a false sense of security which was suddenly shattered by the unexpected, forceful Arab attack. The new sense of insecurity was exacerbated by a series of internal conflicts, political events and changes which left many Israelis with a growing sense of 'the inability of the society, its leadership and institutions to deal adequately with some of its basic, central, internal and external problems'.[18]

After 1973, discontent grew amongst Labour Zionists, not only in response to developments in the broader society – which were basically beyond the government's control – but also in response to developments that were considered to be the responsibility of the government and within the realms of its control. In the wake of the Yom Kippur War the Labour government came to be seen, by many Labour Zionists, as being corrupt and incompetent. They were dismayed by a series of scandals involving cases of corruption of high-ranking Labour Party officials – the climax of which came when the Minister of Housing committed suicide, following reports that the police and Attorney-General were investigating his contravention of foreign exchange regulations. Soon after the war, the country was hit by rocketing inflation; repeated industrial conflicts, especially in the public sector; and the intensification of ethnic and religious-secular conflicts, none of which the government seemed able to handle.

Labour Zionists were also disturbed by Israel's rapidly changing image abroad. The continued occupation of the territories, which Labour had begun to settle, undermined Israel's international image as an innocent David bravely confronting an Arab Goliath. The world had come increasingly to see the Palestinians as the victims, subject to Israel's military might and, at times, brutality. Israel's isolation was made greater when most African countries severed diplomatic relations. All these factors contributed to the growing sense of disillusionment and to the belief that the Labour alignment was no longer able to govern effectively. The growing sense of dissatisfaction amongst all Israelis was made evident by the increase in emigration from Israel to the West. In the first few years following the 1973 war, emigration actually exceeded immigration – a highly sensitive and politically explosive issue, given Israel's claim and aspiration to be a place of refuge and a national home for the Jewish people.

THE FAILURE OF PARLIAMENTARY PROTEST

Not surprisingly, the years following the 1973 war were marked by an escalation in public protests of all kinds, illustrating the general mood of dissatisfaction. The time was now ripe for the formation of a social movement. Yet, between 1973 and 1977, the peace movement remained largely unmobilised. This was partly because, although protest was widespread, it was highly dissipated, covering the wide range of issues already referred to. Furthermore, protest was not entirely extra-parliamentary. The Labour alignment was still in power and, to a certain extent, discontent could still be directed through party channels in the hope of effecting the desired change. But, perhaps of greater significance, a large number of Labour Zionists were directing their energies into the establishment of two new political parties which were to compete with the Labour alignment for the Labour Zionist vote. They were to sap the strength of the Labour party and, in 1977, contribute to its electoral defeat.

The first of these parties to be established was Ratz (the Citizens' Rights Movement). It won a respectable 2.2 per cent of the nation's vote (3 seats out of 120) in the 1973 elections. Standing against the occupation, against religious coercion and for citizens' rights – with a special emphasis on women – Ratz gained the support of many discontented Labour Zionists.

The second political party, formed in 1976, was Dash (see Chapter 1). It drew its support partly from existing political groups which had emerged out of the post-1973 waves of public protest, but the majority of its activists and supporters came from within the ranks of the

Labour party. They were dissatisfied with the corruption and incompetence of Labour rule, disturbed by the exhaustion of Labour Zionism's ideological vision and frustrated by the ossification of political leadership which limited participation in the political centre to an established élite.

Dash, under the apparent dynamic leadership of Yigal Yadin (who had previously not been involved in politics and was hence 'untainted'), offered the possibility of reforming and rejuvenating the political centre *without* deviating from the basic tenets of Labour Zionism. The party's electoral platform was not significantly different from Labour's, except for its emphasis on the need to reform the electoral system. Yet, in the 1977 election, the new party won an unprecedented fifteen seats, most of which came off Labour.

Following the elections, the party was faced with the choice of sticking to its electoral platform – and remaining a part of the opposition – or of entering into a coalition with Begin's Likud on the best possible terms. For four months, the party did neither. This allowed Begin time to reach a coalition agreement with the religious parties. Then suddenly, Yadin declared that the 'political state of emergency' necessitated that the party drop all its terms and enter the government.[19] The decision to join the Likud-led government was unacceptable to the Shinui (Change) faction which, within a very short time, left the party. Not long after the split, the party broke up, having bitterly disappointed its supporters who had placed their hopes, and their votes, in the party's ability to renew Labour Zionism. Its only 'achievement', in its short life, had been to help bring down the Labour party – a most unintended result for those who had seen their vote for Dash simply as a 'protest' vote to signal their discontent to a re-elected Labour party.

The absolute failure of Dash as a parliamentary 'protest' party, coinciding with Labour's loss of control of the corridors of power, greatly contributed to the willingness of many Labour Zionists to participate in an *extra-parliamentary* protest movement. In fact, a number of Dash local branch leaders were soon to become prominent members of the peace movement.

ZEITGEIST IN 1977

While the conditions of discontent and frustration in 1977 were right for the emergence of a protest movement, the mood of the country was far from right for the development of a *peace* movement.

The news, in the early autumn of 1977, had been dominated by Arab–Israeli disagreement and bickering over the procedure by which the Geneva peace conference could be reconvened. With the two sides disagreeing on fundamental issues, the chances of reconvening the conference in 1977 seemed negligible. Egypt and Israel exchanged warnings of war, with President Sadat publicly stating that Egypt, with the support of Arab oil states, would launch a war against Israel to liberate the occupied Arab territory. Prime Minister Begin responded in kind, saying that Israel would not be intimidated and would launch a pre-emptive strike if the Arabs appeared to be preparing an attack.[20] Soon after, violence erupted when Palestinians rocketed a northern Israeli town. In response, Israel bombarded Palestinian positions in southern Lebanon from the air. As analyst Arnold Lewis points out, these events are congruent with the episodes which have dominated Israeli life for many years. The result is that Israeli images of 'social order' in the Middle East have been permeated with a fear of further war with Arab states and terrorist attacks. In his words:

> Decades of conflict and intermittent warfare have ingrained in the Israeli consciousness a deep-seated national consensus regarding Arab–Israeli relations. Dominating this world view is a strong distrust of Arab intentions and a disbelief in the possibility for the Jewish state to live in trust and amity with its neighbours. It is assumed that the Arab states are unwavering in their wish to annihilate the Zionist state. Radical Arabs are seen as wishing to accomplish this goal through warfare while their more moderate comrades are seen to think more in terms of Israel's social destruction through economic warfare and political pressure. . . . Reflecting this point of view 90 per cent of the urban Jewish population in June 1977 believed there would probably be yet another war with the Arab states in the future.[21]

Israeli leftists and peace activists, who did not accept this view, were unable to make much impact; their argument that certain Arab leaders would be prepared to live in peace with an Israel *willing to coexist with a Palestinian entity in the occupied territories,* was totally at odds with the dominant Israeli view outlined above by Lewis.

THE IMPACT OF SADAT'S VISIT

In November 1977, the dominant Israeli view of Arab intentions towards Israel was shaken by the dramatic declaration by President Sadat that he was prepared to travel to Israel to negotiate peace publicly with Israeli leaders. The magnitude of Sadat's gesture cannot be overestimated. In a single speech, he ruptured a long-standing Arab accord not to recognise or negotiate with the State of Israel. The suspension of diplomatic relations with Arab states, and the expulsion of the PLO representatives from Egypt, underlined and dramatised Sadat's determination to achieve peace, despite the costs to Egypt as a leader of the Arab world. The impact that Sadat's visit had on Israelis was unmistakable. In fact, such is the significance of the visit to the formation of the peace movement that it warrants full quotation from the works of those who have studied its impact in depth:

> ... by going to Jerusalem, in what was to be the biggest media event of the century, when hundreds of millions of viewers saw on their television screens Sadat shaking hands with his former enemy, while thousands of Israeli school children waved the flags of both countries and as the Israeli army band played the two national anthems, he [Sadat] gave the Israelis a taste of peace which thirty years of warfare and praetorian statehood had denied them until then. For, through his action, Sadat set into motion *an evolution in Israeli attitudes* – among the masses and at least [among] some of the leaders, like Defence Minister Ezer Weizman – which is a necessary precondition for the emergence of any peace formula. ... His accomplishment was to make some ... limited ... break in both Arab rejectionism and Israeli suspicion. ... In Israel, once peace became a credible alternative, the earlier consensus about the value of territory for security started to erode.[22] (emphasis added)

Although no statement made during Sadat's stay, by himself or Begin, departed from past positions, the very fact of his presence in Jerusalem was enough to set in motion an extraordinary about-turn in Israeli attitudes to their past enemies. When Sadat returned home, attention shifted to Cairo where preparations began for Begin's reciprocal visit. Israelis were presented with nightly television features of journalists' impressions of life in Egypt; they were introduced to almost every aspect of Egyptian life: history, folklore, economic and social problems, hopes and fears. Thus, the stereotype of the enemy, based on years of suspicion and lack of knowledge, was transformed with factual information.

Ordinary Israelis' participation in the new peace process was not limited to following developments on television. Here Arnold Lewis reveals the impact the two leaders' visits had on the lives of the 'average' Israeli.

While observing this drama on television, Israelis sought avenues for private expression of their desire for brotherhood with the Egyptian people. Some deposited money with travel agents for trips to see the pyramids, as others attempted to open correspondence with Egyptian counterparts in pursuit of commerce and cultural exchanges. The Minister of Education expressed his wish that Arabic become the primary foreign language in schools, even above English. On 18 December, over 100,000 persons gathered in a spontaneous outpouring at the Tel Aviv city hall to sing for peace and fellowship with the people of Egypt. The idea of joining Tel Aviv and Alexandria as sister cities was put before the public. In ceremonial procession the hopes, fears and aspirations shared by Israelis and Egyptians were acted out.[23]

Following Sadat's initiative, over 50 per cent of Israelis expressed their belief that there would be no more war between Israel and the Arab states – compared with less than 10 per cent six months earlier.[24]

SINKING HOPES

Israeli hopes in a possibility of peace had been raised to an unprecedented level by the visit of Sadat to Israel and that of Begin to Egypt; a new vision of brotherhood in the Middle East had been born. Then, as the two sides sat down to attempt to translate this vision into reality, as the flag waving and anthem playing were replaced by hard negotiations and as discussions proceeded on the 'structure' of peace, 'each side began to move away back from a universal vision of peace towards attitudes inherent in the traditional social order which existed before Sadat's visit.'[25] The mood of euphoria declined – hopes were threatened and pessimism began to set in. Politicians in Israel demanded that Jewish settlements remain part of any agreement; Gush Emunim established new settlements on the West Bank; the government announced its intention to strengthen the existing settlements in the Rafiah approaches, while Begin restated the exclusive Jewish claim to sovereignty over the West Bank and the Gaza Strip. Disagreements and insults grew until finally, on 18 January, President Sadat broke off the diplomatic talks in Jerusalem.

It seemed at the time that a unique chance for peace was about to be missed. It was feared that peace was to remain a distant, virtually unobtainable dream. Those Israelis whose attitudes and beliefs had been transformed by the visit of Sadat and those who had always believed that 'moderate' Arabs would negotiate – *if* Israel demonstrated a willingness to cede the occupied territories – feared that their dream of peace was about to turn into another Middle East nightmare. They soon came to see Begin as the culprit. They placed the blame for the breakdown squarely on his shoulders, which is not surprising considering Begin's past record and association with Gush Emunim. These Israelis believed that Begin's intransigent determination to hold on to the West Bank – a determination obviously motivated primarily by religious-nationalist sentiments – was responsible for torpedoing the new peace process.

THE SPARK IN THE OFFICERS' LETTER

At this crucial point in the history of the country, an obscure ideological peace group, that had hitherto had no impact on public life, decided to write an 'officers' letter' to Begin. One of the officers, Yuval Neriya, later described the thinking behind the decision to write the letter. In his words:

> Other letters had been written to the Prime Minister, . . . they had been treated with patronising contempt . . . so we decided that the PM would find it hard to ignore a letter written by combat officers who had proved their worth in action, and had already made a contribution to Israeli society . . . [Neriya was one of the few Israelis to have been awarded the *Itur Hagvura* – Israel's highest award for valour]. Our idea was to show the PM that he did not have the nation behind him when he refused to negotiate over Judea

and Samaria (the West Bank) to get peace . . . We also wanted to
show him that we, the combat soldiers, would be placed in a very
difficult moral position if the chance to achieve peace is lost and
another war breaks out. It was a problem of conscience. If we have
to fight again we have to be sure that everything possible has been
done to avoid war and get peace; that there really is no alternative.[26]

The letter, which was eventually signed by 350 reserve officers
before being sent to Begin, stated the following:

> We write to you with a profound anxiety. A government that
> prefers the establishment of the State of Israel in the borders of a
> Greater Israel (that is, including the West Bank and the Gaza Strip)
> above the establishment of peace through good neighbourly
> relations, instills in us many questions (doubts).[sic]
> A government that prefers the establishment of settlements
> beyond the green line (the pre-'67 border) to the elimination of the
> historical quarrel and the establishment of normal relations in our
> region will awaken in us questions about the justice of our cause.
> A government policy that will encourage the continuation of
> control of approximately one million Arabs may damage the
> democratic, Jewish character of the State and make it difficult for us
> to identify with the State of Israel.[27]

The letter, coming as it did from reserve army officers – whose
Zionist credentials were unquestionable – struck a chord which rever-
berated in the hearts and minds of the many thousands of Israelis who
were still hurt and disappointed by the apparent failure of the peace
process. It was evident to them that the officers, who were all
'graduates' of the 1973 war and who had always done the 'right thing',
were not criticising the government for ulterior or questionable
motives (such as support for the PLO), but rather because they
genuinely cared about the future of the Zionist state. The response to
the letter was immediate and massive. Reporters with links to the
group rushed to publish it. Israel's national television network
interviewed two members of the group. Within hours, the small group
was overwhelmed by a flood of telephone messages from around the
country from well-wishers and sympathisers wishing to join. The

officers' letter proved to be the necessary spark to set alight the tinder-box of discontent which had been smouldering amongst Labour Zionists since the Six-Day War.

3 The Rise and Fall of Peace Now

The small Jerusalem group which had initiated the officers' letter were totally taken aback by the response. None of them had foreseen the results of the letter. Previously the group – known as the Other Zionism Group – had done little, besides discuss their ideas for an alternative (or 'sane') view of Zionism to the one propounded by Gush Emunim which was sweeping the country; their time had been taken up writing and rewriting platforms which nobody read.

At one point the group had come together with an equally obscure 'bohemian' group from Tel Aviv, called Peace Now, to discuss taking out an advertisement in a national newspaper (with money provided by the peace journal *New Outlook*). The Jerusalem group had opposed the use of the name Peace Now, and so left the Tel Aviv group to take out a half-page advertisement, appealing for peace, in a weekend paper. The advertisement had the misfortune to coincide with the news (and vivid photographs) of a terrorist attack on a bus inside Israel. The juxtaposition of the two produced disastrous results – no public response.

Given the failure of the advertisement, the Jerusalem group decided to write a letter to the Prime Minister. As Neriya points out, other groups had done this; there had been teachers' letters and social workers' letters. The ingenuity of the group had been (a) in correctly realising that an officers' letter would have an impact quite unlike that of the others and (b) in focusing their attention on the government's attitude to the West Bank, which was seen as the prime obstacle to a full peace accord with Egypt. It should be pointed out that the decision to send an *officers'* letter, was only taken after intense discussion. Members of the group were well aware that they would be accused of manipulating their army status to gain attention. The supreme value placed on military service in Israel ensured that the credibility of the officers would not be in question. They were well aware of this and made use of it.

The group, it should be noted, was a solidly Zionist group, but their vision of Zionism, which maintained universal and particular values, was radically different from the 'New Zionism' of Gush Emunim and Begin. In the letter they were not stating that they were no longer willing to fight for the Zionist state; they were simply making it clear that, if called to fight, they would go with 'a heavy heart' – believing that their government had sacrificed a chance for peace on an altar of territorial expansion erected on religious-nationalistic beliefs. By placing loyalty to the state first, the group were assured a positive response from Labour Zionists, which would not have been forthcoming had they worded the letter in such a way as to cast doubt on their faith in Zionism. Four years later, when Israel invaded Lebanon, the question of loyalty (and obedience) to the state versus military willingness to fight in a war which could have been avoided, would no longer be simply theoretical.

Events moved remarkably fast once the tinder-box had been ignited by the letter. In keeping with the sociological predictions about the formation of social movements, the new Israeli peace movement formed in a remarkably 'spontaneous' manner. Nothing was planned – it 'just happened'. In response to the thousands of phone calls, the group decided to hold a demonstration; the organisers were stunned when an estimated 35,000 people turned up. The Tel Aviv 'bohemian' group was there with posters and stickers bearing their name: 'Peace Now'. The name caught on and henceforth the new movement was known by it. In response to the many requests to join or to do something, the small Jerusalem core group told the people calling from around the country to form local groups, or to do whatever they pleased, as long as it was in keeping with the spirit of the officers' letter. Any activity carried out in the name of Peace Now which went beyond the spirit of the letter, would be denied.[1]

The letter, which some 250,000 Israelis eventually signed, became the uniting force of the new movement – beyond it there was very little agreement on specific issues relating to future borders or negotiations with the Palestinians. In other words, from the outset, the movement developed the characteristics of an 'inclusive movement organisation' as described earlier, allowing considerable ideological variation and flexibility in interpreting the social order. Indeed, the officers' letter united a wide range of people who opposed the Likud's policy to settle and maintain the occupied territories. It assembled Israelis who feared that this policy would take precedence over a rare opportunity to achieve peace with an Arab leader who had gone to extraordinary lengths to initiate negotiations. Because the letter did not propose an alternative to the occupation, this enabled diverse opinions to coexist within one movement. One Peace Now activist later described the movement as a slow-moving train, allowing people to get off at different ideological stops. Some would go as far as the last stop – advocating a Palestinian state along the pre-1967 border; others would stop off earlier, determined not to cede Jerusalem; yet others, unwilling to accept a Palestinian state, would get off at the 'Jordanian option stop' (Palestinian autonomy in confederation with Jordan).[2]

Not long after the formation of Peace Now, Tzali Resheff, a leading spokesperson, pointed out that the movement had no intention of forming a new party or of supporting any existing party. It had been decided that Peace Now was to remain an extra-parliamentary movement. Although Peace Now was later to develop close links with different dovish political parties, the fact that it remained an extra-parliamentary force exempted it from having to draft a detailed electoral platform on a wide range of issues – many of which would not be related to peace. This meant that there was, in fact, no need for unanimity. Resheff stated that Peace Now did not intend to draft a detailed, hard and fast programme, much less to draw maps of the kind of settlement they advocated. Instead he outlined the three basic positions held by the movement. Firstly, Peace Now opposed any policy that involved perpetuating Israeli rule over $1\frac{1}{2}$ million Arabs; secondly, it held that borders should be based only on security considerations and not on the location of existing (Jewish) settlements; thirdly, it proposed that Israel should be ready to make territorial concessions for the sake of peace. These positions could hardly be seen as radical.

Clearly Peace Now's intention was to maintain broad public support – 'to keep the train moving' – rather than to put forward a clearly defined alternative vision for the future. In this respect, Peace Now established itself as 'a reform social movement', accepting existing universal values and norms within the society and using them to criticise and oppose 'defects' – in this case, the placing of religious-nationalist territorial desires above an opportunity for peace with the Arabs.

The activists from the original Other Zionism Group were well aware that Peace Now was becoming a unique 'grassroots' movement with support emerging most rapidly amongst Labour Zionists – the political centre of the nation. As Peace Now grew, these activists were faced with the decision (that confronts all successful MOs) of either advocating their own ideological positions (which tended to be well left of centre) or maintaining a moderate, centrist position, more in keeping with public opinion than their own views. They chose, at times, to sacrifice their own ideals (or ideological purity) by not crossing certain lines which they knew demarcated the bounds of Zionist legitimacy. They consciously chose to take the opportunity afforded to them, by the massive response to the officers' letter, to become a 'mass social movement' – albeit reformist rather than revolutionary, inclusive rather than exclusive, but with the clear opportunity of mobilising large enough numbers of Israelis to make some impact on national life and political decision making. As activist Yuli Tamir put it, 'We'd had enough of talking to ourselves.'

Peace Now's determination not to step beyond certain well-defined limits, which would jeopardise their legitimacy with moderate Labour Zionists, is well illustrated by an event which took place about four months after the publication of the now famous letter. A group of about one hundred reserve soldiers wrote a public letter to Prime Minister Begin, saying they would not be able to defend or guard Israeli settlements in the West Bank and the Gaza Strip because they considered them to be 'an expression of annexationist aims and of the rejectionist policy of the government'. Government policy, the letter stated, was based on 'mysticism' which led to the domination of another people and which contradicted the 'secular needs of the state' thus thwarting peace efforts and endangering 'the Zionist endeavour'.[3] Setting aside questions of precise terminology, the letter's content was not that different from the officers' letter. Both objected to the government's continued occupation and settlement of the territories in lieu of negotiating for peace. Yet the soldiers carried their objection a step further – they threatened not to carry out their military duties in the territories as a concrete form of protest – and in doing so, they brought into question their loyalty and obedience to the state. Peace Now responded immediately, announcing that it had 'no connection with the reserve soldiers' letter'. It strongly condemned the attempt to attach conditions to military service and stated that, even if one disagreed with the premier's political path, 'military service is over and above any political debate'.

As we shall later see, Peace Now's drawing of distinct 'boundaries', beyond which it was not prepared to step in its protest, may have helped maintain the support of large numbers of moderate Labour Zionists, who were 'ripe' for participation in a basically Zionist extra-parliamentary protest movement; but, it also inevitably led to sharp divisions within the peace movement and the establishment of new movement organisations which were prepared to over-step the boundaries of presumed Zionist legitimacy. Before going on to examine t.ie structure that the movement assumed, as a consequence of these differences, I shall briefly outline how Peace Now developed between its first demonstrations in April 1978 and January 1985.

PEACE NOW'S RECORD

As a demonstration-by-demonstration account of Peace Now's history would be tedious, a graph has been compiled from newspaper reports and Peace Now's own record of events. Table 1 places each demonstration ever held by the MO (over a period of seven years) along a time-scale in weeks. Each demonstration is represented by a column which gives a rough indication of the number of people who attended the event. Estimations of the size of any large crowd always vary considerably. Nevertheless, although people may disagree over whether there were 20,000 or 30,000 at a demonstration, their estimates are usually a fairly accurate guide to whether the demonstration was 'small' (under 1,000), 'medium' (between 1,000 and 10,000), 'large' (between 10,000 and 50,000), 'very large' (between 50,000 and 100,000) or 'exceptional' (over 100,000). In addition to giving an indication of size, the columns also give an indication of what the main focus of the demonstration happened to be. Again, this does not pretend to be a precise scientific tabulation of events, but rather an indicator of broad trends. Evidently, a number of issues may be raised by numerous speakers at one particular demonstration; the question of governmental policy towards the occupied territories may be raised in conjunction with calls for the government to negotiate with the Arabs. Nevertheless, demonstrations usually have a primary focus which can be recognised. Table 1 thus shows a series of shifts in the focus of attention, which took place during Peace Now's most active years.

Table 1a   Peace Now activities. April 1978 – April 1979

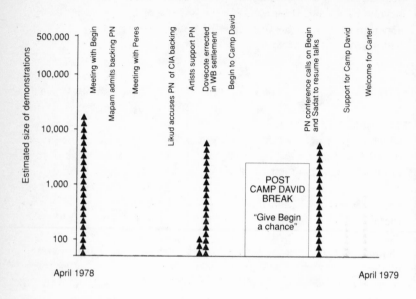

April 1978   April 1979

Key to the nature of the demonstrations

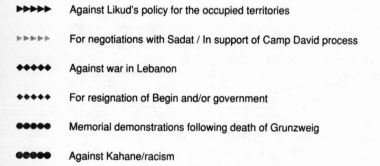

▶▶▶▶▶	Against Likud's policy for the occupied territories
▷▷▷▷▷	For negotiations with Sadat / In support of Camp David process
◆◆◆◆◆	Against war in Lebanon
◆◆◆◆◆	For resignation of Begin and/or government
●●●●●	Memorial demonstrations following death of Grunzweig
●●●●●	Against Kahane/racism

Table 1b   Peace Now activities. April 1979 – April 1980

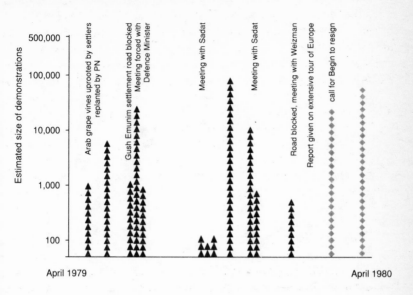

Table 1c   Peace Now activities. April 1980 – April 1981

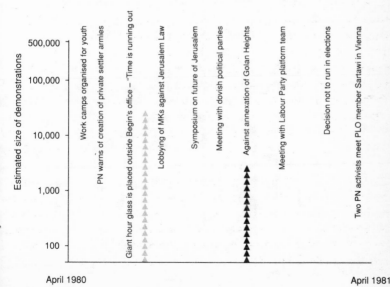

Table 1d   Peace Now activities. April 1981 – April 1982

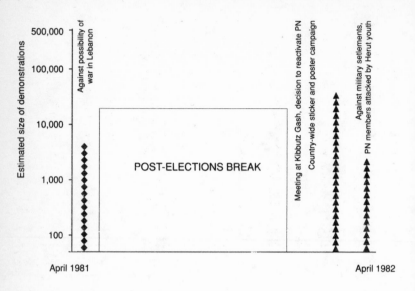

Table 1e   Peace Now activities. April 1982 – April 1983

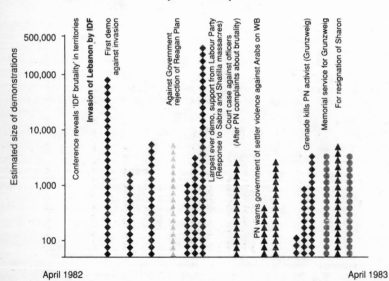

Table 1f   Peace Now activities. April 1983 – April 1984

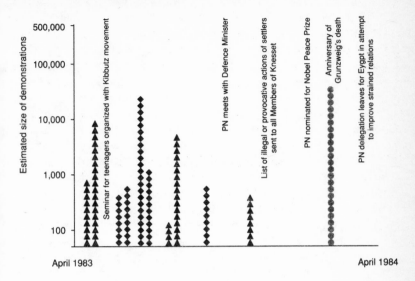

Table 1g   Peace Now activities. April 1984 – April 1985

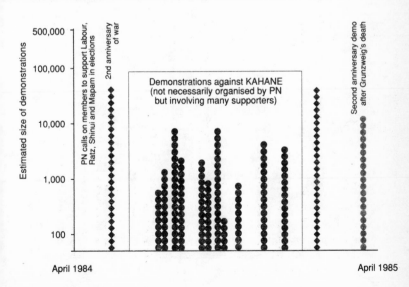

In addition to providing an account of the nature, number and size of demonstrations, the table also includes a partial account of newsmaking events involving Peace Now. These include meetings with important political leaders, conferences, campaigns, press releases and so on, illustrating the fact that its activities are far broader than the demonstrations which are most visible to the public eye. This record provides fertile ground for analysis. To begin with, it is immediately evident that Peace Now was a 'successful' social movement from a number of perspectives. Firstly, Peace Now mobilised a significant percentage of the Israeli public. It became, almost immediately, the central hub of the peace movement. Activists from a wide range of MOs, which pre-dated Peace Now, attended its demonstrations *even if they did not agree with its position or approach*. The demonstrations attracted large numbers of political party activists from the Labour party's left, as well as many moderate Labour Zionists who had previously been uninvolved in parliamentary or extra-parliamentary politics.

Its second major achievement was that it came to represent an alternative, universal view of Zionism, which challenged the increasingly particular view of Gush Emunim and the ruling Likud. Henceforth, when important political events took place, the media would typically contact Gush Emunim and Peace Now for their different responses, recognising that these two extra-parliamentary movements represented (perhaps more unambiguously than the elected parties) the views of a highly polarised society.

Peace Now was successful in coming to represent an alternative (albeit 'reformist') view of Zionism because it was able to attract *constant* media attention. As the table illustrates, this coverage extended beyond demonstrations; other Peace Now events, such as seminars, meetings and symposia, which are not usually considered to be particularly newsworthy, were also covered. Furthermore, due to the fact that many journalists were sympathetic to the aims of the group, Peace Now was able to gain relatively positive coverage.

If positive media coverage is taken as the third major success of Peace Now, the fourth would be governmental response. The response may not always have been favourable to Peace Now demands; nevertheless the government was forced to recognise the importance of the movement as an extra-parliamentary political force and to make some kind of response. The most evident response, which can be gleaned from Table 1, came in the form of meetings with top-ranking members of government. Within weeks of its formation, Peace Now members gained an audience with Prime Minister Begin. Begin was not sympathetic to the movement's claims of widespread support. He claimed the government was receiving letters 'by the thousand' to counter the 60,000 signatures of Peace Now. In fact his Herut party attempted to counter Peace Now opposition to the government by organising a series of massive demonstrations in support of Begin. These were supposedly organised by a new extra-parliamentary, pro-government, 'peace' organisation called the Movement for Peace and Security. It soon became evident that the group was simply a cover for Herut when journalists discovered that Herut branch offices were being used to organise activities. Peace Now claimed that the counter demonstrations were actually being organised from the Prime Minister's office and being financed by Herut. Being an artificial 'movement', it vanished once party funds dried up.[4]

Given Begin's apparently unsympathetic response to Peace Now, it is difficult to judge what impact the movement had on his decision making during the crucial years he was in office. It is clear, however, that after the massive pre-Camp David demonstrations marked on Table 1, Begin could not claim to have a national consensus for his West Bank policy. He had to take this into account when negotiating with Sadat. There is some evidence to suggest that he was disturbed by the extent of opposition to his policies. He is said to have written to author Amos Oz, claiming to have 'walked along Camp David's pathways ruminating about the vast numbers who days before had gathered in Kar Malchei Yisrael' (the site of the demonstrations held in Tel Aviv before his departure).

Not only did Peace Now activists meet with high-ranking members of the Israeli government, they also met leading Palestinians (notably PLO representative Issam Sartawi) and Egyptians (notably President Sadat). In fact, Peace Now claimed to have 'given heart to the Egyptians when the [peace] talks stalled'. In addition to this, they claimed to have legitimised criticism of the government, provided an outlet for 'a large section of the Israeli public which until then had watched mutely from the sidelines' and, by so doing, to have 'directly influenced the Cabinet's position'.[5]

If Peace Now was successful in obtaining meetings with prominent members of the government, it should be stressed that such meetings were not always obtained through 'the right channels'. Indeed, Peace Now proved to be ready to use the most unorthodox of methods to force meetings with an appropriate minister. Although the MO never used violence as a means to achieve such meetings – or any other objective – it was willing to use non-violent methods of civil disobedience when it deemed it necessary. This can be well illustrated with the case of Eilon Moreh.

Eilon Moreh was one of the most controversial West Bank settlement sites chosen by Gush Emunim. Because the settlement was to be established in an area with a large Arab population (and on land seized from Palestinian farmers), Peace Now was strongly opposed to it from the outset. This opposition increased when the settlement received backing from the Likud government and construction got under way. It became a focus of protest, a symbol of the whole process of settling the occupied territories, a sign of 'creeping annexation' designed (in the words of Ariel Sharon) to stop the 'establishment of a second Palestinian State'.[6][sic]

On 9 June 1979, between 3000 and 4000 Peace Now activists held a demonstration at the site of the new settlement. They blocked the access roads with large boulders and began 'squatting' as an act of protest. The army declared the site 'a closed area' (making it illegal for the demonstrators to be in the vicinity) and ordered the Peace Now demonstrators to leave. They refused to do so and were subsequently surrounded by hundreds of soldiers. Even though the soldiers threatened confrontation, the 'squat' continued and, at 2 a.m., the Military Commander of the West Bank arrived on the scene. The demonstrators, supported by two Members of Knesset (Yossi Sarid and Meir Pail) demanded to see Defence Minister Weizman, who arrived at 8 a.m. by helicopter. During this unscheduled meeting, he assured the demonstrators that he would report to the Cabinet their grievances concerning the seizure of 800 dunam of land from Arab owners for Eilon Moreh. Peace Now spokesperson, Tzali Resheff, warned Weizman against the starting of work on the site of the settlement while the demonstrators were still there. Weizman halted work and, in return, they promised to leave the site after a rally that afternoon.[7]

Six months later, Peace Now activists had a less productive encounter at Eilon Moreh with another Likud Minister – their 'arch enemy', then Minister of Agriculture, Ariel Sharon. Sharon was busy escorting two bus loads of families from the north of the country and the Negev around the settlement 'in an effort to persuade them of its strategic importance'. While Sharon was guiding the visitors around the site, an estimated 500 Peace Now activists arrived in trucks and blocked the entrance road. They off-loaded large concrete blocks and then chained themselves to these and to the trucks. Sharon and his guests were stranded for five hours while the Peace Now activists negotiated with the West Bank military commander (Ben Eliezer). They once again demanded to meet Defence Minister Weizman. Eliezer travelled to Nablus to contact Weizman, who eventually agreed to meet the Peace Now activists 'to hear their complaints about the government settlement policy'.[8]

Peace Now's success in eliciting meetings with the Defence Minister through the use of non-violent civil disobedience, does not necessarily prove the effectiveness of such methods of protest in Israel. More radical MOs (and Palestinians), who attempted to use similar methods, were treated quite differently by the military. It was above all Peace Now's moderate stance and 'well-connected' position (made evident by the support of Members of the Knesset) that produced such a restrained and reasonable response from the authorities.

SURVIVING THE DOLDRUMS

A significant indicator of social movement success is the ability of a MO to overcome setbacks and periods of apathy which often take place when a movement fails to achieve its goals. Although Peace Now achieved a number of immediate goals, such as the meetings with Weizman described above, its overall goals of ending the occupation of the West Bank and negotiating a settlement of the 'Palestinian Question' and peace treaties with Israel's neighbours, remained as elusive as ever. Nevertheless the movement, perhaps encouraged by the achievement of immediate goals, succeeded in surviving the doldrums of periodic inactivity without becoming becalmed. Table 1 clearly illustrates how periods of intense activity were followed by periods – sometimes lasting months – of virtual inactivity. At times these breaks were intentional: after the series of large demonstrations in the months preceding the departure of Begin for Camp David, Peace Now decided to call a halt in activities to give the negotiations a chance. It was only after talks broke down, and after it became apparent that Begin was continuing his policy of settling the West Bank, that Peace Now once again became active. At other times, the break in activity was not intentional, but due rather to extraneous factors. For example, in 1981, there was only one Peace Now demonstration (compared with fourteen in 1979 and at least ten in 1982). How can this be explained?

Inactivity appears to be due partly to 'battle fatigue'. The two preceding years had been filled with the organisation of a large number of massive protests directed firstly against the settlement of the West Bank, and then against the government itself, in an attempt to bring about its resignation. Activists were worn out and many were disillusioned by the failure to achieve either goal. However, the break in activity was probably due more to the fact that 1981 was an election year. Peace Now activists who were also involved in the dovish political parties (see Chapter 8), gave most of their free time to the election campaign.

METHODS OF ORGANISATION

From the start, it was agreed that Peace Now would be totally voluntary; the movement had no paid officers, no formal leaders and no '*apparatchiks*' – except for a treasurer, because somebody had to deal with the bank. The MO was run by a national council composed of representatives of its three big city forums (Tel Aviv, Jerusalem and Haifa) and delegates from towns and kibbutzim where there were local supporters. The local forums met once or twice weekly as events required. Anyone could attend but, as it was the activists who went most regularly, their word inevitably carried most weight. Policy and activities were decided at these meetings and each activity or demonstration was run from start to finish by a team of *ad hoc* volunteers. There was no executive and no actions' committee. Peace Now came to an agreement with a number of major newspapers whereby they could place an advertisement in the paper for a demonstration, and then pay for it later with money collected from supporters at the demonstration. To mobilise a maximum number of people as rapidly as possible, Peace Now activists established a mobilisation system modelled on that of the IDF. The small group of volunteers organising a particular demonstration would each telephone ten to twenty known activists. These in turn would telephone a similar number in their area, who would in turn telephone friends and supporters known to them. Within a very short space of time, a large number of people could be informed about a forthcoming event with virtually no cost at all to the MO. The MO also made good use of petitions as a way of contacting supporters. Often people who had signed a certain petition would receive a call from a Peace Now activist asking them to help in making placards, distributing leaflets, putting up posters or simply to announce a forthcoming demonstration. Such people would often assist Peace Now by selling T-shirts or stickers – thus improving the MO's finances as well as spreading its name.

Given the voluntary nature of Peace Now, it is not surprising that the MO went through a lull in activity during the election period when so many activists were giving their time to political parties in the hope of defeating Begin at the polls. Table 1 shows that, at the end of 1980, Peace Now met with the Labour party's electoral platform team. A few months later, Peace Now formally announced its decision not to attempt to run in the elections; instead it asked its supporters to vote for those dovish parties which shared Peace Now's basic view of the conflict.

What is significant is that, after the elections, when Peace Now had been inactive for some months and just when it seemed that its days were over, activists succeeded in pulling it out of the doldrums and reactivating it by organising a large demonstration (estimates range from 50,000 to 80,000) against government policy in the occupied territories. This was supported by all the Zionist dovish parties, which had recently failed to defeat Begin during the elections. The demonstration was preceded by a 'March for a Sane Zionism' which began in the north of the country and ended, on the day of the demonstration, at the Tel Aviv Museum. The choice of the museum is an interesting one because it reflects the nature of Peace Now (which could appropriately be described as 'a movement for a sane Zionism'). The Tel Aviv Museum is where Israel's Declaration of Independence was signed. It was chosen as the site for the demonstration to 'remind the nation of the forgotten principles of the Declaration of Independence'.[9] The Declaration recalls the history of the Jewish people's relationship to the Land of Israel, declares that the State of Israel will be based on 'freedom, justice and peace', that it will ensure 'complete equality of social and political rights to all its inhabitants' and that it will be 'faithful to the principles of the Charter of the United Nations'. By upholding the document, which is a symbol of Labour Zionist

achievement, Peace Now was in effect calling for a restoration of the
universal principles contained in it – without rejecting those principles
particular to the Jewish people which the Declaration upholds. The
movement was reactivated with a broader focus than that of
opposition to governmental policy in the occupied territories, although
this remained its primary focus.

PEACE NOW AND THE WAR IN LEBANON

The invasion of Lebanon marked a new and intensive phase in the
history of the peace movement. Although the whole peace movement
deplored the invasion of Lebanon, the various MOs responded quite
differently to it. Peace Now, maintaining a solidly Zionist position,
immediately placed 'loyalty to the State' above all other considerations. Many of the MO's leading activists argued that it was their duty
to serve their nation in its hour of need. They pointed out that the war
had been started by a democratically elected government and that it
was the duty of all loyal citizens to obey the decisions reached by their
government – at least until such time as the government was changed
through the electoral process. Because Peace Now refused to demonstrate while the fighting was still in progress, it lost the initiative to
more radical MOs that were prepared to demonstrate. Within hours of
the invasion small *ad hoc* demonstrations broke out in the major
Israeli cities and before long the radical MOs held large and well-
organised demonstrations against the war (see Chapter 8).

As it happened, the leading activists of Peace Now had underestimated the strength of opposition to the war amongst their own
'rank and file'. Many peace activists, who had previously been
supportive of Peace Now, believed that the war was unjustifiable –
quite unlike both the Six-Day War and the Yom Kippur War which
were fought in defence – and that circumstances called for a high level
of confrontation with the government. As Peace Now was initially not
willing to protest against the war, these activists gave their support to
the more radical MOs that organised the first anti-war demonstrations. Once these had broken the 'taboo' of criticising the government
during a war, and had given an indication of the extent of opposition,
Peace Now did a turn-around and put its full weight behind the
anti-war effort.

As Table 1 shows, Peace Now's opposition to the war produced demonstrations which were unprecedented in their size and frequency. The MO drew in ever greater numbers of protesters. Yet, at the same time, the war gave rise to new MOs who opposed the war but were unwilling to join Peace Now. Reasons for this varied considerably: some refused to join Peace Now because they did not agree with its broader political position concerning the occupied territories; others believed Peace Now to be too moderate. The war also saw the emergence of Israel's first MO made up of Mizrachim as well as the formation of a new religious peace group. Both felt unable to work with Peace Now although they shared similar objectives. The differences that emerged during this intensive period of anti-war activity are the focus of following chapters.

In spite of the differences betwee the MOs, Peace Now continued to act as the 'hub' of the peace movement until at least the official end of the war in Lebanon. It remained the only MO capable of bringing together activists, from a wide range of MOs in the peace movement, for massive demonstrations against the war. Even members of Israel's small anti-Zionist MOs, who are fiercely critical of Peace Now's unambiguous commitment to Zionism, joined Peace Now's anti-war demonstrations.

PEACE NOW'S PINNACLE AND DECLINE

The peace movement's opposition to the war peaked with the Sabra and Shatilla demonstration. Even though demonstrations continued until the withdrawal from Lebanon was *officially* complete, the Sabra and Shatilla demonstration stands out as a watershed. This was not only because it was, without a doubt, the largest demonstration (of any kind) ever seen in Israel, but also because it was the one time that the government was clearly forced to accept a Peace Now demand. Peace Now insisted that a full inquiry into Israel's role in the massacres be held. Begin's government was forced to bow to the public pressure brought to bear on it by the demonstration; it established the Kahn Commission of Inquiry into Israel's role in the massacres. The establishment of the Commission, which 'implicated the Israeli civilian and military élite in the massacre and recommended that Sharon should be relieved of his post as Defence Minister',[10] was seen by many activists to be Peace Now's greatest achievement.

Despite this achievement, the war in Lebanon continued for

another two years and slowly, demonstrations declined in size and frequency. Nevertheless, as Table 1 illustrates, even when the presence of Israeli troops in Lebanon was the main concern of the peace movement, Peace Now never lost sight of its goal to force the Likud to end the occupation and settlement of the West Bank: anti-occupation demonstrations were interspersed with those against the war. However, as the war dragged on, as activists tired and as the 1984 elections grew close, Peace Now activities slowly began to diminish. Table 1 clearly shows the gaps between demonstrations progressively growing larger: in the first eight months of 1983, there were no fewer than sixteen Peace Now demonstrations – compared with only two in the first eight months of 1984.

Certain Israeli intellectuals believe that Peace Now demonstrations declined after the 1984 elections because the MO's close association with the Labour party made it difficult for activists and supporters to demonstrate against Prime Minister Shimon Peres whom they supported. Once Begin was out of power (thanks, at least partly, to the efforts of the peace movement), and had been replaced by a Labour premier, many felt that the country was once again in 'sane' hands and that the time for extra-parliamentary protest was over. But there is another important reason for Peace Now's decline.

In the 1984 elections, the outspoken, overtly racist leader of the extreme Kach group, was elected to Israel's parliament. The triumph of Rabbi Kahane, who made no effort to hide his extreme particular views, shocked those Israelis who could hardly believe that it was possible for a Jew, with a basically fascist platform, to be elected to the centre of Israeli democracy. Kahane's election was an indicator of increasing racist trends; he made visible, through his unexpected electoral victory, the strength of particularistic forces which had been on the rise since 1967. Demonstrations against Kahane and 'Kahanism', and programmes designed to counter the rising tide of racism – especially amongst Israeli youth – soon overshadowed concerns about the settlement of occupied territories. Peace Now activists dedicated much of their time to this new cause – the details of which are considered in the next chapter. The general shift of attention, away from the occupation to the broader problems of racism and democracy, may be explained in part by the dramatic electoral victory of Kahane – but there were other important factors at play.

Sociologists specialising in the study of social movements have noted that, if a movement is unable to attain its goals, it is likely to shift its focus, replacing its specific goals with more diffuse ones. Having failed to achieve a halt to the specific problem of the settlement of the West Bank, Peace Now shifted its attention to the more diffuse goals of confronting racism and promoting democracy. Furthermore, after the 1984 elections, Peace Now began to move away from being the entirely voluntary, intentionally unstructured MO described earlier, to being a partially institutionalised organisation with paid officers.

Peace Now's shift was marked by the establishment of its 'Education for Peace Programme'. The programme is designed to reach the hundreds of thousands of Israeli youth who have grown up since the 1967 war. In an appeal to American Jews for financial help for the programme, Peace Now pointed out that the Israel of these young people 'has fought two brutal wars and a constant battle with terrorists . . . has always ruled over more than a million Palestinians in the occupied territories – most of them hostile to Israel's presence . . . has seen the emergence of Jewish terrorists – many of whom are leaders of Gush Emunim.' The appeal noted that, under these circumstances, 'many young Israelis have given up hope of living in peace with their Arab neighbours' and asked: 'If the Arabs decide to talk about peace, will Israelis be prepared to listen?' In order to prepare young Israelis 'to listen', Peace Now appealed for finances to pay the salaries of two full-time staff who, with the help of volunteers, would enter Israeli schools to carry out their education programme. The programme aims firstly to 'explore with students the many possible military and political arrangements which would protect Israel's borders while giving Palestinians some form of self-rule on the West Bank and Gaza'. Secondly, it would teach students about the 'moral dangers of occupation and unnecessary wars'. For this it would use Biblical, Talmudic and Zionist sources to 'examine the rich Jewish tradition which offers guidelines for avoiding unnecessary wars and for strengthening relations with neighbours'. A third stated objective was the breaking of stereotypes by encouraging the reading of Arab literature, arranging meetings with Palestinians the same age as Jewish participants, and by role-playing in workshops thus helping young Israelis to 'realise that Palestinians are human beings, not abstract enemies'. Finally, the programme aims to encourage the pursuit of peace by teaching students 'how they can participate in the national debate on Arab-Israeli relations. They will discover how Israeli democracy enables them to make their voices heard.'[11]

In adopting an educational strategy aimed at more diffuse goals, Peace Now appears to have begun a shift away from being a 'cause' (or protest) group, expecting the government to act in response to demands, to adopting a 'do-it-yourself' approach to Jewish–Arab peacemaking. The assumption behind this approach is that the political consciousness of the public, notably the youth, has to be developed so as to eliminate racist attitudes and prepare the way for peace because, whatever political arrangements are made, Jews and Arabs will still have to live together in Israel. Instead of putting pressure on the government to act, MOs undertake themselves to work for peace through education and positive Jewish–Arab contacts. As we shall see, this approach to furthering Jewish–Arab coexistence has been practised by a large number of MOs.

The shift of focus from the occupation was regarded by the radical anti-Zionist MOs as a retreat. They argued that the occupation was the prime cause of racism because it perpetuated a cycle of violence (oppression-resistance-oppression). One of the most active and vocal organisations which continued to focus exclusively on the occupation was the Committee Confronting the Iron Fist (CCIF). The CCIF was founded shortly after the arrest of a Palestinian employed at the East Jerusalem Arab Research Society. The director of the Society, Faisal Husseini, enlisted the aid of Gideon Spiro, the spokesperson of the radical (predominantly Jewish) Birzeit Solidarity Committee (see Chapter 8). Some days later a meeting was held between Palestinian activists, mobilised by Husseini, and a much smaller number of radical Israeli activists mobilised by Spiro. Those present resolved to dedicate themselves to a campaign of protest against the Israeli government's 'iron fist' policy in the occupied territories and formed a committee as the first step in their campaign. While the numerous 'moderate' MOs in the Israeli peace movement were caught up in the fight against racism, the CCIF, made up predominantly of West Bank Palestinians (with the participation of a small number of radical Jewish Israelis), continued to protest against the occupation. Through demonstrations, seminars, the distribution of fact sheets and press releases as well as visits to the sites of 'iron fist' targets, the group drew attention to deportation, administrative detention, house or town arrest, collective punishment involving the demolishing or sealing of houses, the closure of Palestinian institutions (newspapers, unions, committees) and, in particular, the mistreatment of Palestinian political prisoners.

In April 1986, Peace Now held a remarkable demonstration in Hebron which seemed to indicate that the shift in focus and activity discussed above was not permanent. This was not only reminiscent of 'old times' – it also broke some new ground for the MO. The demonstration was held at the Park Hotel, site of the first Jewish settlement attempt in 1968. It marked eighteen years of settlement in the occupied territories and, at the same time, was organised as a protest against the extreme right-wing Tehiya party being allowed to hold a convention in the Arab city.

On the road to Hebron Peace Now activists, supporters and invited guests were confronted by angry and aggressive Jewish settlers who set up roadblocks of cars, stones and burning tyres. The peace activists were forced to run a gauntlet of insult and fury: Mapam leader Victor Shemtov's car was stoned; Members of Knesset Yossi Sarid and Shulamit Aloni were pushed around and cursed; *Haolam Hazeh* editor Uri Avnery was knocked to the ground and spat upon before being pushed off a 3-metre ledge. Had it not been for the reportedly reluctant intervention of the army, it is likely that the confrontation between settlers and peace activists, reminiscent of earlier confrontations in years gone by, would have resulted in serious injury and the cancellation of the Peace Now meeting in Hebron. Justifying the confrontation, settler leader Eliakim Haetzni told *The Jerusalem Post*: 'Whoever comes here to hug them [the Arabs] is in effect creating a united front of terrorists and Jews. This is tantamount to stabbing us in the heart.'[12]

With the way cleared for them by the army, the peace activists made their way to the Park Hotel which was under tight security. Here an unprecedentedly radical face to Peace Now emerged. For the first time the MO had invited West Bank Palestinians, sympathetic to the PLO, to share the platform. Amongst them was Hanna Siniora, editor of the East Jerusalem paper *Al Fajr*, who openly called for the establishment of a Palestinian state in the West Bank and the Gaza Strip. Peace Now spokesperson Tzali Resheff called on the government to allow free elections in the occupied territories to enable Palestinians to elect their own representatives and demanded that the Prime Minister declare his willingness to meet with any Palestinians willing to talk to Israel – *including the PLO*. In making these demands Resheff was situating the movement's political position well to the left of Labour – which consistently refused to allow open elections or to meet with PLO representatives or supporters.

Expectations were high that the MO would confront the Labour party and launch a new campaign for an end to the occupation and for the resolution of the conflict through mutual recognition of the right to self-determination. However, in the months that followed, Peace Now was once again inactive.

To a large extent, the development of Peace Now, outlined in Table 1 and in this chapter, correlates closely with theoretical predictions about a 'successful' social movement. The MO emerged suddenly in a spontaneous manner. It mobilised a significant percentage of the Israeli population who were alarmed that their hopes would be shattered by religious-nationalist ideals. Carried by the spirit of the day (*Zeitgeist*), it organised demonstration after demonstration, receiving positive media coverage and obtaining certain, albeit limited, concessions from the government. Then, after about six years, Peace Now's activities began to decline. Various reasons for this have been cited. The government and the mood of the nation both changed. It became increasingly difficult to mobilise large numbers of supporters to demonstrate for specific goals – such as an end to the occupation – which remained as elusive as ever. These were replaced with more distant and diffuse goals – an end to racism and the promotion of democracy. Large demonstrations gave way to occasional conferences which in turn became fewer and further between. The MO did not disband, it did not die a sudden death – it simply went to sleep. The question of whether or not it will ever 'awaken' again is one of continued speculation. Despite its dormancy, debate about what the movement achieved and failed to achieve continues. Peace activists outside Peace Now are highly critical of the MO while supporters remain defensive of most of the steps taken. The intense debate and profound divisions within the peace movement (many of which centre on Peace Now) form the bulk of the remainder of this book.

4 Against Racism and for Dialogue

As we saw in the previous chapter, the election of the racist Rabbi Meir Kahane to the Knesset provoked a massive public outcry. The danger of racism and even fascism becoming real factors *in Israel* soon overrode concerns about the occupation. This chapter explores the rise of racism amongst Israeli Jews and describes the struggle against it, which was to involve not only public protest but also new legislation. Ironically, legislation against racism was linked (in the Knesset) to legislation aimed at preventing peace activists from engaging in a dialogue with the PLO – hence a chapter dealing with both the struggle *against* racism and the struggle *for* dialogue with the PLO.

I

RACISM AMONGST ISRAELI JEWS

The problem of overt racism amongst Jews in Israel was hardly discussed until early 1983 when tension mounted in Nazareth. Nazareth is the one large Palestinian town in Israel from which few inhabitants fled in 1948. The presence of a large Palestinian majority in the Galilee created public concern amongst Israeli Jews and consecutive governments adopted a policy of 'Judaisation' of the Galilee. To increase the number of Jews in the area, a new Jewish town was built on the hills overlooking Arab Nazareth. Known as Upper Nazareth, the town grew to number 25,000 by 1983. At this point about 3,000 Arabs had moved into apartments in Upper Nazareth due to an acute housing shortage in the crowded old city of Arab Nazareth. The presence of Arabs in the new Jewish town was opposed by an overtly racist group called Mena which, with the enthusiastic co-operation of Kach, demanded the expulsion of all Arabs from Upper Nazareth. With the tension mounting, a number of liberal Jews living in Upper Nazareth joined with a group of Arabs from the lower town to form the Committee for Upper and Lower Nazareth Co-operation (number-ing approximately fifty members).[1] This small group was to be the first of many new groups that formed in the early eighties to confront the overtly racist trends emerging amongst Jews in Israel.

CALLS FOR A LAW TO DEAL WITH RACISM

In January 1984 the idea of a law against racism was aired by Latan Lerner, a lecturer in Law at the University of Tel Aviv. Although in 1978 Israel had ratified the 'International Convention on the Elimina-tion of All Forms of Racial Discrimination', Lerner and others felt that a law was needed to enable the authorities to respond to the increasing number of overtly racist acts in Israel.

With the election of Kahane to the Knesset in 1984, the call for an anti-racist law was heard from many new and influential quarters – including those of Teddy Kolleck (Mayor of Jerusalem) and Haim Cohen (retired Supreme Court judge). People were concerned that the election of a proud racist to Israel's highest legislative body would legitimise the public expression of racist sentiments that had previously only been expressed under the cloak of privacy. A member of the faculty of Rabbinics of the Jewish Theological Seminary of America in Israel voiced the fears of many:

> If such a man and his position are legitimised by election to the Knesset, every fanatic in the population is vindicated, every impulse to violence, every excuse to hatred is admissible. All of the extremism that was hidden and therefore under control is released and freed to come out into the open under the covert if not overt tutelage of the Member of Knesset who represents it.[2]

In short it was widely feared that Kahane's election had opened a Pandora's box releasing all the demons of racism into Israeli society. Within weeks 'Kahanism' became an Israeli synonym for racism. The bills that he sought to introduce into the Knesset were compared to the anti-Jewish laws of the Nazis. They called for the forcible deportation of non-Jews unwilling to accept the status of second-class citizens; the prohibition of their residence in Jerusalem; the prohibition of sex between Jews and non-Jews and so on. Many Israelis, who recalled the fact that Hitler had been elected to power, feared that Kahane's successful election marked the emergence of a fascist movement in Israel. Such fear prompted rapid anti-racist action.[3]

THE RISE AND FALL OF PROTEST ACTION AGAINST KAHANE

In Jerusalem a petition was started for the passage of an anti-racist law directed against Kahane. Professors at the Hebrew University united to condemn 'Kahanism'. When Kahane provocatively attempted to enter the largest Arab village in the Galilee – Um el Fahm – to set up an 'emigration office', he was prevented from doing so by 5,000 Jewish and Arab protesters. On 14 August 1984, 2,000 demonstrators confronted Kahane at the opening of the Knesset, protesting against his entry into the heart of Israeli democracy. Two weeks later another 3,000 people again demonstrated. In fact, each time Kahane appeared in public, he was confronted by anti-Kahane demonstrators who frequently clashed with his own Kach members.

Many of these demonstrations were organised by a new Jerusalem-based group called Citizens Against Racism (CAR). It formed quite spontaneously, following the television appearance of two Jeru-salemites – Mike Levine and Nava Fuchs – on a popular television news programme. They openly discussed their fears arising from the election of Kahane and their concerns about the apathetic response of Israeli citizens. Neither Levine nor Fuchs were well-known political activists; neither could be regarded as leftist (Levine was actually a member of Herut). Both were surprised when they were inundated by telephone calls and messages following the broadcast. As was the case with the famous officers' letter, they had managed – almost uninten-tionally – to touch a chord which resonated in the hearts of many Israelis, leading them to act promptly on their feelings.

Levine and Fuchs suggested that those concerned should join them in the formation of CAR which became the centre of opposition to Kahane in Jerusalem. Jerusalem was not the only place where the anti-racist movement took form; new anti-racist groups formed in Tel Aviv, Acre, Haifa and in many of Israel's smaller towns. What is clear is that the new groups, under whatever name, formed because neither Peace Now nor any of the other MOs responded rapidly enough to appease the fears which came to the fore with the election of Kahane. This does not mean that Peace Now activists were not involved. On the contrary, activists from Peace Now and all other MOs were very involved in the formation of the different anti-racist groups. In fact, the Israeli Left as a whole seemed to forget about the occupation as all attention shifted to focus on Kahane and his racist followers.

The anti-Kahane snowball gathered force well beyond the usually confined circles of the Left and the peace movement. Even the army announced that it intended to 'do its bit' in fighting racism by 'teaching democracy' to conscripts. Then the Minister of Education announced that 'education for democracy' would be given priority in schools over the next two years. At about the same time the various MOs that had emerged to combat racism joined to form an umbrella organisation called Ma'aneh (Answer).

The initiative for this came mostly from the United Kibbutz Movement (UKM) which had been under pressure from its members to do something to confront Kahanism. With Ma'aneh largely under the control of the kibbutzim, with the Knesset beginning to consider anti-racist legislation and with 'education for democracy' under way in many schools, the number of demonstrations against Kahane and racism suddenly declined. It appeared that the many 'moderate', 'liberal' Israelis who had joined in demonstrations believed that things were now 'in good hands' and once again 'under control' – despite the fact that polls continued to show that Kahane's popularity was rising, *especially* amongst the young.

A number of the more radical activists became disillusioned with Ma'aneh. The new umbrella movement had refused to allow the participation of the communists. This had disturbed activists like Levine, who though not communists themselves, believed that it was absurd to exclude a political party with a large Arab majority from the struggle against racism – especially as the communists were often the majority at street demonstrations against Kahane. Furthermore, Levine and others were disappointed that Ma'aneh was not prepared to consider protests against apartheid and Israel's links with South Africa. They were also concerned by the lack of activity of the movement. The institutionalisation of the anti-racism movement had produced exactly the opposite result than that hoped for by many of those who had been involved from the start. It had produced a belief that all was in good hands and that 'ordinary people' now had no need to act – in short it produced complacency and a lack of action that left many activists disillusioned.

Although the anti-racist movement was short-lived, it need not be regarded as a failure. For a start it mobilised many thousands of previously uninvolved Israelis, increasing their awareness not only of the rise of racism and possibly fascism in Israel but also of the need, above all in a democracy, to act visibly in order to force elected representatives to legislate decisively. The movement was also successful in capturing media attention and thus making it evident that a large number of Israelis were not prepared to stand by idly while Kahane and his followers spread their poison. There can be no doubt that, as mentioned, the movement prompted legislators to act. Ironically, those left of the Israeli centre – who had pushed hardest for anti-racist legislation – were to be the most disappointed with the results that were finally produced by the Knesset.

LEGISLATION AGAINST RACISM – THE KNESSET MAKES ITS MOVE

Legislators, spurred on by the rising tide of public protest, began to seriously debate the legal means available for curtailing the likes of Kahane. It was widely agreed that an anti-racist law of some kind was needed but the actual passage of such a law proved to be a lengthy and complicated affair. The Attorney-General, Itzhak Zamir, began by warning that curtailing Kahane's freedom to operate could easily pose a threat to the civil liberties of others. He nevertheless accepted that existing legislation was insufficient for an effective battle against racism. Indeed, the word 'racism' did not even appear in the law; incitement to racism was not specifically laid down as an offence; establishing an organisation to inculcate racism was not explicitly prohibited, nor was it illegal for such an organisation to run for the Knesset.

In November 1984 the House Committee of the Knesset empowered the Speaker to strike from the record a racist remark, to expel a member for racist remarks and to prevent racist draft legislation from being tabled as a private member's bill. Five days later the Speaker made Knesset history when he disqualified a bill (submitted by Kahane) on the grounds that it was racist. Ironically, the High Court of Justice was eventually to overturn this decision. The Court went out of its way to acknowledge that the bill in question was a threat to Israeli democracy and recalled racist legislation enacted by the worst enemies of the Jewish people. However, at the same time, it pointed out that by Israeli law, any Member of Knesset was entitled to submit bills in accordance with his or her platform and that the Speaker only had the power to approve or disapprove bills on strictly technical or procedural grounds – not on their socio-political contents. Not to be deterred the Knesset voted (with a majority of only twenty-two) to deprive Kahane of the freedom of movement granted to Knesset members – thus curtailing further provocative attempts to enter Arab villages to 'encourage' the departure of Arabs from Israel.

Shortly after Kahane's election, the Ministry of Justice took a decisive step towards the creation of an anti-racist law by drafting two bills dealing with the problem. The one aimed to make it illegal for anyone to publish material which incites racism, while the other laid down that electoral lists which supported incitement to racism would be prohibited from running *as would lists that negated the existence of the State of Israel as provided for in the Declaration of Independence.* Thus, from the outset, the anti-racist legislation was linked, like a Siamese twin, to legislation aimed at the non-Zionist Israeli Left. This was largely because, in the 1984 elections, the Progressive List for Peace (PLP) was perceived as being the left-wing equivalent of Kach – an extremist movement threatening the existence of the State of Israel by advocating the creation of a Palestinian state and negotiations with the PLO. The Israeli Right was clearly as keen to eliminate the PLP as the Left was to eliminate Kach. Consequently pressure was placed on the Minister of Justice to draft bills which would deal with what was considered to be the 'extremes' of the Israeli political spectrum.

CONTRADICTORY RESULTS

It took the Knesset almost a year to pass the first piece of 'anti-racist' legislation. This empowered the Knesset's Central Elections' Committee to disqualify lists likely to incite racism as well as those which 'might' negate the existence of the State of Israel as the state of the *Jewish* people.

The law immediately drew heavy criticism from Palestinians and from the Israeli Left. Palestinians saw that law as yet another denial of the fact that 16 per cent of Israel's citizens are not Jewish. They tended to regard the law as racist itself – a denial of their basic rights as 'non-Jewish' Israeli citizens. Noam Chomsky, a long-time observer of the Israeli scene, pointed out that the new law had brought the emerging conflict between Zionism and democracy a step closer – a conflict which he believes will inevitably force Israel to choose between being Jewish and being democratic. Numerous left-wing commentators pointed out that, instead of dealing simply with the issue of racism, legislators had introduced a clause aimed at *preserving the Jewish character* of the State of Israel. In doing so they had made the entire law unacceptable to those most concerned about the rights of Palestinians in Israel and the nature of Israeli democracy. Indeed, to many in the peace movement, the new law seemed to undermine Israeli democracy rather than protect it.

The next step in the saga of legislation against racism came when, after yet another year of 'wheeling and dealing' between Labour and Likud, a second 'anti-racist' law was passed. This made the publication of racist material an offence – with one very important exception: on the insistence of the orthodox religious parties, a clause was added to the law excluding from prosecution the publication of material that aimed at 'preserving the character, uniqueness of worship of a religion'.

The inclusion of this clause caused considerable protest. The entire left-wing opposition voted *against* the law they had originally fought so hard for while Kahane himself voted for it – with both hands raised above his head and with a smug smile on his face. Abba Eban, a well-known 'dovish' Member of Knesset, later remarked that it was like watching Casanova voting for the Seventh Commandment – prohibiting adultery. Shulamit Aloni of Ratz argued that the clause itself constituted incitement to racism while Ruth Gavison of the Association for Civil Rights in Israel expressed her fear that the new law would make little legal difference when it came to prosecution. In her words: 'The secular racists are slightly worse off now. The religious racists are better off. I'm afraid the rhetoric of religious racism will become more eloquent and more vocal.'[4]

Disillusionment was widespread at the result of months of work for anti-racist legislation. *The Jerusalem Post*, considered to be slightly left of Labour, expressed the views of many on the left and in the peace movement in an editorial entitled 'Kahane has Last Laugh'. It was pointed out that:

If the Knesset had actually intended to promote racism by seeming to ban incitement to it, it could not have done better. For what it has legislated is the grant of a Kashrut certificate to all racists who put a religious label on their wares ... All that the country's Kahanists need to do is what Rabbi Meir Kahane has been doing all along: pluck, even if out of context, a scriptural figleaf – and not only cover their racist shame but stay within the law.

As an example the editorial referred to the infamous 'pastoral' letter of the army chaplain in 'Judea and Samaria' in which he called for the genocide of Israel's enemies. He named the Germans and implied the Arabs – 'since they represented a latter-day incarnation of the Amalek, which the Children of Israel were bidden in the Bible to wipe off the face of the earth.' As the editorial went on to point out, under the new law it would be unlikely that the publication of such a document – blatantly inciting the most extreme form of racist action (genocide) – would result in prosecution because it included Biblical reference.[5]

THE LAW PROHIBITING CONTACTS WITH THE PLO

No less than four hours after the Knesset voted against the law prohibiting publication of (non-religious) racist material, it passed a law which struck at the efforts of an important segment of the Israeli peace movement. The law prohibited contacts between Israeli citizens and the PLO. In the words of one observer: 'The stupidity of the Left was stupendous.'[6] The Left had, since the election of Kahane, pushed hard both within the Knesset and on the streets for a law that would effectively curb 'Kahanism' and make it impossible for any racist to operate openly in Israel. Instead they obtained a law so blatantly weak and ineffectual that Kahane himself voted for it and only hours later a law which would end dialogue with the PLO.

To understand how this absurdity occurred, one has to remember that the laws were passed by a 'National Unity' government. The government depended on agreements between the two major coalition parties – Labour and Likud – for the passage of any law and was strongly influenced by the position of the orthodox religious parties. Once an agreement had been reached there was very little the small, left-wing parties in the Knesset could do. Observers tended to agree that the genius of the Likud, on seeing how keen the Left was to oppose Kahane, was to insist that the anti-racist laws should be linked with legislation that would exclude non-Zionist parties from the Knesset and end contacts with the PLO. Why, however, was the Likud so keen to end peace activists' dialogue with the PLO and why did Labour acquiesce so easily? To understand this we must briefly consider the extent and the implications of the Israeli–PLO dialogue.

II

ENEMIES TALK – THE STORY OF ISRAELI–PLO DIALOGUE

RADICAL ROOTS

Secret talks between PLO officials and Israeli peace activists go back at least as far as 1970. At first such talks involved only the most radical elements in the Israeli peace movement – Trotskyites, Maoists and other anti-Zionists. They amounted to little more than an exchange of political views which had little impact on the Israeli public. This was the case until a certain Udi Adiv of the Revolutionary Communist League (RCL) was arrested and charged with treason, violation of state security and meeting foreign agents. Adiv had been persuaded to accompany a group of Palestinians to Syria in order to be introduced to PLO representatives. The trip was a failure. Adiv met no PLO representatives but rather Syrian agents. He returned to Israel only to be arrested, along with four other members of the RCL and twenty-five Palestinians. He received a jail sentence of seventeen years – the most ever meted out to a Jew for a political 'crime'. The media had a field-day giving full coverage to the trial. Adiv was labelled as a 'super-spy', a 'saboteur' and a 'terrorist'. Thereafter, the establishment fully exploited Adiv's case by branding all Israelis who entered into dialogue with PLO representatives in a similar way.[7]

CHANGES IN THE RANKS OF THE PLO

The involvement of less radical activists came about in response to a change in the outlook of high-ranking PLO officials that occurred after the 1973 Yom Kippur War. The war produced neither victory nor defeat on either side; the failure of military might to achieve a solution apparently led numerous PLO members to reconsider political solutions. Another factor which influenced their attitudes to the problem of considering relations with Israel was the rise in popularity of Rakah (the Israeli Communist Party) in Israel and in the occupied territories. In the early seventies, while the PLO was struggling to survive in crisis-ridden Lebanon, the Palestinian community were in the front line of opposition and resistance inside Israel and across the 'Green Line'. Their involvement in strikes and demonstrations – often resulting in imprisonment – boosted the party's prestige amongst Palestinians. Thus, as Maxim Ghilan reports, 'the PLO mainstream was faced with the fact that besides the PLO there existed a force fighting for Palestinian national and civil rights *but accepting the physical and political existence of the State of Israel provided that Israelis withdrew to pre-1967 borders.'* [8]

The development of political thinking within the PLO (or at least within Fatah, the dominant group within the organisation) was also influenced by certain PLO intellectuals who knew Israel well, from the inside. Sabri Jiryis, an ex-Israeli citizen, a lawyer and the author of *The Arabs in Israel* (written in Hebrew), left Israel in 1970 for Beirut where he became the Deputy Director of the PLO Research Centre. From there he began to publish his view that the PLO should accept statehood in the West Bank and the Gaza Strip thus compromising the official (and exclusive) PLO position calling for the establishment of a Palestinian state in *all of historical Palestine*. Jiryis' views made him a marked man and he was once kidnapped by Palestinian 'rejectionists' only to be released after the intervention of Arafat himself. [9]

At about the same time that Jiryis began making his views known in Beirut, two articles appeared in *The Times* of London. The first (16 November 1973) stated the following:

> Many Palestinians believe that a Palestinian state on the Gaza Strip and West Bank . . . is a necessary part of any peace package. Such a Palestinian state would lead to the emptying and closing down of the refugee camps, thereby drawing out the poison at the heart of the Arab–Israeli conflict. It is no small thing for people who have been wronged as we have to take the first step towards reconciliation for the sake of a just peace that could satisfy all parties.

A second article (17 December 1973) argued that the Israeli Jews and the Palestinian Arabs were the only two parties that could lay the foundation stone for a peaceful future in the Middle East. As a first step towards this goal, the author called for mutual recognition: 'The Israeli Jews and the Palestinian Arabs should recognise one another as peoples, with all the rights to which a people is entitled.' The articles were signed by none other than Sa'id Hammami, the PLO's official London representative.

AVNERY MEETS HAMMAMI

The call, from a high-ranking PLO official, for a political solution based on mutual recognition and a Palestinian state alongside the State of Israel, caused considerable excitement amongst Israeli peace activists who had advocated the same solution for some time. One such activist was Uri Avnery, editor of the popular weekly *Haolam Hazeh*, who shortly after the Six-Day War had called for the establishment of a Palestinian state in the newly-occupied territories. Through the intermediary of Edward Mortimer, the Middle East expert of *The Times*, Avnery arranged a secret meeting with Hammami in a London hotel. Avnery was not the first Israeli Hammami had met. He had already met a number of anti-Zionist Israeli exiles linked to the anti-Zionist group Matzpen. Avnery was, however, the first Israeli he had met who was not an anti-Zionist. It is unlikely that such a significant meeting could have taken place without the authorisation of Arafat and the support of leading members of the PLO. Evidently part of the PLO leadership had come to the conclusion that meeting only with anti-Zionists, who were despised in Israel, would hardly have any positive influence on Israeli public opinion and consequently would not enhance the possibility of negotiations over the future of the occupied territories.[10]

Although PLO Chairman Yasser Arafat never officially and publicly stated his willingness to recognise the State of Israel and to accept limited Palestinian statehood in the occupied territories, he was to hint at such a possible solution many times. In his famous speech at the UN he described the official PLO view of a 'democratic, secular state in all of historic Palestine' as a 'dream' and offered Israelis a choice between a gun and an olive branch. In the months and years to come, in numerous communications to diplomats and journalists (which were made known to the Israeli government), Arafat was repeatedly to suggest that the PLO would be willing to accept a 'mini-state' alongside Israel. Arafat did not unequivocally recognise

Israel because this would be unacceptable without Israel recognising the Palestinians' right to self-determination – a unilateral act which would totally discredit his leadership amongst Palestinians.

PEACE ACTIVISTS RESPOND

Despite the fact that the recognition Israelis so desired was not forthcoming, numerous peace activists responded to the steps towards dialogue and peace which had been made. In March 1974 Maxim Ghilan, the Israeli editor of the Paris-based journal *Israel-Palestine*, met with Sa'id Hammami – as did Shalom Cohen, the ex-secretary-general of the Black Panthers (see Chapter 5). In December 1974 a meeting took place in Prague between Mapam's secretary-general, Naphtali Pered, and an unnamed member of the PLO executive. In May 1975 a conference for 'a just and peaceful solution to the Middle East problem' was held in Paris. This brought together Israelis, members of the PLO and international observers concerned about the conflict. The conference succeeded in producing a joint declaration signed by both Israeli and Palestinian participants.

From the outset, the development of PLO–Israeli dialogue was encouraged by a small number of influential individuals, living outside Israel, who worked as mediators. They included very well-known people such as French ex-Prime Minister Pierre Mendès France and Austrian Chancellor Bruno Kreisky. They used their prestige and influence to facilitate private meetings between Israelis and high-ranking members of the PLO. Lesser-known mediators included Maxim Ghilan and a most remarkable Egyptian-born Jew called Henri Curiel. Curiel was a founding member of the (largely Jewish) Egyptian Communist Party. In 1948 the party – which supported the partition of Palestine as did the Soviet Union – demonstrated against Egyptian intervention. As a result Curiel and others were expelled from Egypt. Curiel became a stateless exile based in Paris where he became what Uri Avnery describes as a 'one-man centre for international liberation movements'.[11] While Curiel certainly expended a great deal of his energy assisting different liberation movements, his prime concern remained Arab–Israeli peace. He remained convinced that the Arabs had to recognise Israel and that Israel had to recognise and make peace with the Palestinians; towards this end he was to work tirelessly promoting Israeli–PLO dialogue as the prime means.

In the first months of 1975, while the pace of PLO–Israeli dialogue was quickening in European capitals, various MOs in the Israeli peace movement were holding a series of meetings in Tel Aviv aimed at unifying the movement. Endless debate resulted only in disagreement. Uri Avnery and others who were aware of the changes taking place in the PLO became increasingly frustrated by the lack of unity and fruitless discussion. 'The sole result', according to Avnery, 'was a renewed feeling of impotence.'[12] Convinced that an organised response from the peace movement was essential to encourage the moderates within the PLO, Avnery decided to invite a few like-minded activists to join him in publishing an unequivocal statement which they would call on others to sign.

On 10 June 1975 Avnery, Yossi Amitai and the well-known Israeli author Amos Kenan published a statement which declared (in part) that the only road to peace was through 'the coexistence of two sovereign states – the state of Israel and the state of Palestine'. It continued: 'the establishment of the sovereign state of Palestine alongside the state of Israel will be the outcome of negotiations between the government of Israel and the PLO, as the recognised national representatives of the Palestinian people.' The statement called on like-minded Israelis to join in establishing The Israeli Council for Israel–Palestine Peace (ICIPP) which would 'take part in a dialogue with all Palestinian elements who are ready to promote contacts between the two peoples of this country'.[13] The statement, published in Israel's prominent daily *Ha'aretz*, attracted considerable interest in Israel and abroad and within six months Avnery and company had collected the signatures of over one hundred fairly prominent Israelis – including those of Matti Peled, David Shaham, Arieh Eliav and Elishu Eliashur. On 10 December 1975 they became members of the new ICIPP, a MO committed to peace with the Palestinians through dialogue and the mutual recognition of the right to statehood.

THE TERRIBLE PRICE OF DIALOGUE

In the years to follow, the ICIPP was to be at the forefront of dialogue with the PLO, assisted enormously by the sympathetic and hard-working intermediaries mentioned earlier. It was to be a dialogue wrought with joy and pain, hope and disillusionment, trust and treachery, success and failure and more than one death. Indeed,

Israelis, Palestinians and intermediaries were to become the victims of 'rejectionist' assassins violently opposed to dialogue with the hated enemy. Only days before the founding of the ICIPP, Avnery was stabbed several times by an attacker whose knife only narrowly missed his heart. In January 1978 an unknown assailant entered the London office of Sa'id Hammami, the pioneer of Israeli–PLO dialogue, and fired a volley of shots into his victim killing him instantly. Four months later Henri Curiel was assassinated in Paris. In April 1983 a terrible blow was dealt to the cause of Israeli–Palestinian dialogue when Issam Sartawi (who had been especially appointed by Arafat to engage in PLO–Israeli dialogue) was assassinated by a hit-man from the rejectionist Abu Nidal splinter of the PLO. The dramatic and often painful story of Israeli–PLO dialogue has been told in detail by one of the key participants – Uri Avnery. In his book, *My Friend the Enemy*, Avnery gives an intricate, personal account of how the dialogue developed from a highly secretive affair to his much publicised encounter with Yasser Arafat behind the lines of fire in war-torn Beirut.[14] Such encounters – of which there were many – would hardly have been possible had it not been for the brave and relentless efforts of Sartawi. Totally dedicated to peace through dialogue (which he hoped would lead to real negotiations), Sartawi worked tirelessly to convince his comrades in the PLO Executive of the need for dialogue. In this he had the support of Arafat – but even this was not enough to prevent the rejectionists' bullets ending his life.

Sartawi's work, along with the creation of the ICIPP, resulted in the 'broadening' of Israeli–PLO dialogue. The number of participants (on both sides) as well as the number of meetings increased considerably after 1976. For some time excited participants believed that their dialogue would soon bear fruit. The Israeli government was informed of all important developments by Avnery and other Israeli participants, while the PLO Executive was kept in touch by Hammami, Sartawi and others who had been given the responsibility of contact with 'progressive' Israelis. The Israeli government under Rabin adopted a 'wait and see' attitude – allowing the talks to take place as if to 'test the temperature of the water'.

Within the leading ranks of the PLO, it seemed as if the 'moderates' (those in favour of dialogue with Israelis who were not anti-Zionists) had won the day and that the 'rejectionists' (those opposed to dialogue or at least only in favour of meetings with anti-Zionists) had lost their battle. Yet, opposition to dialogue remained strong and was soon to come to the fore, shattering the hopes and aspirations of many.

THE DEBATE OVER DIALOGUE IN THE PEACE MOVEMENT

Ironically, opposition to dialogue in Israel often came from within the ranks of the peace movement. Although this never reached the extremes of political assassination (as it did within the PLO), criticism from within the peace movement underlined the complexities and contradictions inherent in Israeli–Palestinian dialogue. For some activists, such as Avnery, dialogue is considered to be:

> a political act which has its own value in that it shows that the two sides can conduct a dialogue and therefore can eventually live in peace. It also helps both sides gain a perception of the other side. This is essential to the decision-making process of the people – not just the leadership . . . [It] changes everyone who engages in it. Our side gains a perception of Palestinian feelings, political realities, psychological realities, and emotional realities which are absolutely essential to any struggle for a solution. The same is true – even more so – on the other side.[15]

Avnery, and other like-minded activists, have such a belief in the value of dialogue that they have never set preconditions to their participation. This has not been the case for less radical activists. Peace Now has in the past 'supported' Israeli–Palestinian dialogue but only on the condition that the Palestinians are not members of the PLO. This attitude has angered the likes of Avnery. As he points out:

> You can't have conditions to dialogue. In a way, it's a contradiction in terms. [Dialogue is] a coming together of minds, an exchange of perceptions, feelings, political information and so on. If you put conditions to this you are really saying that you want to put the outcome ahead of the process. The conditions to be met, whatever they are, can only be the outcome of the dialogue.[16]

Some activists in the peace movement have opposed dialogue on the grounds that it has become an end in itself. In other words the event itself is given all importance while the content and outcome are disregarded. In a news and headline-oriented society such as Israel this is partly because the press often reports the event but does not enter into the details of what took place at a given meeting. More important is the fact that often very little is achieved at Israeli–Palestinian encounters and that results are few and far between. Occasionally joint declarations may be published but these rarely have any impact on the Israeli (or Palestinian) public. Activists critical of 'non-productive' dialogue would rather wait until such time as they are sure that their efforts will produce 'results'. The obvious question is: will such a time exist without preparation being made for it?

Perhaps the most serious criticism launched from within the peace movement is that Israeli–Palestinian dialogue is asymmetrical. This is true in the case of dialogue between Israelis and Palestinians from the occupied territories. Such meetings are often presented as a dialogue between equal individuals – equally interested in peace. Yet, participants cannot escape from the fact that they are engaged in what is a dialogue between occupier and occupied; between powerful and weak; between oppressor and oppressed. Indeed, should participants choose to attend a demonstration together, the asymmetry of their positions in Israeli society would be immediately apparent: the Israelis, who enjoy the privileged right of dissent, would not be likely to face police (or army) harassment or prosecution; the West Bank Palestinians, who certainly do not enjoy this privilege, would quite possibly be harassed or arrested. Time and again non-violent Palestinian demonstrations in the occupied territories have been broken up by the IDF, their participants have been detained, injured and not unoccasionally killed. This stands out in sharp contrast to the way in which Israeli Jewish demonstrators (whatever their political views) are treated by the IDF. The usual tack of the IDF, when confronted with an 'unofficial' Jewish demonstration on the West Bank, is to declare the area 'closed' and then to request demonstrators to leave.

Dialogue between ordinary Israeli citizens – not representing their government – and the PLO is also asymmetrical. It takes place on unequal terms partly because Israelis represent the victorious nation in the struggle for Palestine/Eretz Yisrael and the Palestinians the vanquished. The Israelis are free, after engaging in dialogue in a neutral country, to travel home to a state which is their own and which ensures their protection and survival. The members of the PLO remain stateless refugees – exiles whose very survival, in an often hostile environment, is a daily struggle. The dialogue is also one between unequals because the Israelis who meet with high-ranking PLO officials do not represent anyone except themselves or, at the most, peace groups whose membership is unlikely to be more than a few hundred. By contrast the Palestinians are officials of a quasi-governmental organisation widely recognised as the 'sole legitimate representative' of the Palestinian people. Then, while the Israeli participants are not in any position to enter into real negotiations which could lead to a resolution of the conflict, the PLO officials are. In fact evidence suggests that the only reason why the PLO engages in dialogue with peace activists is because it hopes that such 'preliminaries' may pave the way to a real match between it and the Israeli government. As Avnery puts it: 'They [the PLO] are not really interested in having a dialogue with Uri Avnery because he's such a nice guy, they want to use us as a conductor to the Israeli government.'[17]

With this clearly understood by both parties, Avnery began 'conducting' information to the Israeli government from as early as 1975. Not only did he report on the growth of dialogue and on much of what took place at the meetings but he also conveyed messages from the PLO directly to the Israeli government. In other words, the government of Israel was well aware of changes taking place within the PLO *vis-à-vis* their attitude towards recognising Israel in exchange for negotiations leading to Palestinian self-determination in the occupied territories. The question which must then be asked is: why did Israel not respond?

WHY THE GOVERNMENT TRIED TO END DIALOGUE

The answer to this complex question is fearfully simple: no Israeli government has ever been prepared to give up the occupied territories and above all to accept a *Palestinian* state in their place. Rabin did not put an end to dialogue but, as soon as it became apparent to him that such a dialogue might ultimately lead to negotiations – which in turn would have to lead to territorial concessions and Palestinian self-determination if peace were to be achieved – he made his opposition clear. If Labour was opposed to dialogue and its possible outcome, all the more so was the Likud. Yet, their victory in 1977 and again in 1981 did not bring an end to meetings between Israeli peace activists and the PLO as might have been expected. Firstly, this may have been because the dialogue was still limited to a small number of activists. Secondly, it was because the government did not have the legal means to prevent such meetings. However, when a growing number of Israelis began to participate and when it became increasingly apparent that dialogue could only lead to territorial compromise, the Likud's determination to end all Israeli contact with the PLO grew. The opportunity presented itself after the formation of the 'National Unity' government in 1984. Seeing Labour pushing hard for the legal means to combat racism, the Likud cleverly decided to ensure that such a law, dealing a blow to the 'extreme-right', be linked to one dealing a blow to the 'extreme-left' and thus end, once and for all, the 'dangerous' dialogue between peace activists and the PLO and *the subsequent danger of negotiations over the future of Eretz Yisrael.*

5 Ethnicity and the Peace Movement

If tempers ran high amongst Israeli Jews over the future of the occupied territories, they ran even higher over the Lebanon war. The clashes that took place between Peace Now and Gush Emunim on the West Bank soon faded in significance compared with those which took place between supporters and opponents of the Lebanon war. In the gravest incident, a hand-grenade was thrown into the midst of a Peace Now anti-war demonstration, killing Peace Now activist Emil Grunzweig. Although no arrest was made in the immediate aftermath of the attack, it was fairly evident to all that the grenade had been thrown from the midst of a group of counter-demonstrators who were presumed to be Mizrachim.

The attack, which left an acrimonious cloud hanging over the peace movement, had two significant effects. Firstly, it deepened the resolve and determination of many Peace Now activists: this was made evident by the large numbers who attended the memorial demonstrations held one week and one month after Grunzweig's death. He became the martyr of the movement; a memorial was erected near the place where he was killed and huge commemorative demonstrations were held on consecutive anniversaries of his death. Secondly, it led to a marked increase in inter-ethnic tensions, which soon resulted in the fragmentation of the peace movement along ethnic lines. This complex and vital question of ethnicity and the peace movement is the focus of this chapter.

THE FORMATION OF EAST FOR PEACE

The assumption that Mizrachim were responsible for the attack led to a wave of anti-Mizrachi rhetoric. A well-established stereotype, depicting Mizrachim as 'primitive, violent, haters of Arabs and

opponents of peace'[1], was once again unearthed and used to depict all
Mizrachim – regardless of their diverse attitudes and political positions. This greatly disturbed a number of Mizrachi peace activists who
had been at the demonstration – *on the Peace Now side of the barricades*
– and who were in fact long-standing supporters of the peace movement. Evidently, while it is not wrong to characterise the peace
movement as a *predominantly* Ashkenazi social movement, it is
certainly not *exclusively* so. This was made evident in the months
following the attack: Mizrachi peace activists made a concerted effort
to counteract the hawk stereotype by attending all the Peace Now
'memorial demonstrations' which followed Grunzweig's death. But to
no avail. Their presence apparently went unremarked. One leading
Mizrachi activist later complained: 'We were present but our presence
didn't change the stereotype. The fact remained, as it were, that all
Oriental Jews were in the other [pro-war] camp.'[2]

These Mizrachi activists felt that they had to act to save their
'dignity and honour' which had been brought into question when they,
as Mizrachim, were lumped together with the perpetrators of the
attack and accused of being Arab-haters and opponents of peace. To
counter the accusations, a group of Mizrachi activists organised a
series of meetings to prepare a text for publication emphasising their
commitment – *as Mizrachim* – to peace. These meetings generated
intensive discussion, attracting new Mizrachi participants as well as
media attention. It soon became clear to participants that they could
not simply refer to the 'hawk stereotype', as they felt this was only one
aspect of a complex range of issues confronting Mizrachim in Israel.
Although the intention had simply been to prepare and publish a
statement on peace, the stimulation of the discussion, the high degree
of consensus about general principles and the attention given by the
media, all led to the decision to form a distinct Mizrachi peace group
which would militate not simply for peace but also for social justice
and for nothing less than a fundamental reorienting of Israeli culture
and values.

The ideas of the new Mizrachi MO – called East for Peace – will
later be examined in depth. First, basic questions raised by the
violent attack on Peace Now, the depiction of Mizrachim as hawks
and the formation of an ethnic MO must be examined. What are
the origins of the hawk stereotype? What evidence is there to
support such a stereotype and, if it contains an element of truth,

what are the reasons for this? Why, indeed, is the peace movement predominantly Ashkenazi?

THE HAWK STEREOTYPE

A number of factors contributed to the depiction of Mizrachim as 'predisposed to parochialism, traditional religion, charismatic leadership, chauvinism, irrationality, messianism and intransigence'.[3] These can often be traced back to the first years of Israel's existence when the population was more than doubled by large 'waves' of immigrants. The majority of new immigrants were Mizrachim from different Arab countries (for a breakdown of numbers and countries see Figure 1).

Figure 1   Mizrachi Immigrants to Israel 1948–1972

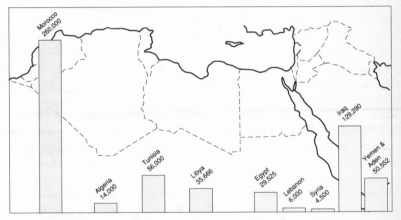

Source: M. Gilbert, *The Arab–Israeli Conflict: Its History in Maps*, (London: Weidenfeld and Nicolson, 1979).

They differed in fundamental ways from the Ashkenazi refugees from Europe and from the Ashkenazi 'old-timers' who handled their 'absorption'. Firstly, Mizrachi families tended to be large and extended; they placed far greater emphasis on the status of the father and strongly resisted changes in types of employment (often necessitated by the move to Israel) which threatened to undermine this status.[4] This resistance earned Mizrachim the reputation of being 'intransigent' and 'irrational'. The second factor which encouraged a negative stereotype was that many of the Mizrachi communities came without their secular intellectual élite. This was certainly the case with the North Africans. The well-educated, the trained technicians and the business men had chosen to make their homes in the West while Israel drew those who lacked both possessions and resources. This point is well illustrated by the fact that, by 1962, the University of Paris had among its *faculty* eighty-five Mizrachim of North African origin, while the Hebrew University of Jerusalem counted less than half that number of North Africans in its *student* body.[5] This, coupled with the low levels of modern, secular education of Mizrachim from Yemen, Kurdistan and rural North Africa, led absorption officials (and other Israeli Ashkenazim) to depict Mizrachim, in general, as 'primitive' and 'uncultured', with 'no appreciation of modern society'.

This aspect of the stereotype was reinforced by pronouncements made by prominent Ashkenazi leaders. Ben-Gurion, for example, called for the younger generation of Mizrachim to be 'imbued with the superior intellectual qualities of those who created the state' (that is the Ashkenazi socialist élite). He continued: 'If, Heaven forbid, we do not succeed, there is a danger that the coming generation may transform Israel into a Levantine state.'[6] Expressing a similar negative view of Mizrachim and a fear of 'Levantinisation', Abba Eban is quoted as having said: 'So far from regarding our immigrants from Oriental countries as a bridge towards our integration with the Arab-speaking world, our object should be to infuse them with an occidental spirit, rather than to allow them to drag us into an unnatural orientalism.'[7] Not only did Israel's élite portray Mizrachim as inferior and as part of a backward Levantine, but also they associated them with the Arab enemy. This appears to have occurred most frequently during the heat of the election campaigns. For example, in 1981, Labour party leader, Mordechai Gur, threatened Mizrachi hecklers saying: 'We will beat you as we beat the Arabs', while Shimon Peres called them 'Khomein-ists' and advised them to return to their countries of origin.[8]

In 1959, discontented Moroccan immigrants rioted in Wadi Salib – a poor (formerly Arab) quarter of Haifa. Although many Ashkenazim were apparently shocked to discover the extent of deprivation and discontent in some Mizrachi neighbourhoods, they were, perhaps, most taken aback by the actual outbreak of violence (Jew against Jew). After the riots the word 'Moroccan' became almost synonymous with 'aggressiveness' in the minds of many Israelis.[9] The 1959 riots, and other periodic outbreaks of violence in the Mizrachi neighbourhoods, greatly contributed to the development of the notion that Mizrachim were aggressive and prone to be violent.

Finally, once Mizrachi discontent began to translate into electoral support for the right-wing opposition, this was pointed to as firm evidence of their hawkish attitudes. The fact that people may vote for a party for reasons other than support for its ideology and electoral platform did not affect the development of the hawk stereotype – a stereotype which has been given a certain degree of credibility by some academic studies. These have unquestioningly accepted certain assumptions and have led to attempts to explain *why* Mizrachim are hawkish without first adequately proving that this is indeed the case. Before considering how East for Peace responded to the hawk stereotype, branded on Mizrachim *en masse*, the assumptions behind (and the basis for) the stereotype need to be examined.

PAST SUFFERING AND PRESENT ATTITUDES

In Israel, it is often said that Mizrachim as a whole are hawkish (or anti-Arab) because they suffered under Arab rule. As it stands, this simple explanation has considerable appeal and is frequently repeated. What truth does it hold? Is it at all valid? To answer these vital questions the history of Mizrachim in their countries of birth must be briefly explored. The intention here is not to offer a comprehensive historical account, but rather to illustrate the diversity of Mizrachi experience and to question the above argument.

DHIMMI IN SUNNI AND SHIITE LANDS

The first thing that emerges out of even the most casual reading of Mizrachi history is that their situations varied enormously from one region to another, in accordance with the economic and political conditions which prevailed. Their fortunes were closely tied to those of the local population. Under Islam, Jews, as a 'people of the book', were accorded a special status designed, on the one hand, to protect and, on the other, to humiliate. They shared this special status (*dhimmi*) with Christian minorities. Both were theoretically obliged, amongst other things, to wear distinctive clothes; were forbidden to carry arms or ride horses or build high houses (lest they looked down upon Muslims); and were obliged to pay a special poll-tax exempting them from military service. In practice, however, these Islamic laws were not strictly implemented in all Muslim lands. The extent of their implementation varied not only from country to country but also from ruler to ruler.[10]

To begin with, a clear distinction can be made between Sunni and Shiite lands. In the two areas where a Shiite majority governed – present day Iran and Yemen – the *dhimmi* laws were implemented with vigour. Furthermore, in these two areas, Jews were considered unclean. This increased their isolation, as communities, from the wider society. At times, imprisonment and torture followed refusals to convert. In one incident, in the seventeenth century, the Jews of Yemen were expelled for refusing to convert; they were later allowed to return when the craft industry collapsed as a result of their departure.[11] The Yemenite Jews were, with little doubt, amongst the most impoverished, mistreated and poorly educated (in modern western terms) of the Mizrachi communities. The fact that, before 1948, virtually all the women were illiterate illustrates how traditional the community had remained.

In the Sunni-dominated countries, the Islamic laws governing the treatment of the *dhimmi* were generally not implemented. Under the Ottoman Empire in particular, a Jewish commercial and diplomatic élite prospered. A certain class of Jews benefited from being part of a dispersed people. Their international links enabled them to trade profitably with the Christian lands of the North. In places like North Africa, the urbanisation of the Jews was encouraged by the Sultans who asked wealthy Jews to help them develop commerce. Not only did the Jewish élite serve the Sultans as traders and bankers, they also played the role of diplomats, forming an essential 'neutral' bridge between the Muslim lands of the South and the Christian North.[12]

The commercial importance of the Mizrachim was also recognised and exploited by European nations competing for commerce and influence in the Middle East and North Africa. They valued the language skills and knowledge of the countries which the Jews were able to use to bring commercial success. In return for their services, the consuls afforded the Jews 'consular protection', which applied to matters of 'personal status, worship and trade as well as guaranteeing fiscal and legal privileges'. In this way the Jews became instruments of European penetration into Muslim lands.

In 1839, the Ottomans extended equal rights to all minorities. Under this decree, Turkish Jews received appointments as judges and university lecturers and as civil servants in the police, treasury and ministry of education. It is reported that government and private banks were sometimes closed, on Jewish holidays, at the request of the Jews and that, in 1864, 'the Turkish authorities made a grant for the purchase of Passover *mazzot* (unleavened bread) and wine for the poor, notwithstanding the fact that wine is forbidden to Muslims and Turkey was at that time a religious Muslim state.'[13] This event was obviously highly exceptional and is cited only because it underlines the vast differences between Jewish life in Sunni and Shiite lands.

Admittedly, the privileges the Sultans accorded to a Jewish élite in Sunni lands led to a degree of popular resentment. It was in the Sultans' commercial and diplomatic interests to foster close relations with a Jewish élite. They knew they could depend on the loyalty of Jews, who were unarmed and sought their protection, and they often used trusted Jewish officials to exploit the local population. The people, who already resented the fact that the *dhimmis* had been allowed to assume high office, ride horses and prosper economically, were known to take vengeance against an exploitive Sultan by attacking 'his' *dhimmis*.[14] Matters were not helped by the Jewish élite's relations with foreign Christian powers. Given the occasion, they would openly side with an invading European power: the local Jews supported Napoleon when he conquered Egypt in 1798; they supported the French in 1830 when they invaded and colonised Algeria and they celebrated the arrival of the British in Iraq. In Egypt, the French employed Jews and Copts as translators and tax collectors and permitted them to sell wine, which later led to rioting in Cairo. When French rule abruptly ended in 1801, the local Muslim population, not surprisingly, took vengeance on the Jews.[15] Such attacks were, fortunately, few and far between.

Mizrachi Jews were, on the whole, tolerated as a *religious* minority. The expulsion of the Jews from Yemen in the seventeenth century is the only recorded case of mass expulsion of Jews from a Muslim country before the creation of the State of Israel.[16] The contrast between this and Europe's long history of expulsions is striking. Generally speaking, it would seem that *religious* minorities were tolerated in Muslim countries while *national* minorities – such as

Greeks, Armenians and Kurds – were not. This point can be illustrated by the example of Iraq.

In Iraq, religious minorities were not harmed, while nationalist minorities, such as the Kurds and the Assyrians (with possible foreign loyalties and/or separatist tendencies) were perceived as a threat and were hence more likely to be mistreated. The Jews of Iraq were, for centuries, considered to be a religious minority. They were amongst the most ancient and prosperous of Mizrachi communities. The Ottoman laws of 1839 regarding minorities applied in Iraq, thus enabling Jews to become citizens. They ceased to pay the special poll-tax, were represented in parliament, appointed to government courts and municipal councils. They served as civil servants and judges. In fact, a Jew was appointed Minister of Finance from 1920 to 1925. There were no restrictions on religious practices or on entering institutes of higher learning. From 1921 until 1929 the government even allowed an active Zionist society to function.

The arrival of refugees from Palestine in the late 1920s led to anti-Zionist demonstrations (one of which was broken up by the government in 1928) which sometimes resulted in attacks on individual Jews. Aware of these events and concerned by their implications, thirty-three Jewish dignitaries in Baghdad expressed their open opposition to Zionism in an attempt to dissociate the Iraqi Jews from the Zionist activities in Palestine. In 1941, events in Palestine and the presence of Palestinian refugees and of German Nazis, led to a rise in anti-Jewish sentiment which became most clearly manifest in the Baghdad Pogrom which left 170–180 dead. Although the pogrom was an exceptional event, which took place during a transition of government and was comparatively minor in European terms, it marked a clear change in the Arab perception of the Jews, from a religious to a nationalist minority. The change was perhaps most radical at the level of government; their previously protective attitude changed rapidly following the rise of Zionism, the conflict in Palestine and finally the creation of the State of Israel.

With the declaration of Israeli independence, martial law was imposed throughout Iraq. Iraq was at war with Israel and the Jews of Iraq, who had been part of the nation since the destruction of Jerusalem and the exile of their forefathers to Babylonia in 568 BCE, became, overnight, potential Zionists and hence enemies of the nation. The Iraqi government acted to prevent Jewish banks from engaging in currency transfers; import and export licences were reduced and many suspected 'Zionists' were arrested.

This dramatic change in the attitude of the government was to contribute largely to the sudden mass exodus of the Iraqi Jews to Israel, in 1950, when the government permitted them to leave. Within weeks, over two and a half thousand years of Jewish cultural achievement and prosperity came to an abrupt end, bringing 129,290 new Mizrachi immigrants to Israel.[17]

THE SPECIAL CASE OF MOROCCAN MIZRACHIM

While the Jews in the Arab states closest to Palestine may have suffered as a direct result of the outbreak of hostilities, those in the Maghreb were less affected. However, even here conditions differed considerably from one country to another.

In Algeria, which became a full French colony, the Jews were eventually rewarded for their decision to support the French invasion of 1830 when, in 1870, they were awarded full French citizenship. This gave the Algerian Jews considerable political influence, often resented by the Radical and Socialist parties because the Jews tended to vote for the rightist parties. Despite periodic waves of *French* anti-semitism, the Algerian Jews prospered politically, economically and socially. Very few left Algeria after the creation of the State of Israel. Most stayed there until their sudden departure, with the French, in the last few weeks preceding Algerian independence.[18]

In Morocco things were very different. The country became a French protectorate rather than a colony. The Jews, during the years of French rule (1912–56), did not acquire French citizenship and were almost completely excluded from the country's political life. Nevertheless, in socio-economic terms, French rule began a period of rapid transition for the Moroccan Jews. Industrialisation brought rapid urbanisation and proletarianisation. Jewish petty craftsmen were ruined by the competition of large-scale manufacturers – leading to widespread unemployment. These developments, plus the growth in French education, led to a breakdown in the traditional Jewish social structure: extended patriarchal families were broken up, learning became divorced from religion; spirituality and mysticism were challenged by materialism and rationality.

Despite the difficulties brought by rapid change, the overall situation of the Jews improved under French rule – certainly *vis-à-vis* the Arabs. However, because they were not fully accepted by the French, the Jews became a monolithic block caught between the French élite and the Muslim masses – accepted by neither but a vital link between the two.[19] There can be little doubt that these rather unique circumstances left their mark on the Moroccan Jews, who later became the largest Mizrachi immigrant group to move to Israel (260,000).[20]

Once in Israel, the Moroccans reacted in a distinct way to the experience of 'absorption' – as it was optimistically called by the Ashkenazi establishment. They observed that, once again, they were caught between two ethnic 'blocks' to which they did not belong – the Arabs and the Ashkenazim. They appeared to be more conscious of their status *vis-à-vis* the Arabs than other Mizrachim and resisted more strongly the transition to manual work that occurred for many in Israel. One Moroccan immigrant said to Eisenstadt: 'I do not want to do here all the things that only the Arab riff-raff did in Morocco. I did not come to Israel to be like one of them. We are better than them. We are stronger – why should I do all this manual labour . . . at home they would laugh at me for this.'[21] Indeed, although most Mizrachi immigrants experienced harsh economic conditions on arrival in Israel, the Moroccans appear to have felt particularly bitter about their position. This was recorded by the historian André Chouraqui who noted at the time:

> There is a difference between being poor and being the most poor. In North Africa the Jews, as a group, had been the poor but they had not been the most poor. The poorest, the most famished, the worst off, the sickest, were the Arabs. Even the most miserable Jew might feel himself king in comparison with the penury he could see all around him. And, even for the most wretched among them, there was always the hope that he might profit on some little deal with an Arab . . . In Israel, however, the North African Jews are, as a group, the poorest. The Arabs of Israel are much better off. The North Africans, perhaps because they were the last to arrive, are the poorest, and the least accepted. As such they feel themselves entrapped with no apparent escape.[22]

Unlike the Yemenites, who came with high messianic expectations, the Moroccans, whose upward social and economic mobility had been blocked by the French, came to Israel with high expectations for social and economic success. In Israel they found no resolution to the problems faced in Morocco, partly because they were inadequately equipped to exploit opportunities, and partly because of their disdain for manual labour. Objectively, conditions may have been better in Israel but, because their expectations and aspirations were high, disappointment and dissatisfaction were great. With this in mind, it is not surprising that, when riots eventually broke out in 1959, they were primarily Moroccan.

With such varied backgrounds, what conclusions are we to reach about the alleged link between past suffering and present day attitudes of Mizrachim?

Although cases of mass expulsion were rare in the Muslim world, it is not difficult to catalogue lists of periodic attacks on Jewish life and property, which escalated dramatically between 1941 and 1948, as well as cases of harsh injustice and the rigid and humiliating implementation of the *dhimmi* laws. This has, in fact, been done in different Israeli-backed publications (distributed by Israeli Embassies abroad) which stress Jewish suffering in Arab countries to score political propaganda points. Yet, even these admit that Jews were sometimes treated better in Arab countries than they were in Europe.[23] There is hardly any point in over-emphasising this fact by providing an account of the mass expulsions, pogroms and acts of genocide perpetrated against the Jews of Europe; however, it might be appropriate to recall that, at different times, Muslim countries became places of refuge for European Jews fleeing persecution. The best-known example of this is, of course, the expulsion of the Sephardim from Spain, where they had prospered for generations under tolerant Muslim rule. They spread throughout the Middle East, bringing new life to ancient Mizrachi communities. A lesser-known case is that of Turkey, which not only received a large number of the Sephardim expelled from Spain, but went on to serve as a place of refuge for centuries, for Jews fleeing Eastern European pogroms. On the eve of the Second World War, the government refused to yield to pressure to prevent Jewish refugees coming to Turkey – or passing through it on the way to Palestine.[24] Suffering there may have been, but equally there was considerable tolerance, security and even, for an élite, prosperity.

The sudden departure of the Mizrachim for Israel has often been attributed to persecution, which can then be used to explain hawkish attitudes. Writer Maurice Roumani suggests that the Mizrachim left for Israel *because* they were confronted with a political and social climate of intensified and unbearable hostility.[25] This may have been true for certain Mizrachi groups (such as the Iraqis) but it conceals the fact that this was not universally the case. Indeed, research done precisely on reasons for emigrating to Israel demonstrates that only 23 per cent of the largest Mizrachi immigrant group (the North Africans) moved to Israel because of political events or out of fear of the Arabs. The majority emigrated for a wide variety of reasons unrelated to persecution or suffering: 7.1 per cent for economic reasons or children's education; 8.9 per cent because 'everyone else' was moving; 5.8 per cent to join family already in Israel; 6.8 per cent because of 'Zionist propaganda' and the remaining 33.2 per cent for 'ideological reasons'.[26]

EXPLAINING THE ATTITUDES OF ISRAELI-BORN MIZRACHIM

Those who blindly accept the assumption that Mizrachim as a whole suffered before immigrating, are left with the difficulty of explaining why those Mizrachim who have never lived under Arab rule hold hawkish attitudes. One would expect to find a softening of attitude amongst the Israeli-born generation; however research reveals that this is not the case: on the contrary, a hardening of attitudes has taken place *vis-à-vis* the Arabs amongst young Israelis as a whole.

When compared with their parents, young Israelis are clearly more hawkish. They hold more negative attitudes towards the Arabs and the establishment of personal and social relations with them; they are more inclined than the population as a whole to retain the occupied territories and show a high degree of consensus on annexation. Research reveals a clear relationship between parents' education and children's attitudes: the higher the level of parents' education, the more moderate and open the attitudes of the children. Lower education is correlated with more hawkish attitudes in the second generation.

Despite a growth in the standards of education, intergenerational shifts in attitude have tended to be from dovish to hawkish rather than the contrary. Researchers have come to the conclusion that attitudes of young people are heavily influenced by 'immersion in the continuing state of tension, violence and war with the Arabs'. All their evidence indicates that hawkishness, far from being related to country of origin, is directly related to socio-economic factors and more so to growing up in a society at war with its neighbours, where tension and violence prevail.[27]

Following in-depth interviews with over six hundred Mizrachim in 1986, researcher Amiel Alcalay did not find even one case of parents who were more right-wing than their Israeli-born and educated children. He noted that the children viewed their family's past experience (in their countries of origin) more negatively than their parents and affirmed that the hawkishness of young Mizrachim is related to their Israeli upbringing. This, he argues, stems from their 'insecure identity and ambivalence about their place in Israeli society' which leads to a tendency to 'overcompensate', to be 'more Israeli than the Israelis'. In other words, 'once this generation perceives that hostility towards Arabs is not only condoned but may, in fact, serve as a kind of extrance ticket to the mainstream, they use their vague and incomplete picture of their family's past . . . to assert that they really know "how it is with the Arabs"'. As Alcalay so correctly concludes, research does not prove that anti-Arab attitudes are handed down from one generation to the next within the family; rather, it demonstrates that, 'people mould one aspect of an imperfectly grasped past experience in order to assert their own status within the given and prevalent stereotypes and biases of the society at large.'[28]

If suffering was not universal for Mizrachim living under Islam, if reasons for departure to Israel do not always correlate with persecution and if Israeli-born Mizrachim are more hawkish than their parents, we may reasonably conclude that the allegation that Mizrachim are hawkish because they suffered under Arab rule is a gross and misleading over-simplification.

MIZRACHI ELECTORAL SUPPORT FOR THE RIGHT

Another frequently heard argument, used to 'prove' that Mizrachim are hawkish, is that they vote for right-wing parties. That the majority of Mizrachim support right-wing parties – most notably the Likud – is beyond question. The steady rise of Mizrachi electoral support for the Likud since the early sixties, resulting in the defeat of Labour in the political 'earthquake' of 1977, has been noted and discussed by social scientists at great length.[29] While *electoral* support for the right is indisputable, a number of facts should be noted. Firstly, not all Mizrachi immigrant groups support the right. In fact, 54 per cent of the Iraqi Jews voted for the Labour alignment in the 1981 elections.[30] Secondly, many Mizrachim who voted for the Likud opposed the party's hawkish policy of settling the West Bank.[31] Clearly, voting for a party with hawkish policies does not prove an individual's adoption of that party's position: people vote for a particular party for a wide variety of reasons – some of which have little to do with the party's official platform. One simple reason is that the rest of their community votes for that particular party. Researchers studying the 1981 elections – when voting along ethnic lines intensified – noted that great pressure was exerted upon members of the community to vote as the majority did. Once voting patterns begin to polarise along ethnic lines, the process tends to perpetuate itself.[32]

Professor Shlomo Elbaz, a founder of East for Peace, holds that Mizrachi support for the right has 'no ideological weight', but is rather the outcome of 'passing circumstances'. Pointing out that the great majority of Mizrachim are not even familiar with the doctrines of Jabotinsky, Elbaz asserts that Mizrachim 'went to Herut in protest against the entire Labour regime which had generated embitterment and frustration among them.'[33] The long-term durability of Mizrachi electoral support for the right remains to be tested. However, in the meantime, a significant body of literature has emerged, affirming the assertion that the shift of Mizrachi votes to the Likud developed as a form of protest against the Labour establishment – not because the Mizrachim necessarily endorsed the hawkish policies of the opposition.

From these works, a general consensus emerges depicting the following: Mizrachi families and communities suffered years of humiliation and relative deprivation in transit camps, isolated 'development towns' and impoverished urban quarters while Ashkenazi immigrants, with the help of Ashkenazi Labour party members, moved rapidly on from transit camps to prosperity in kibbutzim and the upper-class suburbs of Tel Aviv, Haifa and Jerusalem. The Mizrachi fathers' skills were very often not adapted to the needs of the Israeli economy, forcing them to give up cherished forms of self-employment and become salaried manual workers; unemployment and the low income of the fathers led to their children giving up school at an early age to supplement family income – thus perpetuating the disadvantages of the Mizrachim into the second generation after immigration. The Mizrachim did not share the Ashkenazi socialist notion of the 'redemptive' power of manual labour and found the manual work they were expected to do demeaning. At the same time, little respect was shown for Mizrachi culture while the religious authority of their rabbis was undermined by secular Ashkenazi school teachers and absorption officials. With dissatisfaction, they observed the growing affluence of Labour kibbutzim. They began to resent Labour's control, not only of government but also of institutions such as the Histadrut (Israel's massive trade union which also runs the health service and is itself an industrial giant). They came to feel increasingly alienated by the dominant, secular version of Zionist ideology, advanced by the Labour establishment and rooted in Ashkenazi experience which they did not share. In time Mizrachim threw off the yoke of their dependence on Labour – rejecting at the same time Labour's socialist version of Zionism which had been 'forced' on them – and turning instead to support the strongly nationalistic Herut led by Begin.

Although Mizrachi support for the Revisionists can be traced back to the days of the Mandate, the bulk of Mizrachim only began to vote in large numbers for the right in the late sixties and seventies.[34] This 'delayed reaction' against Labour is attributed to a number of factors.

To begin with, the occupation of the territories opened up new markets and provided a vast cheap labour reserve. This led to an economic boom which provided a degree of economic independence and upward mobility for many Mizrachim, which had interesting results. Firstly, they came to favour the occupation, *not because they desired to settle the territories* but because the influx of cheap Arab labour meant that many of them no longer had to do the work of the 'Arab riff-raff'. In ten years the number of Arab migrant workers increased tenfold to 215,800.[35] The majority of these were unskilled labourers who found work in agriculture and construction, where they replaced what had previously been a predominantly Mizrachi work force. Author Amos Oz recorded the remark of a Mizrachi worker that appears to reflect popular Mizrachi thinking on the question of the occupation: 'If they give back the territories, the Arabs will stop coming to work, and then you [Ashkenazim] will put us back into the dead-end jobs, like before. If for no other reason, we won't let you give back those territories.'[36] Fearing that Labour might make territorial concessions for peace, Mizrachim began to vote against the party in subsequent elections. Then, economic betterment diminished their personal dependence upon Labour-run governmental and administrative organisations with regard to matters of employment, housing and social services.[37] This newly-found freedom allowed them to express their resentment politically.

Delayed protest is also attributed to Mizrachi observations of how Ashkenazi newcomers, who arrived in the 1970s from places such as the Soviet Union, seemed to fare very much better than they had after immigrating. A third reason given is that the Yom Kippur War exposed the military unpreparedness and weakness of the Labour regime. This shocked Israelis as a whole, but it appears to have dashed much of the remaining trust that Mizrachim had in Labour. At the same time, the war produced new military heroes – notably General Ariel Sharon, who was acclaimed as 'King of Israel' by many Mizrachim.[38]

As past suffering and right-wing voting are not adequate explanations for the alleged hawkish and anti-Arab attitudes of Mizrachim, we must look elsewhere.

IDENTITY, INTEGRATION AND ATTITUDES

On arrival in Israel, many Mizrachim suffered something of an identity crisis. Not only was the world that they had left often totally different from the one to which they had come, but it was frequently at odds – and occasionally at war – with their new homeland. The world from which they had come was regarded with disdain by the Ashkenazi establishment. Not only did they come from the land of the enemy, they often actually resembled him. Many were 'cursed' with the mother tongue of the Arabs; they came wearing similar dress; they ate the same kinds of food and enjoyed 'Oriental' music. Speaking Arabic may have served as an advantage for those who found work with the security forces but, for the majority, it appears to have been little more than an embarrassment. This was particularly true of the second generation who usually refused to use Arabic to communicate with their parents, thus revealing to what extent they had accepted and 'internalised' the prevailing negative view of things 'Oriental'.

From the point of view of the Ashkenazi establishment, the 'absorption' and 'integration' of immigrants was a top priority. The 'ingathering of the exiles' is a central value justifying the very creation of the Jewish state, and underlying this value is the belief that the Jews form a single nation. Ethnic differences, more than any other, threatened to undermine the basis of Jewish nationhood: the antidote adopted by the state was the 're-socialisation' of immigrants which was intended to result in their successful 'absorption' and 'integration'.

Although all newcomers who arrived in Israel in the decade following the foundation of the state 'were treated as diaspora Jews who needed to be taught to be Israelis', Mizrachim were considered to be in 'greater need of re-socialisation' than others.[39] For some, this process began with literally being disinfected on arrival. From there followed a lengthy process at the end of which they were implicitly expected to have adopted the norms and values of the dominant group.[40]

With their own cultural heritages 'denigrated as contemptible products of Diaspora, or as retrograde superstitions, unworthy of the new, modern Israeli', many Mizrachim confined expressions of their own cultures to religious or family spheres of activity, or altogether rejected any aspects of their culture.[41]

The close association of Mizrachim with the Orient and the culture of the Arab enemy, combined with their own desire to integrate into the mainstream of Israeli life, led many Mizrachim to distance themselves as much as possible from the Arabs; this was particularly true for the Moroccans who, for reasons already explained, were highly conscious of their status *vis-à-vis* the 'Arab block'. In fact, the adoption of visibly hawkish attitudes appeared to many Mizrachim to be 'a golden opportunity for integration, a chance to prove that they are genuine patriots, clinging to their [new] homeland's central mores'.[42]

With the weakening and delegitimisation of the Labour regime, Mizrachi electoral support began to shift to the right-wing Ashkenazi leaders who stressed patriotic values, military prowess, the need to 'keep the Arabs in their place' and to unite all the Jews in a 'Greater Israel'. At the same time Mizrachim began to reject the notion that their participation in Israeli society was conditional upon their re-socialisation and their adoption of the predominant value system. This went hand in hand with the rejection of many of the universal components of Labour ideology which had their roots in European socialist thought. Many denied that 'in order to become Israelis, Oriental Jews should first uncritically embrace Western values and abandon and denigrate their own culture.'[43] Mizrachim began to redefine the criteria for participation in the national community; no longer was it necessary to adhere to the universal aspects of European Zionism; now, to be a Jew – of whatever culture – was enough. This rejection of the universal components of Zionist ideology, while stemming from quite different motives, converged with the growing particular outlook in other sectors of Israeli society discussed in the first chapter. In stressing particular values, Jewish unity, Israeli patriotism and strength *vis-à-vis* the Arabs, the Ashkenazi leaders of the Likud were able to capture the support of the hundreds of thousands of Mizrachim disillusioned not simply with economic hardship, but with Labour's whole policy of re-socialisation and 'absorption' into an Ashkenazi-moulded society with a 'built-in' socialist ideology.

MIZRACHI DOVES

If anything can prove that Mizrachim are not 'innately conservative' or universally hawkish, it is the various examples of Mizrachi left-wing or 'dovish' protest groups.

The Black Panthers

The best-known Mizrachi protest group is probably the Israeli Black Panthers. Although their story is fairly well-known, it is worthy of special attention here for a number of reasons: firstly, they were one of the first radical protest groups in Israel to attract national and international attention. In fact, they inaugurated an age of extra-parliamentary protest politics which has yet to end; secondly, their revolt was distinctly left-wing and dovish – quite contrary to the right-wing shift amongst other Mizrachim discussed previously; thirdly, they were one of the first groups to strongly condemn the poverty of Mizrachim and the degradation of their culture. Finally, the group was primarily Moroccan. As we shall soon see, all these characteristics (other than the first) can be attributed to East for Peace, with the essential difference being that the Black Panthers were not middle class or intellectuals – far from it.

The Black Panthers emerged out of one of Jerusalem's poorest Mizrachi neighbourhoods – Musrara. All came from large, impoverished families. Most had police records for petty crimes and long associations with special institutions and social workers – technically speaking, they were delinquents. Having police records, they were rejected by the army; having not been in the army they were often refused employment. None of the Black Panthers had any formal education worthy of mention. Like many Mizrachim of their class, they felt frustrated and rejected.

A small group of these young 'delinquents' used to meet to read the newspapers to keep abreast of events. One day, they were struck by an article on the kidnapping of an ambassador carried out by slum dwellers in Tupamaros, Uruguay, whose conditions of poverty they felt were the same as theirs. According to Sa'adia Marciano, who later became a leading member of the Black Panthers, they were struck by the fact that the ambassador had not been kidnapped for a ransom, but rather to demand that their neighbourhood be cleaned up and that food be brought in for the poor. Marciano and his friends were amazed that a group of poor 'delinquents' could put pressure on their government to obtain something for themselves.

This realisation of the possible uses of protest action to affect government policy, was the grain which eventually germinated and grew into one of Israel's most successful protest groups. After reading the article, a number of the friends suggested forming a group to be named 'Tupamarocanos' because the majority of them came from Morocco. This was rejected because the group did not want to exclude non-Moroccans. Later, the name Black Panthers was chosen (after the American group), primarily for its shock appeal.

At about this time, a friend of Marciano's was caught trying to sell a set of stolen records by a friend of the rightful owner. Marciano was taken with his friend to confront the owner. Much to their surprise the owner, instead of taking them to the police, invited them in for coffee. They sat and talked. Marciano explained that his friend (the thief) had no records of his own and that he came from one of the poorest houses of their neighbourhood. Again, to their surprise, the owner seemed to understand. He told Marciano that he knew about their poverty and began to discuss with them problems which interested them greatly. According to Marciano, the Ashkenazi record owner told them they should 'organise' in their neighbourhoods to create groups. Marciano and his young friend began to appreciate that outsiders could understand their problems and were interested in helping them. The discussion lasted a few hours and they became friends. This rather remarkable friendship led to introductions to a wide circle of people (mostly Ashkenazi leftists) the likes of which the 'delinquents' had never met before: students, academics and journalists. They played an important role in the politicisation of the Black Panthers, encouraging the group to organise in the poor Mizrachi neighbourhoods and to demonstrate in the city to draw national attention to the plight of the Mizrachim. The result was to be a series of demonstrations and Robin Hood-type, media-oriented events, inspired by the original Tupamaros. On one occasion the Black Panthers stole milk from the affluent Ashkenazi suburb of Rehavia – which they then distributed in the poor, predominantly Mizrachi neighbourhoods.

From the outset the group was highly successful in capturing media and official attention. Within weeks of the first demonstration, Golda Meir, then Prime Minister, along with the Ministers of National Education and Social Affairs, arranged to meet with the Black Panthers. Their demonstrations had touched upon an ultra-sensitive political minefield – social and economic inequality along ethnic lines and possible Mizrachi revolt in response to it. State officials, with the co-operation of some traditional Moroccan leaders, attempted to defuse the situation by co-opting the leadership of the Black Panthers. They were offered 'financial aid' (basically an official bribe) if they dropped the name 'Black Panthers' and joined the 'Alliance des Immigrants du Maroc'. Others were invited to join neighbourhood councils or work on youth and community projects. Some Panthers accepted, but the majority refused and the demonstrations continued.[44]

Certain aspects of the Black Panther revolt are pertinent to our discussion. Firstly, their protests often ended up in violent confrontations between police and protestors and between demonstrators and counter-demonstrators (the Black Panthers clashed with members of the extreme right-wing Jewish Defence League as early as 1972).[45] Israel had never before witnessed anything of the kind. Although they were highly successful in drawing attention to the problems of poverty, low education, delinquency and lack of political representation experienced by Mizrachim (and in promoting government action), they also succeeded in reinforcing the stereotype that Mizrachim were violent.

Secondly, the Black Panthers never took an anti-Arab stance. On the contrary they linked their immediate conditions of poverty to the broader Arab–Israeli conflict and the cost of the conflict. In 1975, four years after their appearance on the national political stage, the Black Panthers called for the establishment of a separate Palestinian state 'with Sephardi Jews, possessing a cultural background strongly influenced by living among Arabs, acting as a bridge for co-existence between them'.[46] It is interesting to note, however, that the Black Panthers were critical of left-wing, Ashkenazi-dominated groups which attempted to gain the support of the Mizrachim by linking their poverty to the expense of the Arab–Israeli conflict and the settlement of the West Bank, *but* did little to combat the actual conditions of poverty. The Panthers claimed to first tackle the questions of immediate poverty before talking to people about the links between their poverty and the broader questions of war and peace.

Thirdly, it is worth noting that, besides condemning expenditure on the occupation and settlement of the West Bank – in lieu of social development in Israel – the Black Panthers went on to raise questions about the suppression of Mizrachi culture which was virtually official policy. In 1974 a leading Black Panther activist, Shalom Cohen, stated: 'One of Israel's mistakes years ago was to get Oriental immigrants to break away from their Islamic culture . . . it was a fatal mistake, for Western Israeli culture hasn't succeeded in replacing what they gave up.'[47]

The Black Panther movement began to lose momentum in the mid-to-late seventies. This was due, in part, to political differences which split the leadership three ways during the 1977 elections. Some joined Rakah, which then became the Democratic Front for Peace and Equality; Marciano joined the left-wing Sheli party and eventually obtained a Knesset seat through a rotation which was to split the party; others joined Dash – none joined right-wing parties.

As individuals, the Black Panthers continued to be active in various ways. Some joined a new radical organisation called Ohel which, between 1979 and 1980, actively opposed Begin's policy of settling the West Bank. Like the Black Panthers, Ohel made use of dramatic media-oriented events to press home their demand that money be spent on poor Mizrachi neighbourhoods in Israel proper – and not on Jewish settlements in the occupied territories. In August 1979, Ohel activists occupied an abandoned Youth Aliya school on the outskirts of Jerusalem, claiming that: 'Settlement is the only way to get money out of this government.'[48] In June 1980, they organised a pre-dawn Gush Emunim type settlement, consisting of tents, on government-owned land (within the 1967 line) declaring: 'We have decided to act in the only way effective in Israel . . . the way of Gush Emunim, courage, *hutzpah*, ignoring certain norms, faith in one's goal, and settlement.'[49] In 1985, Marciano and others devoted their energy to the production of two short anti-racist films (funded by the Jerusalem municipality and the Labour party) designed primarily to alert Mizrachim to the degree of Kahanism. In an interview about one of the films (entitled 'Kahanism and the Cuckoo's Nest'), Marciano argued that:

> Kahanism is a social disease and the saddest thing is that so many [Mizrachim] don't realise they're infected. . . . Don't they realise he [Kahane] is our enemy as well as that of the Arabs? . . . We speak the same language, enjoy the same music and eat the same foods. Whoever thinks that Kahane will stop at Moslem and Christian Arabs had better think again; the Jewish Arabs are the next on his list.[50]

East for Peace

As noted at the beginning of this chapter, East for Peace began with the coming together of Mizrachi intellectuals whose initial aim was to publish a manifesto that would challenge the hawk stereotype. It is important to stress that the MO has not developed much beyond the original circle of intellectuals who helped prepare the manifesto. The MO has not been able to 'mobilise the masses' as it hoped and sincerely believed it would. There are numerous reasons for this. The reason given by group members is invariably lack of funds. They claim that, without funds, they cannot campaign on a large scale for members and, without members, they cannot raise money to campaign. This may indeed be a good reason; however, it seems that even with sufficient funds, the group would be unlikely to expand significantly. It does not require funds to start a successful social movement. Social movements form in a spontaneous manner – they cannot be orchestrated. The problem with East for Peace is evidently not simply a lack of finances as its members suggest.

The first reason why East for Peace has been unable to 'mobilise the masses' is because the MO was immediately (and correctly) perceived to be dominated by intellectuals. Even 'natural allies', like Black Panther leader Marciano, were reluctant to join the MO even though it advocated ideas which the Black Panthers had promoted. When Marciano was asked why he hadn't joined, he described East for Peace as an intellectual Moroccan 'salon', whose members had bought a few Moroccan carpets and now sat around drinking mint tea talking about 'Eastern Culture'![51] East for Peace believed that it would succeed in mobilising Mizrachim where Peace Now and others failed because, as Mizrachim, they were accepted in the Mizrachi neighbourhoods as 'part of the people'. According to poetess Shelly Elkayam, a founding member: 'They accept us as their representatives because we are part of them . . . we don't patronise them or tell them what to say. We discuss with them as equals and listen.' While the MO's founders may have felt a sense of acceptance, they failed, as did other MOs before them, to bridge the class divide between them and working-class Mizrachim – who may have accepted them, but were certainly not prepared to join them.

Although the founders of East for Peace were 'part of the people' in ethnic terms, they were not a grass-roots neighbourhood group. Unlike the Black Panthers, East for Peace was made up almost exclusively of outsiders. Shlomo Elbaz and others in the group arrived in Israel in the early 1960s. They formed part of a group of young Moroccan intellectuals (called Oden) who were recruited by Ben-Gurion's government to come to Israel to study and ultimately, it was hoped, to act as the leaders of the North African community. Jacques Pinto, who was brought to Israel on the Oden programme and later joined East for Peace, believes that Oden members made the mistake of looking down on the Panthers as the 'violent ones' instead of helping them. This may explain why East for Peace has received little support from neighbourhood groups.

Pinto recognises the fact that East for Peace has had virtually no impact on the political scene and that it remains primarily an intellectuals' 'salon'. Yet he continues to support the group for two significant reasons. Firstly, because the mere fact of its existence challenges the prevailing stereotype. Secondly, because of what he calls the 'Mediterranean element'.

This idea was inspired by the writings of Albert Camus who, after

the Second World War, opposed the division of states into two major
super-power blocs. According to Pinto, Albert Camus 'wanted to find
a third way, that of Mediterranean man; the man who would not be
caught up in the ideology of the *goulag* (a Soviet-term for a
concentration camp); the man for whom there exists a certain limit –
a human limit.' Pinto considered the idea of 'Mediterranean man' as a
way to link the diverse people of the Mediterranean shores, as a means
of transcending the boundaries of nationalism dividing Israel from its
neighbours.

His original idea was to create a Centre for Mediterranean Studies
'to approach the countries that surround us some way other than with
a gun'. Pinto argued that, to survive, Israel had to recognise that it was
an integral part of the Orient, not the Occident, and accept that its
destiny was linked to that of its neighbours, not to Europe or
America.[52]

This idea emerged as one of the two key ideas that were to
distinguish East for Peace from Peace Now and the main body of the
peace movement. In their manifesto, East for Peace declare their
loyalty to Jewish and Zionist values; while denouncing oppression and
racism towards the Arabs as well as 'every act of settlement likely to
endanger the chances for peace'. Like Peace Now, they insist that the
'physical borders of Israel shall be determined in such a way as to
maintain its Jewish nature and democratic character.' However, to
these basic ideas, the group attach two further dimensions which other
groups have largely ignored. The first of these is social justice. Quite
simply, it is felt that there can be no social justice for the Mizrachim
without peace, and that peace itself is dependent on social justice. This
is evidently not a radical new idea. As we saw, the Black Panthers
stressed the link between their poverty and the costs of the larger
conflict. East for Peace could hardly ignore the 'social gap' between
Mizrachim and Ashkenazim and expect to attract popular support. But
they went a step further: they argued that, while social justice and peace
are interrelated, both are *dependent* on what the group calls the
'Eastern dimension'. In the words of Shlomo Elbaz: 'There is no peace
possible, whatsoever, there is no social justice possible without the
recognition, without the acceptance of what we call the "Eastern
dimension" of our existence.'[53]

The 'Eastern dimension' is contrasted with the Western character
that Israel has come to assume. East for Peace insists that Israelis must

recognise that their country is an integral part of the East and must cease to deny facts that are determined by geography and history. Elbaz made the point that:

> As long as we reject the East, we will never be able to do what has to be done towards peace. As long as we see ourselves as Western . . . in defiance of the simple, visible facts of life . . . our neighbours will see in us a foreign body, and so it's indispensable and urgent that we change orientation and let it be oriented Orientally!

It is not easy to ascertain in practical terms exactly how one becomes a 'Mediterranean man', or exactly what an acceptance of the 'Eastern dimension' implies. To begin with, for East for Peace, it appears to imply a concerted effort to oppose the negation of all things Oriental – including the 'Orientals'. Anti-Mizrachi public statements, made by Ashkenazi politicians and leaders, are most strongly condemned. The MO strives to combat all anti-Mizrachi sentiment (which it tends to see as being an extension of anti-Arab and anti-Oriental sentiment) by improving the image Israelis have of the East.

The first concrete step the group took in this direction was the establishment of a small publishing house which markets publications promoting a positive view of the East. The group attempts to persuade Mizrachi educators and members of the media to do likewise. They also hold symposia to analyse and discuss problems emerging from the 'Levantisation' of Israel. They stand for the promotion of complete bilingualism, believing that,

> as long as the Arab language is not spoken by Jews to the extent that the Hebrew language is spoken by Arabs, we will never reach equality in the Middle East . . . we define peace not as a piece of paper, but as peace between peoples. And peace between peoples can't begin without a common language and human contacts.[54]

East for Peace believes that Mizrachim are in a unique position to form a bridge between the two peoples, but that they cannot do so as long as one side (the East) is looked upon with disdain, while the other (the West) is idealised, virtually beyond recognition. Members of the MO feel that there is something 'unhealthy' in the way the West is regarded in Israel. It is seen as the 'paragon of excellence – Auschwitz,

Hiroshima and moral decadence are too easily overlooked.' They argue that the view of the West, which has been adopted by many who have no *experience* of it (notably Eastern Europeans and Mizrachim), is, in the words of Elbaz, 'mythic . . . a pseudo-West'.

Elbaz argues that the 'unnatural, unauthentic . . . pro-Western inclination' in Israel was first introduced by Eastern European Jews who idealised the West and adopted an extreme pro-Western position when they first arrived in the country. In laying blame on the Eastern Europeans for mythologising the West, Elbaz overlooks an important point: Eastern Europeans did not only idealise the Occident – but also the Orient. This evident tension between Orient and Occident is worth exploring further, not only because it is interesting in itself but because it reveals how certain ideas are passed on from one ideological group to another.

ORIENT OR OCCIDENT?

The growth of Zionism in Eastern Europe awakened a nostalgic, mythical longing for the Orient. This was made most evident in the literary works of writers such as Bialik and Freierberg. In his novel *Whither?* Freierberg describes the longing of a young Russian Jew for a return to the Orient. In the book he delivers a fiery sermon to a Zionist meeting:

> Europe is sick; everybody senses that its foundations are rotten and its society is crumbling. Our destiny lies in the East . . . the East will reawake and will rule the world, replacing western hegemony . . . Then new vigorous peoples will emerge and will establish the new society . . . and you, my brethren, when you now go eastward, you must always remember that you are Oriental by birth . . . that the worst enemy of the Jews is the West and that, therefore, it is unnatural that we, the Hebrew, Oriental people, should put our lot with the nations of the West . . . if it is true that the people of Israel have a mission, let them bear it and carry it to the Orient . . . My brethren, inscribe on your flag: Eastward![55]

This extraordinary passage reveals a desire amongst Eastern European Jews to be free not only of the bonds of their physical Diaspora but also of the culture of the Diaspora; a desire to 'establish a new society' with 'new vigorous peoples'. Their lost 'Hebrew, Oriental' identity is emphasised rather than their 'Jewish, European' identity.

In the first decades of this century, two opposing views of Zionism emerged in Europe. One was expressed originally by Herzl in *Altneuland*, in which Zionism was portrayed as a 'civilising movement' bringing the Western enlightenment to an underdeveloped region. The support of Western European powers was sought for the endeavour and it was argued that the local Arab population would welcome the Zionist European settlers because they would bring Western skills and great prosperity. The opposing view which might be described as an 'integrationist' view, held that the Jews must return to Palestine as an Oriental people and forge a new culture with their long-lost Semitic brothers, the Arabs. Some argued that unless such a *rapprochement* took place between Arab and Jew, the whole Zionist enterprise would be doomed to failure.

At first it seemed as if the 'integrationist' view would win the day: in 1914, Nahum Sakolov, president of the Zionist Organisation, called for a joint Arab–Jewish effort to build 'a great Palestinian culture which will replace the civilisation of the earlier era'.[56] Many early settlers, including prominent leaders such as Ben-Gurion, believed that many of the local Arabs descended from prominent Jews who, in times of strife, had preferred to convert to Islam or Christianity rather than go into exile. Early writings portrayed these 'distant relatives' as the authentic residents of the land of the Bible, free-spirited and worthy of emulation. Many settlers adopted Arab dress, some went so far as to advocate 'intermarriage with the Arabs as means of quick merger'.[57] This attitude had certain concrete effects. For example, in 1911, Ben-Gurion decided that the Jews of Palestine should renounce their foreign citizenship and become subjects of the Ottoman Empire. He believed that it was important to establish a leadership that spoke Turkish and knew Ottoman law. Consequently, he himself left for Turkey in 1911 to study Turkish and law at the University of Constantinople (his studies came to an end when the First World War broke out).[58]

The longings of European Zionists to integrate into the Orient were somewhat shattered by the Arabs' reluctance to welcome the settlers as 'long-lost brothers'. With the outbreak of open hostility, notably the riots of 1929 in which whole families of Jews were killed by Arab mobs, the romantic view of the 'noble Arab' was gradually replaced by a more negative one and the scales tipped against those Zionists advocating an 'integrationalist view' in favour of those who saw Zionism as a 'civilising mission' in a backward and hostile land. Clearly East for Peace's 'integrationalist' platform is not new.

The desire to be an integral and accepted part of the Orient strongly influenced other groups. One such group that deserves special mention was the Canaanites. They were a small group of Israeli intellectuals who attracted a fair amount of attention in the 1940s and 1950s. They sought to dissolve the connection between the State of Israel and the Diaspora; between 'Hebrew' (or Israeli) identity and Jewish identity. They believed a new 'Hebrew' nation would emerge in the Fertile Crescent if Israel stopped insisting upon a Jewish conception of national identity 'which kept any sense of history developing among peoples in the region'.[59] The Canaanites believed it was the task of the new 'Hebrew' nation to help the 'Arabised' peoples of the region – the Maronites, the Druze, the Alawis, the Kurds, the Bedouin and others – to throw off the pan-Arab yoke and forge together a new nation in the Fertile Crescent. In this respect their ideas resemble those of the Russian Jew in Freierberg's novel and are not far removed from the idea of 'Mediterranean man'. The Canaanites dreamt of recreating a 'golden age', which they believed existed prior to the creation of distinct Arab and Jewish identities. This was based on the belief that the ancient Israelite tribes merged with the inhabitants of the land of Canaan to create the synthesis that was 'Hebrew' culture. In certain respects the Canaanites were anti-Zionists; they believed that 'the Zionist revolution defeated its own purpose (independence) by clinging to the umbilical cord of its birth: the religious-cultural background inherited from the Diaspora days.'[60] It failed because it did not become an integral part of the Orient. The Canaanites believed that mass immigration was responsible for tipping the scales in favour of an exclusive Jewish identity: 'If the State of Israel had not assimilated so many immigrants in so short a time the Diaspora would not have assimilated Israel to its Zionist fold.'[61] This is of course slightly different from the East for Peace view. East for Peace does not reject 'Diaspora culture' outright, but rather denounces the artificial elevation of *Western* Diaspora culture and denounces the intentional degradation of Mizrachi culture which developed in an Oriental Diaspora.

6 New Mizrachi Initiatives and Dialogue

Although East for Peace did not grow rapidly, it was successful in raising Mizrachi interest in the stereotype branded on them as a whole. However, many of those who wished to confront the stereotype – or to engage in a dialogue with the Palestinians – were reluctant to join East for Peace.

Newly-formed peace groups in Israel rapidly gain reputations for themselves both within the peace movement and the country at large. East for Peace proved to be no exception. It soon gained the reputation of being 'intellectual', 'well-mannered' and 'overly concerned with a mystical notion of Mizrachi culture'. Whether or not there is any truth in these labels is not the point. The point is that the labels stick, despite strenuous efforts on behalf of the 'victims' to be rid of them. On the third anniversary of the founding of East for Peace, Shlomo Elbaz was asked by an interviewer: 'Does the intellectual and "well-mannered" image you have bother you?' Elbaz replied:

> I totally reject this image. It's natural that there are intellectuals among us – every movement for social reform has a nucleus of thinking people who are referred to as intellectuals. But if such a formation lacks broad public support it is destined to failure. In contrast to this image, we have persistently worked to expand our movement and incorporate popular forces and authentic protest groups.[1]

Despite such persistent denials, East for Peace has failed to shake off its 'intellectual' label and many would-be peace activists have kept at arm's length.

THE COMMITTEE FOR ISRAELI–PALESTINIAN DIALOGUE

In January 1986 a number of Mizrachim in this position moved to form a new 'popular' Mizrachi MO which would concentrate on bridging the widening gulf between Mizrachim and Palestinians – the Committee for Israeli–Palestinian Dialogue. East for Peace participated fully in the founding of the new committee. This is interesting for it well illustrates the way in which members of one MO will help establish and participate in another *while still maintaining the separate integrity of their own MO*.

The new Committee was launched at a press conference in Jerusalem. (An American Quaker who spent some time working with the peace movement concluded that organising press conferences and press releases was the prime activity of the movement with very little being done 'on the ground' to achieve peace – an observation not far from the truth in many cases!) At the press conference the new Committee made public their declaration of principles signed by one hundred Mizrachi personalities from different walks of life. Ironically, the list included a large number of professors, teachers and students – all 'intellectuals'. It also included public figures, members of municipal councils, lawyers and doctors – hardly more proletarian than East for Peace. It reads as follows:

> We, a group of Israeli citizens of oriental origin, are full of anxiety regarding the condition of both peoples in their common homeland of Eretz Yisrael/Palestine. . . . We recognise their inalienable right to live in peace each under its own sovereignty. It is our obligation, then, to make our contribution to the struggle for peace and democracy in Israel. We, therefore, call for: (1) An uncompromising struggle against all forms of national and ethnic discrimination in Israel, to support a peaceful coexistence and to repel the racism which threatens our very existence. We reject the vile generalisation that all those of Oriental origin are Arab haters. None of the leaders of the nationalistic-chauvinistic camp in Israel come from among the Jews of the Orient. Israelis of Oriental origin possess the ability and the desire to build a bridge between the Arab world and Israeli society, and to renew the centuries-old tradition of cultural partnership as a step towards our integration in the region. An uncompromising struggle to achieve a peace agreement which will

put an end to the destruction, suffering and bloodshed. We appeal to both sides to immediately enter political negotiations on the basis of mutual recognition of the right to self-determination of both peoples. This agreement, when it is reached, will guarantee a prosperous future for our nation and the nations of the region.[2]

The driving force behind the new Committee was the head of Mapam's Arab Affairs Department, Latif Dori. There are some who believe that Dori (an Iraqi-born Mizrachi) initiated the new Committee because 'he wanted to run his own show' and that he wanted to carry out activities which went well beyond official Mapam policy. There may be some truth in these allegations. Dori is a dynamic character who has been described as one of the peace movement's 'solos' – energetic individuals who find it difficult to submit to the pressure arising from working in a group where decisions are reached laboriously through consensus. (The presence of such 'solos' has certainly been a factor which has led to splits within existing MOs and the formation of new ones.) Setting aside speculation about Dori's character and ambitions, it is possible that the new Mizrachi Committee would have done little more than write declarations and hold press conferences had it not been for Dori's outright opposition to the new Israeli law forbidding Israeli citizens to meet with members of the PLO and his *personal* willingness to defy it. Indeed, even while the new law was being debated in the Knesset, Dori travelled to Vienna to represent the Committee at the third United Nations NGOs meeting on the 'Question of Palestine' (2–4 July, 1986). There he gave a paper which emphasised the growing role of Mizrachim in the Israeli peace movement and which presented his own MO's platform for peace in the Middle East. Dori also took the opportunity (as did other Israeli peace activists attending the conference) to meet with PLO representatives.

THE ANTI-CONTACTS LAW AND MIZRACHI GROUPS

Seven weeks later, when the law against contact with the PLO was passed, Dori's Committee immediately called a press conference where he was joined by Shlomo Elbaz, Hanna Siniora, Mustafa Natshe (deposed mayor of Hebron) and others. Speaking on behalf of the Committee, Dori declared:

We know what the whole world knows, that the overwhelming majority of the Palestinian people, and first and foremost the residents of the Occupied Territories, consider the PLO to be their only legitimate representative. The purpose of this law is to try to break off all contact and to prevent all dialogue between us and them. According to the law, we are forbidden to meet with our friends the Palestinians who are here with us today, because they identify with the PLO . . . Just imagine what would happen if the law would be applied retroactively to 1 July, I would be sent to prison for three years for a dialogue for peace which I carried out in Vienna with PLO members. I would like to announce here that I would be ready to pay that price – and I'm sure that many other people would be ready to act in the same way. We cannot forget the fact that Palestinian personalities have given their lives for peace and dialogue with us, beginning with Said Hammami, and including my friend Issam Sartawi, and they were joined by our friend Emil Grunzweig. They were all murdered by wicked hands. We will honour their memory by increasing the struggle and deepening the dialogue between us and the Palestinians in the Occupied Territories and outside them. We declare that no power in the world can prevent the dialogue between the Israeli and Palestinian peace seekers, which will continue at all times in all places.[3]

Latif Dori was quite correct in his assessment that many people would be prepared to pay the price of prosecution in order to continue the dialogue with the PLO. In fact, many rank and file peace activists who had never previously considered meeting with members of the PLO now contemplated such meetings – primarily to demonstrate their opposition to a law which they believed could only undermine the achievement of peace. The initiative came to rest with such activists partly because the PLP, with its considerable experience of contact with the PLO, was reluctant to defy the law. The party had to carefully calculate the political implications of defying the law. It realised that if it broke the law, it would then be difficult to criticise right-wing groups which took the law into their own hands. More significantly, defying a law enacted by the Knesset could lead to a ban on the party's own participation in the next elections for the Knesset. As for Peace Now, it adopted a position not far removed from the one it held on fighting in Lebanon: 'The law was passed by a democratically elected government and we must confront it using only democratic means – no defiance.'

East for Peace actively supported Dori's attempt to organise a meeting with the PLO in defiance of the new law. At the same time a relatively new Mizrachi group, organised towards the end of 1985 by radical Mizrachim from the poor neighbourhoods, began its own initiative. The Oriental Front (OF), as the group was called, was formed by an ex-Black Panther leader, Kochavi Shemesh, with the participation of Yosef Shiloh, a well-known Mizrachi actor. Although the composition of the OF was basically working-class – and in this respect quite different from East for Peace – its basic ideology was not any different. It too stressed the urgency of smashing the 'hawk stereotype' and of linking the resolution of social problems in Israel to the settling of the 'Palestinian question'. Why the neighbourhood activists did not simply join East for Peace may again be attributed to the MO's intellectual image and to the apparent desire of Shemesh to 'go solo' as well.[4]

With three Mizrachi MOs attempting to set up a meeting with the PLO, attention suddenly came to focus on the involvement of Mizrachim in the peace process – an aspect which was virtually as new as the intentions to defy the law banning contact with the PLO. Unfortunately the involvement of so many different individuals and groups made the whole process exceedingly complex. Individual, party and ethnic differences all conspired throughout against the success of the endeavour.

BUILD-UP TO THE ROMANIAN MEETING

To begin with, there were a number of objective constraints which complicated the desired meeting with a PLO delegation and worked in an unfortunate way to undermine the unity of Israeli participants. Desiring to meet with the PLO was all very well but, in order to do so, certain concrete obstacles had to be overcome. Firstly, in order to meet the PLO, Israeli activists had to leave the country. Then they had to find a neutral country which would accept both them and a PLO delegation. This country not only had to agree to allow the meeting to take place on its soil but also had to provide adequate security arrangements for both delegations – either of which could be a target for extremists opposed to Israeli–Palestinian dialogue. In addition, the country would have to be willing to help sponsor the meeting as Israeli peace activists are not known for their wealth. Air tickets and lodging would have to be provided if the meeting was to be open to all who wanted to go. Given these requirements, it became evident that there was really only one suitable country in which the meeting could take place – Romania. Following the Six-Day War, most Eastern bloc countries followed the example of the Soviet Union and broke off diplomatic relations with Israel. Romania, exceptionally, maintained diplomatic relations and Romanian President Ceauçescu personally became involved in encouraging Arab–Israeli peace efforts. However, the fact that the Romanians were providing the tickets meant that they ultimately had a veto over who would and would not meet with the PLO delegation. In Israel this meant that the person who had the ear of the Romanians held sway over the final composition of the Israeli delegation. That person turned out to be Latif Dori.

Dori worked through European-based intermediaries who had been involved in facilitating Israeli–Palestinian contacts for many years, such as Maxim Ghilan. While Dori was working through these intermediaries, so was Shemesh of the OF. In fact it appeared that the OF was competing with Dori's Committee to become the main delegation to Romania. Soon rumours and counter-rumours were rife and it became difficult to verify exactly what was happening, especially as messages were often passed through different intermediaries hundreds of kilometres away. Things were further complicated by the fact that Dori refused to call a meeting of those interested in going to Romania on the ground that such a meeting could itself be illegal – a conspiracy to commit a crime. However, various potential delegates to Romania (said to total about one hundred) began to suspect that the real reason was that Dori wanted to have a free hand in organising the meeting and was not willing to subject the selection process to democratic restraints.

Political party involvement was a key factor in creating tension and suspicion amongst would-be delegates – especially amongst the Mizrachim, ever suspicious of being manipulated for political ends. Rakah had, at first, limited its involvement; like the PLP it did not want to be implicated in breaking the law. It was also reluctant to become involved in an initiative with uncertain political returns. However when it appeared that the meeting was to become the 'great event' of the Israeli peace movement, Rakah began to reconsider its position.

The party wanted to include Uzi Burnstein (the party's spokesman) in the delegation. When Latif Dori's Committee refused, Burnstein announced that he would be going anyway at the invitation of the Romanian Communist Party. This created a wave of anger amongst potential Mizrachi delegates. The presence of Burnstein in Romania may not have resulted in Rakah control of the delegation but, for Mizrachim, it recalled years of manipulation by all political parties, when, as new immigrants, they were 'distributed' amongst the parties as if they were incapable of choosing their own leaders.

In the meantime competition was building up between Shemesh and Dori over who would lead the delegation. Shemesh apparently got a message through one of 'his' Paris intermediaries that the PLO would welcome as many Mizrachim as possible. Meeting with Mizrachim apparently appealed to two streams of thinking within the PLO – the 'idealists' and the 'realists'. Firstly, the 'idealists' saw the proposed meeting as a confirmation of their Arab nationalist world view. In the early years of Arab nationalism, when the Ottoman Empire's policy of division according to religious community was being opposed, the Arab nationalists forged an ideology which held that all Arabic speakers were Arab – regardless of religious affiliation. The idealists in the PLO, who continue to adhere to this view, regard Arab-speaking Mizrachim as Arabs. (In fact, PLO strategy had at one time been to try to persuade the leaders of Arab states to encourage Mizrachim to return from Israel to their countries of origin where they would, according to the plan, be granted equal rights as Arabs. It was believed that if Israel's 'Jewish Arabs' could be persuaded to 'return home', the rising power of the Likud – and of the state as a whole – would be undermined.) For these 'idealists', the chance of meeting Mizrachim (their 'Arab' brethren) offered new hope for an old ideology with no results to support it.

Secondly, the meeting appealed to the 'realists' within the PLO. They are those members who had had first hand experience of Israel before going into exile and were well aware that Israel's Mizrachim were not about to return to their countries of origin. However they were also aware of the extent of Mizrachi support for the Likud and realised that any new Mizrachi involvement in the peace movement was something to be nurtured and encouraged. So, with encouragement from the PLO (via intermediaries) Shemesh began to sign up as many Mizrachim as were ready to go.[5]

At this point in the saga, someone – it is not clear who – is said to have accused Shemesh of signing up people who were 'immature' and 'not ready to talk to the PLO'. He was further accused of collecting the neighbourhoods' *bara* (a term used for second-rate oranges not fit for export) in order to boost the size and importance of his delegation. To anybody who knows anything of the sensitivities of Israeli Mizrachim, the impact of the words 'immature' and *'bara'* can be imagined. Both immediately recall the early days of immigration when Mizrachim were deemed to be too 'immature' to conduct their own affairs and were dumped in isolated development towns as if they were the *bara* of Israeli society – second-rate rejects. Understandably, the alleged insult caused a storm in Mizrachi circles. Then to add injury to insult, Shemesh was told (via intermediaries) that only thirty of the sixty-five people he had signed up would receive tickets from the Romanians, that only one Israeli delegation would be recognised and that it would be headed by Latif Dori. That, for Shemesh, was the last straw; he, and the Oriental Front, withdrew from the proposed meeting. This prompted East for Peace to do likewise – not because they felt any special sympathy towards the OF but because they felt that Mizrachim were being manipulated and insulted. With two of the major components of the potential delegation out, and with the press and the right-wing parties having a field-day (noting with glee the peace movement's inability to 'make peace with itself' let alone with the PLO), more independent activists pulled out. The result was that, instead of a predominantly Mizrachi delegation of about one hundred leaving for Romania, only twenty-nine delegates went, of whom only two were Mizrachim. The first major attempt to include Mizrachim in a dialogue with the PLO ended in complete failure.[6]

Before leaving, delegates were warned by the Attorney-General that they would be prosecuted. At the airport they were confronted by a demonstration that included the relatives of Israelis killed in the past by PLO terrorists. The Abu Nidal 'rejectionist' splinter of the PLO warned that participants would pay dearly. To underline the threat, the Romanian Embassy in Beirut was attacked shortly before the meeting was due to begin.[7] In view of the circumstances, only fifteen of the thirty-one PLO representatives attended the meeting which lasted no longer than ninety minutes (instead of the planned two days).

THE AFTERMATH

Although the meeting made a point by defying a law believed to be against the interests of peace, it was not particularly notable in any other way. It was the participation of large numbers of Mizrachim that had attracted special interest – amongst both Israelis and Palestinians. Once this attraction was 'removed' the focus of attention diminished and came to rest primarily on the question of whether or not the delegates would be prosecuted. As it happened, only four of the delegates (who had been elected to a steering committee once the delegation reached Romania) were to be summoned by the police and ultimately charged with breaking the law. To this other delegates responded by insisting that they too be tried.

Undeterred by the prospect of prosecution, East for Peace began planning further meetings with the PLO which they hoped would be more successful if managed by Mizrachim alone and without the participation of political parties.

THE FLOW OF IDEAS BETWEEN GROUPS

Sociologists argue that the study of small, 'ideological' groups, which form around the nucleus of shared ideas, provides us with a methodology for the historical and sociological analysis of ideas. The examples studied in this chapter illustrate this well. It has been shown how ideas formulated by early Eastern European Zionists, concerning their desire to forge a new society with the peoples of the Orient, re-emerged amongst the Canaanites in the 1940s. Then, in the early 1970s, the idea took a more specific form with the Black Panthers. They condemned Israel's rejection of the Orient and proposed that Mizrachim form a bridge to link Israel to the Arab world in peace. In the 1980s, East for Peace reaffirmed the Black Panthers' formulation of this idea and proposed a 're-orientation of Israeli culture towards the Orient' as the key to peace between Mizrachim and Ashkenazim, Arabs and Jews. The idea of Mizrachim acting as a bridge reappeared a few years later in the manifesto of the Committee for Israeli–Palestinian Dialogue.

What is interesting about the passage of ideas from one group to the next, is that they are often quite unaware that 'their' ideas have been around for many years; they present them as if they were quite new.

This was certainly the case with East for Peace. In 1917, a group called the Pioneers of the East was established by young Mizrachi intellectuals in Palestine; it aimed, amongst other things, to encourage the teaching of Arabic among Jews and Hebrew amongst Arabs as a way of promoting coexistence. The chairman of the group promoted the idea of Mizrachim acting as a bridge to peace for many years. He was a remarkable Sephardi by the name of Elie Eliachar. Eliachar was a sixteenth generation, Palestinian-born Jew from a prominent Jerusalem family. He studied medicine in Beirut and law in Cairo and was later an officer in the Turkish army. He had a successful commercial and public career; he was elected to the First and Second Knesset (as a leader of the Sephardi List); he served for some time as deputy mayor of Jerusalem and as head of Jerusalem's Sephardi Council. Eliachar always maintained that the Ashkenazi leadership of the Zionist movement, the yishuv and the state, had ignored Mizrachi leaders who were in close contact with Arab leaders, and hence the movement lost many opportunities to avoid outbreaks of violent conflict.[8] A bridge *which existed* had not been used by an Ashkenazi, 'Euro-centric' leadership. Shlomo Elbaz said that the first time East for Peace heard of Eliachar and his ideas, was when Eliachar's widow contacted the group after an article on the MO appeared in *The Jerusalem Post*. They knew nothing of the man and his works, yet they had come to express the same basic ideas. How is this possible?

To begin with, as noted, Elbaz and others were outsiders who had only been in the country a relatively short time. More importantly, it is evident that ideas outlive those individuals and groups who formulate (and reformulate) them. They continue to exist, dormant in written form and unspoken thought until, suddenly, a dramatic event (such as the grenade attack) causes a social upheaval which brings new relevance to old ideas, breathing life into their dry bones.

While it is clear that humanity is motivated by outstanding ideas, its ability to use such ideas to achieve predetermined ends is extremely limited. In the same way that the Ashkenazi Labour establishment failed to 'absorb' Mizrachim by transferring their culture from Oriental to Occidental, East for Peace is certain to fail in its bid to 'orient Israel orientally'. The debate over the future cultural face of Israel has escalated in recent years with groups of Mizrachim asserting the Oriental characteristics of their culture with increasing boldness and determination and with many Ashkenazim continuing to deplore the increasing 'Levantisation' of Israel. What is often ignored in the debate is the simple fact that the culture of a nation such as Israel cannot be shaped to fit any particular mould. One person who does not ignore this fact is the writer Nissim Rejiwan who criticises 'those who seem to think of Israeli culture in the black and white terms of "Israel: East or West"; as if somebody, somewhere, somehow, could sit down, draw up and put into effect a cultural plan for the future of any society, especially one which is culturally, temperamentally and traditionally as heterogeneous as Israel's.' The future of Israel is likely to be as painful as its recent past, as long as there is any attempt to plan and create 'an infrastructure of Israeli culture based on an East–West dichotomy'. As Rejiwan points out such attempts are 'bound to lead to something akin to cultural coercion of the worst kind'. Ashkenazi–Mizrachi peace (not to mention Arab–Israeli) will only come with the acceptance of a cultural diversity which is a true reflection of Israel's multi-ethnic, multi-cultural reality.[9]

7 Peace Through Encounters and Education

THE 'STRUCTURE' OF THE ISRAELI PEACE MOVEMENT

Social movements are always extremely 'fluid' and usually quite unstructured in the ordinary sense of the word. Nevertheless, as noted earlier, they manifest themselves in fairly distinct movement organisations. These have recognisable ideologies, modes of organisation and links between themselves. The MOs share common long-term goals (in this case opposition to the occupation and a willingness to negotiate territories for peace); yet, at the same time, they remain independent from one another, being unable to reach agreement on fundamental issues.

The divisions between them are extremely informative: they reveal divergent world views which often reflect similar divisions in the broader society (although the movement is not a microcosm of the society).

The relationships between the MOs are constantly changing. To add complexity to complexity, individual activists are often members of more than one MO, and MOs' activities overlap. Nevertheless, it is possible to artificially freeze the very fluid structure of the peace movement, at a given point in time, for the purposes of 'dissection' and investigation.

Protest MOs, such as Peace Now, are by far the most visible sector of the peace movement. There is, however, more to the movement 'than meets the eye'. The MOs which organise the eye-catching demonstrations are simply the visible tip of an iceberg of popular sentiment from which they draw their support. At times, such as after the Sabra and Shatilla massacres, popular sentiment will rise, revealing the extent of the movement's 'hidden base'. Much of the support

Figure 2   The Structure of the Peace Movement (1982–85)

Sphere 1 – Political Parties

| DFPE | PLP | MAPAM | RATZ | LABOUR |

Sphere 2 – Protest Groups

Anti-Zionist Groups
Revolutionary Communist League
Matzpen
Committee Confronting the Iron Fist

PEACE NOW

Parents Against Silence

Oz ve Shalom/ Netivot le Shalom

East for Peace

Yesh Gvul

Birzeit Solidarity Committee – Committee Against the War in Lebanon

Sphere 3 – IPJACs, Research and Civil Rights Organisations

A. Intervention Programmes in Jewish–Arab Contacts
Reshet
Beit Hagefen
Martin Buber Institute for Adult Education
Beit-Hillel Arab–Jewish Relations Project
Circle for Nazareth–Upper Nazareth Co-operation
Education for Peace Project
Gesher
Interns for Peace
Israel Interfaith Committee
Institute for Jewish–Arab Coexistence
Neve Shalom
Partnership
Ulpan Akiva and others

B. Research and Policy Institues
The International Centre for Peace in the Middle East
The Van Leer Foundation
The Institute for Arab Studies – Givat Haviva

C. Civil and Human Rights Organisations
Association for the Support and Defence of Bedouin Rights
Israeli League for Human and Civil Rights
Committee of Jews and Arabs against Racism
Others

Note: Clear organisational links between spheres are indicated with an unbroken line (——); more ambiguous, *ad hoc* links – often representing dual membership – are indicated with a broken line (– – – –). The blocks (☐) between Peace Now and the other MOs, indicate a barrier – usually ideological – preventing full co-operation. An arrow (——>) gives a **rough** idea of which side is more willing to co-operate should the occasion arise.

comes from individuals and MOs that are not normally engaged in protest, but are nevertheless part of the peace movement in its broadest sense.

The Israeli peace movement may be divided into three broad spheres of activity which reflect an informal division of labour (see Figure 2). The central (or second) sphere is made up of the various protest MOs on which this book concentrates. Their role is primarily extra-parliamentary, but, in their endeavour to influence government, most of the MOs in the 'protest sphere' have forged strong links with one or more of the dovish parties (in the first sphere) which share their basic opposition to the continued occupation. These links will be examined shortly. The third sphere, which also has close links with the protest MOs, is made up of the numerous community, education, academic and human rights groups engaged in promoting Jewish–Arab coexistence or defending Palestinian human rights. These are the focus of this chapter.

INTERVENTION PROGRAMMES IN JEWISH–ARAB CONTACT (IPJACS)

The primary means of achieving peaceful coexistence for the 'third sphere' groups is the bringing of Jews and Arabs together in organised 'encounters' designed to break stereotypes, promote understanding and coexistence. The groups engaged in these 'Intervention Programmes in Jewish–Arab Contacts' (IPJACs) may themselves be divided into different categories. In the first category are the few who work full time on IPJACs. This is their sole *raison d'être*. Such organisations may be supported by volunteers, but they are usually managed by skilled professionals, who work on a full-time basis, often employing the most up-to-date group encounter techniques, drawing extensively from psychological and educational studies related to their work. The more innovative of the professional organisations are often at the forefront of *international* experimentation and research in the field of group encounter and conflict resolution.

The second category consists of MOs which carry out their own IPJACs within the context of their broader work. One such MO, which well illustrates this approach, is Ulpan Akiva in Netanya. The Ulpan (language school) was founded in 1951 to teach Hebrew to new Jewish immigrants. When, in 1967, Israeli rule over more than a million Arabs 'created an urgent need for teaching Arabic', Arabic classes were added for Jews, and Arabs were offered places in Hebrew classes. In addition to simply learning each other's language, Jews and Arabs at the Ulpan participate in a unique IPJAC. Participants, who are required to live in for a 21-day programme, are assigned two to a room – one Jew, one Arab. They take meals together, study together and practise conversation in each other's languages. The assumption behind the programme is that, 'through the hard, dry learning of Hebrew and Arabic, Jews and Arabs can find a common language, a common expression'. In addition to the programme for adults, Ulpan Akiva has organised five-day encounters for Jewish and Arab children which, besides language instruction, include visits to the children's schools and homes. Other examples of MOs which bring Jews and Arabs together, as part of their broader activities, include: Beit Hagefen, a community and youth centre in Haifa (which uses theatre, sports and the arts to attract Jews and Arabs) and the Israeli Interfaith Association, based in Jerusalem, under whose auspices Jews and Arabs meet while discussing or studying religious issues.

In addition to the two categories mentioned above, IPJACs are often carried out by kibbutzim, youth movements and schools. Very often however, these are run on an *ad hoc* basis by well-intentioned teachers and youth leaders – with disastrous results. Tales abound in Israel (at least within peace movement circles) of poorly organised encounters that 'backfired' because they were mismanaged. Young people who are not carefully prepared often have their stereotypes confirmed, rather than reversed, by brief encounters that are poorly planned and badly handled. However, quite frequently, professionals from the first category are invited to run the IPJAC of a school, youth movement or kibbutz.

NEVE SHALOM

Amongst the professional MOs engaged in IPJACs, the best-known and most remarkable is Neve Shalom (Oasis of Peace). Neve Shalom is unique. It is the only MO in the peace movement which is far more than simply an organisation; it is in fact Israel's only Jewish–Arab co-operative settlement – a place where Jewish–Arab coexistence is not only discussed, but lived on a day-to-day basis.[1]

The community was born out of the vision of a multi-lingual,

Egyptian-born Jew, Bruno Hussar. He converted to Christianity and became a Dominican monk before moving to Israel to establish, in the sixties, a Catholic centre for the study of Judaism. Inspired by the idea of establishing an inter-faith community, where the three monotheistic religions of the region would coexist in peace, Hussar acquired one hundred acres of rocky hilltop from the Trappist monastery of Latrun, midway between Tel Aviv and Jerusalem. From there, he hoped to attract Muslim, Jewish and Christian settlers. Living in a converted transport container, with no access road, no water or electricity, Hussar attracted very few, besides the passing globe-trotter who would come to spend a few weeks experiencing communal living with this 'desert prophet'. Occasionally, local Arabs or kibbutzniks would drift up the hill to try to make out what was happening there. Even those who were attracted by his ideas were not prepared to rough it long enough to settle. Hussar, after three or four years of effort, was about to give up. Before doing so, the Dominican Father 'gave God an ultimatum': one year to provide a family who would decide to settle, and the money to start building the inter-faith community he had envisioned.

Within months the 'ultimatum' was met: a family decided to settle and money was received from the Catholic peace group Pax Christi which enabled the nascent community to be connected to the mains water supply, to fix an access road and to acquire an electricity generator. By 1986, Neve Shalom had grown to thirteen families (with twenty-four children) and eleven single people. More families and single people have been accepted by the community's absorption committee and are awaiting the construction of new housing before settling permanently.

Although Hussar had envisioned an inter-faith community, those who came to settle in Neve Shalom (both Jews and Arabs) tended to be secular. They were more interested in creating an 'oasis of peace', where Jewish–Arab coexistence in Israel could be advanced, than in inter-faith dialogue between the religions of the Holy Land.

Once permanent settlers and funds had arrived, the way was opened for the establishment of a 'School for Peace'. The object of the school was to organise encounters between Jews and Arabs from *within* Israel, in order to challenge stereotypes and promote coexistence between the two *national* groups – regardless of religious affiliations. Encounters between Israeli Jews and Palestinian Arabs from across the 1967

'Green Line' were excluded because it was felt that, whatever the future of the occupied territories, Jewish and Arab citizens *of the State of Israel* would still have to learn to coexist. Furthermore, attempting to include Palestinians from the territories could be interpreted as an attempt to coerce them into an acceptance of Israeli domination. Neve Shalom consciously avoided further complicating an already complex problem, by working only with Arabs and Jews of Israel proper. Then, it was soon discovered that bringing Jewish and Arab adults together at Neve Shalom was far from productive; negative attitudes and stereotypes had become too deeply entrenched for brief encounters to change them. So, in 1979, the School for Peace began to work exclusively with teenagers aged between fifteen and seventeen years.

It took a series of day encounters at Neve Shalom before it was realised that a minimum of three or four days was needed if any substantial changes in attitude were to be made. Between 1980 and 1985, approximately 7000 Jewish and Arab teenagers passed through the School for Peace, bringing a wealth of experience to the co-ordinators and educators involved in organising the encounters.

What made Neve Shalom's IPJAC unique was not just its length, but the fact that young people involved in the encounter could see that peaceful coexistence could be put into practice (albeit on a limited scale); the environment in which they were meeting was visible proof that Jewish–Arab coexistence need not remain an abstract, utopian dream. However, while on the one hand being an 'oasis' worked to the advantage of Neve Shalom – allowing for freedom of expression and openness of heart on secure 'neutral' ground – it soon became apparent that it also had disadvantages. Once the four-day seminars were over, the young people would leave the protected environment of the 'oasis of peace', and re-enter the segregated and and conflictual world of Jewish–Arab relationships prevailing in Israeli society.

Realising that young peoples' attitudes could so easily revert soon after leaving Neve Shalom, meetings were arranged between groups of Arabs and Jews who had been there and who lived close to each other. To facilitate these meetings, which would take place on 'home ground', special courses were organised for regional group leaders, as well as for educators interested in IPJACs. With money from the Ford Foundation donated in 1984, Neve Shalom was able to extend its work beyond the 'oasis' and establish a number of regional groups with the intention of forming a Jewish–Arab youth movement which, it was hoped, would enable contacts between young Jews and Arabs to develop into bridges between the two peoples. Within a few years, the School for Peace became a centre for training others to work in the delicate field of Jewish–Arab encounters.

From the outset, Neve Shalom's School for Peace has worked closely with a number of other MOs involved in IPJACs. Although almost all the 'IPJAC MOs' are part of an umbrella organisation called Reshet (Network), co-operation between most of them is limited. The establishment of Reshet was intended to increase co-operation and promote skills-sharing between the MOs concerned. While the idea proved to be attractive, the different MOs failed to turn Reshet into a real 'network'. For one thing, individual activists, both professionals and volunteers, found the commitment to yet another series of weekly or even monthly meetings to be a burden. More importantly, the MOs involved disagreed amongst themselves on fairly substantial issues. Not only did their approaches differ, they were also divided over political questions – and the question of whether or not 'political issues' should be raised during Jewish–Arab encounters.

A number of IPJAC MOs, such as Ulpan Akiva and Beit Hagefen, claim to be 'apolitical'. They refuse, as organisations, to take any position on political issues such as the future of the occupied territories. Furthermore, during their encounters, they shy away from all politically explosive and potentially divisive issues, concentrating on sharing cultural and personal experiences unrelated to the harsh political realities of the Middle East. The 'apolitical' IPJAC MOs will not support the protest activities of Peace Now, let alone any of the more radical protest MOs. Other IPJAC MOs, such as Neve Shalom, tackle potentially divisive political issues in depth, but only after a certain stage in the encounter has been reached. Although even the more political IPJAC MOs are reluctant to openly support the protest MOs, or the dovish political parties (for fear of being too closely associated with them), many individual activists span the two spheres by becoming involved in both IPJAC and protest MOs. The extent of individual and group involvement in protest activities varies considerably from one IPJAC MO to another, limiting the extent of co-operation between members of Reshet, which has all but ceased to exist.

THE IMPACT OF NEVE SHALOM

Although co-operation between the IPJAC MOs *as a whole* is limited, certain MOs, which share common political and organisational assumptions, work closely together. Neve Shalom has, for example, worked very closely with Shutafut (Partnership), a Haifa-based organisation founded in 1979. Together they have developed a methodology for group encounters, giving special attention to the training of group leaders. Neve Shalom has also worked closely with the Kibbutz Hartzi movement which asked for professional help in organising their own IPJAC. Givat Haviva, the Kibbutz Hartzi educational institute, adopted the Neve Shalom model, but applied it slightly differently, using it for larger groups. The Jerusalem-based Van Leer Foundation, an independent research institute with a special interest in promoting Jewish–Arab coexistence, has also drawn on Neve Shalom's experience in writing on the subject of improving Jewish–Arab relations. Another MO that has benefited from Neve Shalom's professional expertise is Nitzanei Shalom (Interns for Peace). This MO, established in 1976 by an American Reform Rabbi, Bruce Cohen, trains young Jewish adults (mostly from the USA) to carry out social development projects in Arab villages, while at the same time arranging IPJACs. The Jews who become 'interns' live in Arab villages where they aim not only to initiate projects which supply a local need, but also to develop contacts with local people and arrange encounters between local Arab school children and their counterparts in Jewish schools. To gain professional training for its interns, Nitzanei Shalom sent them to Neve Shalom. Although the two organisations have different approaches and different views of the role of politics (with Nitzanei Shalom being more 'apolitical'), the two have co-operated. Outside of Israel, Neve Shalom's name has spread. Educators from the community travelled to Northern Ireland where they carried out workshops.

'Graduates' of the Neve Shalom School for Peace have often gone on to initiate their own projects. For example, one graduate became involved in the first attempt to create a Jewish–Arab youth movement, called Re'ut (Friendship). Another graduate, Gershon Baskin, managed to gain governmental co-operation for the establishment of an official Institute for Education and for Coexistence between Jews and Arabs. Baskin's aim was to take the work of Neve Shalom far beyond its limited boundaries to a national level. The only way of achieving this, Baskin believed, was by involving the state. Governmental backing was essential if programmes were to reach the general public.

In 1983, with the backing of the Ministry of Education and the Prime Minister's office, and with financial support from West Germany, Baskin was able to launch his Institute which sponsors a wide range of activities. Joint seminars and workshops are held for Jewish and Arab pupils, educators and community leaders. School seminars have included visits to Arab villages. Work is underway on educational material to be used in schools and other educational institutions; new programmes are being developed for teacher training.

STATE INVOLVEMENT AND THE RADICAL CRITIQUE

The close co-operation of the 'peace institutes' with the state has raised objections from within the peace movement. Baskin evidently had to reaffirm central Zionist values to assure State support. A government press release, explaining state support, argued that Baskin's new Institute was different from the thirty-eight other organisations working on Jewish–Arab dialogue in Israel because of 'the emphasis the Institute places on the philosophy which is its inspiration'. Its 'guiding principle' is the belief that Israel should be a Jewish and democratic state, as embodied in the declaration of independence which guarantees 'full and equal political and social rights to all its citizens regardless of race, sex or creed'.[2]

In the minds of many peace activists, especially those in the radical protest MOs, such a close association with the state discredits the work of any would-be peace organisation. While the assertion of the universal components of the state's ideology is welcomed, it is argued that the accompanying insistence that the state should be *Jewish* undermines and contradicts universal values and the prospects of peace. How, it is asked, can a Jewish state whose name, flag, emblems and dominant language are Jewish, and whose 'Law of Return' allows any Jew of any nation to claim immediate Israeli citizenship (while refusing the right of Palestinian refugees born in the country to return), claim to guarantee 'full and equal political and social rights'?

The radical critique of IPJAC MOs which promote Jewish–Arab coexistence on condition that it takes place within the realms of a

Figure 3   Schematic Reconstruction of the Philosophy behind the Intervention
Programmes in Jewish–Arab Contacts

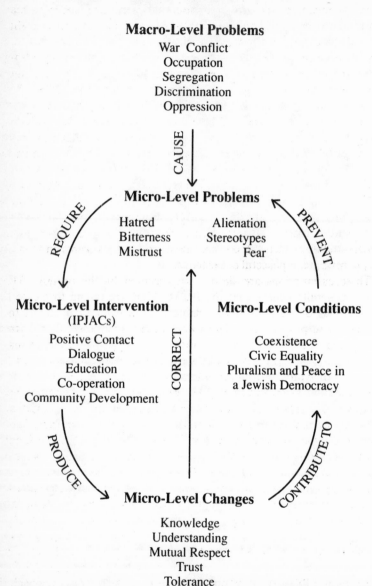

Macro-Level Problems
War Conflict
Occupation
Segregation
Discrimination
Oppression

CAUSE

Micro-Level Problems

Hatred   Alienation
Bitterness   Stereotypes
Mistrust   Fear

REQUIRE

PREVENT

Micro-Level Intervention
(IPJACs)
Positive Contact
Dialogue
Education
Co-operation
Community Development

Micro-Level Conditions

Coexistence
Civic Equality
Pluralism and Peace in
a Jewish Democracy

CORRECT

PRODUCE

CONTRIBUTE TO

Micro-Level Changes

Knowledge
Understanding
Mutual Respect
Trust
Tolerance

Jewish state, is such that MOs are simply attempting to make Zionism more palatable for Palestinians by presenting the universal face of Israel. Instead, it is argued, they should be supporting the Palestinians' right to self-determination (in a state alongside Israel) or their right to live in a non-sectarian, secular Israel.

Criticism of the IPJAC approach, by both anti-Zionist and Zionist protest MOs, also springs from the two spheres' different perceptions of *how* to respond to the Arab–Israeli conflict. The IPJAC MOs believe that, regardless of the political and territorial outcomes of the conflict, Jews and Arabs will continue to live together in the State of Israel; if they are to coexist peacefully, they must overcome the fear and hatred which divide them. These emotions are believed to be the result of ignorance, stereotypes and mistrust. It is thought they can be overcome through 'micro-level intervention' (see Figure 3) involving positive contact, education, dialogue and community development. Generally speaking, the IPJAC MOs assume that such 'micro-level' intervention can produce positive changes (knowledge, tolerance, understanding) which will correct the micro-level problems and in this way contribute to peaceful coexistence.

These assumptions are simply not accepted by the protest MOs. They generally believe that the IPJAC MOs are failing to tackle the *root causes* of the micro-level problems upon which they focus their energy. The protest MOs tend to argue that ignorance, fear, hatred, and mistrust are simply the off-shoot of the 'macro-level' problems of war, occupation, the denial of Palestinian self-determination and the position of Arabs as a minority in a *Jewish* state – which they cannot accept. It is argued that any attempt to alleviate the micro-level problems is futile as long as the macro-level problems exist and continue to fuel the flames of hatred. Attempts to quench these flames with the mere waters of 'dialogue' are considered doomed to failure. For this reason the protest MOs, as we have seen, attempt to tackle the macro-level problems by putting pressure on the government to end the occupation, to allow Palestinians a degree of self-determination and to make territorial concessions which, they believe, will lead to an end of the hostilities between Israel and the Arab world as a whole.[3]

ONE IPJAC MO'S REPLY

In response to the protest MOs' criticism of the IPJAC approach, it should be re-emphasised that many individuals are in fact involved in both the second and third spheres of Figure 2. Furthermore, many of these individuals have become involved in IPJACs because they felt a need to do something 'concrete' other than protest. They felt that the protest groups were incapable of making any real impact on the macro-level problems and that, indeed, their protest actions often simply added to feelings of hostility, thus rendering them counter-productive.

One such person, Rahel Rosenweig, started the MO Shutafut after years of frustrating involvement in protest MOs and dovish parties. In her own words:

> every activity seemed to result in failure. Instead of diminishing Jewish preoccupation with short-range security and stimulating people to think of truly coping with the conflict, so-called 'peace-niks' obviously aroused antagonism and seemed to make things even worse . . . what we were actually doing was fighting and blaming our own people in order to make peace with the enemy.[4]

Rosenweig believed that 'psychological barriers' to peace had to be removed in order to 'create conditions of partnership between Jews and Arabs in the State of Israel'.[5] By turning the Arab citizens of Israel from enemies into partners, she believed it would become far easier to approach the Palestinians outside the 1967 borders and then the Arab states. In order to overcome the psychological barriers to peace, Rosenweig joined with Ibrahim Shim'an to develop the 'partnership way', and establish Shutafut.

THE OBJECTIVE LIMITATIONS OF IPJACS

Although the quantity and quality of IPJACs have grown dramatically since the early seventies, in response to the rise of particular forces described in the first chapter, their impact appears to have been negligible. The growth of extremist, religious-nationalist and racist tendencies has not been stemmed – on the contrary it has continued steadily.

The impact of IPJACs has been limited by a number of factors. Firstly, their development has been hampered by a 'lack of infra-structure and resources, and hence lack of stability and professionality in operation'.[6] Although a number of IPJAC MOs have been successful in developing peace studies curricula for schools (such as 'Neighbours' produced by the Interfaith Association), and although the state has taken certain steps towards encouraging the implementation of such curricula, IPJACs remain extremely limited, reaching only a small percentage of the population.

Secondly, as voluntary organisations, the IPJAC MOs are disadvantaged by a lack of institutional support and nation-wide legitimation from the authorities and the public. This is primarily because Israel's Jewish population tends to regard Jewish–Arab contacts with suspicion. Research indicates that 'most Israelis are interested in "friendly contact" with Arabs only under conditions which confirm their preconceptions.'[7] So, for example, they may be prepared to meet with 'moderates', who describe themselves as 'Israeli Arabs' and who are loyal to the State of Israel, *but* they will not meet with 'radicals', who describe themselves as 'Palestinians' and identify with the struggle to establish a Palestinian state and who may even sympathise with the PLO. This is problematic as a growing majority of Arabs in Israel do identify themselves as Palestinians; in fact, only 20 per cent have come to accept the idea of an independent Jewish–Zionist state with themselves as a minority in it.[8] Furthermore, the largest Arab-dominated political party (the DFPE) advocates the establishment of a Palestinian state in the territories and supports Fatah.[9] Israeli Jews who are ready to meet their 'national minority', the 'Israeli Arab', are often taken aback to discover that: 'The surging Palestinian identity that many Arabs in Israel now embrace and even proclaim has made the compound "Israeli Arab" a contradiction in terms.'[10]

Jewish suspicion of Jewish–Arab contacts and reluctance to meet with Arabs, whose views are perceived as threatening, is paralleled by a growing reluctance on the part of many Arabs to participate in IPJACs organised by Israeli Jews whose motives they suspect. The result is that 'most dialogue groups (IPJACs) are imbalanced in their representation of the two populations, with the Jewish participants "dialoguing" with Arabs who represent only a small, and shrinking, percentage of the Arab population.'[11] This conclusion is reached by researchers Demarest and Abu-Shakrah who argue, in their study of one particular IPJAC, that the 'apparent dialogue' that took place 'had never been between Israeli Jews and Palestinians as two peoples, but rather between a dominant Jewish group intent on preserving the status quo and a fantasised "Arab minority" cleansed of their national identity.'[12]

Considering the lack of institutional support, public suspicion and the imbalance between the two sides engaged in encounters and 'dialogue', Israel's IPJACs are likely to remain ineffectual 'drops in the ocean'. It has been suggested that the gulf between Arabs and Jews in Israel could be narrowed (if not bridged) if the IPJACs run by the MOs of the peace movement were to be superseded by state involvement in the educational system. This would require the institutionalisation of an obligatory, comprehensive and long-term IPJAC, involving all levels within the national education system. Such a proposal has in fact been submitted (by educationalists Tsyona Peled and David Bar-Gal) to the special Committee of Education for Coexistence of the Ministry of Education and Culture.

As appealing as the idea of a state-run IPJAC may sound, it faces huge obstacles. The first and most important of these has been alluded to above: the diametrically opposed Arab and Jewish perceptions of issues as fundamental as the nature of the State of Israel, the position of the 'national minority' and the future of the occupied territories.

Secondly, differences are continually exacerbated by macro-level conflicts such as the war in Lebanon. Evidently, until these basic macro-level conflicts are solved, Palestinians who are citizens of Israel will never identify with a state in conflict with their own people and Israeli Jews will continue to view this minority as a 'security risk' – justifying, in their eyes, certain inequalities in the Israeli state system. It is far from clear how any IPJAC could deal successfully with these fundamental problems. 'Psychological barriers' to peace are grounded in socio-political facts which are not so easily overcome.

As educationalists Peled and Bar-Gal point out, any IPJAC carried out at a national level, within the state education system, would have to be,

> based on strong internal and external consensus with respect to the need for education for Arab–Jewish coexistence, and with respect to its goals and essence. This consensus ought to be shared by officials and educators at the various levels of the system as well as by parents in both sectors. Such consensus is achievable only if based on the assumption that education for Arab–Jewish coexistence is a specific

and important goal within the broader chapter of education for good citizenship in the democratic Jewish State of Israel.[13]

Regrettably, such consensus does not exist in Israel. Not only is it absent, as we have seen, between Arab and Jew, but it is also absent amongst Jews. The lack of consensus was made abundantly clear when, in July 1985, the Labour Minister of Education, Yitzhak Navon, brought out a paper calling for meetings between Arab and Jewish pupils, within the state education system.

The directive created an immediate storm of controversy, even though it had no financial backing to carry out the proposed meetings. Opposition came primarily from the religious orthodox establishment. The head of the Education Ministry's religious education division, Ya'acov Hadani, and the Chief Rabbinical Council came out against Jewish–Arab meetings on the grounds that meetings between the sexes could lead to intermarriage between the two population groups. Hadani spoke in favour of segregation (in Israel and abroad) as a means of protecting Jews from assimilation which he described as 'the greatest danger to the Jewish people in all its generations'.[14] The second objection was based on the fear that Jewish–Arab meetings could lead to a violation of *kashrut* by Jewish children eating in Arab homes. Despite the fact that these problems could easily be overcome (by having single-sex encounters and making special eating arrangements), Hadani issued a directive forbidding any meetings which would bring Jewish pupils of the orthodox school system (which is funded by the state) into contact with their Arab counterparts.

Even with the co-operation of the religious establishment, it would be impossible to institutionalise any comprehensive programme for promoting Arab–Jewish contacts within the school system without the co-operation of the teachers. As pointed out, a successful IPJAC requires 'commitment, involvement and devotion as well as professional qualifications, on the part of the educators'.[15] There are, however, no indications that teachers would be willing to undergo the required training. Peled and Bar-Gal, recognising this difficulty, recommend that in place of direct Jewish–Arab contacts, schools should concentrate on developing curricula with material regarding the language, history, culture and society of the other nation, as well as focusing on Arab–Jewish coexistence per se, possibly using programmes produced by IPJAC MOs which are already being used in a number of schools.

Again, even this would require teachers' co-operation. Unfortunately, research indicates that many teachers are less than willing to promote Jewish–Arab coexistence in any conceivable way. According to one survey, up to 20 per cent of teachers actually support the extreme racist views of Kahane.[16]

THE PROBLEM OF EVALUATION

All in all it appears that the IPJAC organisations are fighting a losing battle. Even though they have been successful in gaining some support from the state – for their approach to conflict resolution – they continue to face seemingly insurmountable obstacles: macro-level conflicts, the rising tide of racist and religious-nationalist sentiments (on both sides) and opposing worldviews, *all* minimise the impact of voluntary and state-run IPJACs. Evaluating the actual success of the existing IPJACs is exceedingly complex. This problem is not confined to the Israeli experience; research from other parts of the world on the effects of organised intergroup contacts is far from conclusive.

There appears to be widespread scepticism amongst Arab educators who feel that any positive change in the attitudes of Jewish pupils will only be reversed by the two or three years they spend in the Israeli Defence Force. So far, to the best of my knowledge, research has not been carried out on the change in attitude amongst young people who have been through a comprehensive IPJAC (such as that of Neve Shalom), before and after military service. Voting patterns consistently demonstrate that the army vote is more hawkish than that of the general population. On the other hand, the army does make some attempt to educate officers 'in the process of peace making in the Middle East conflict'. The scope of this programme is, however, extremely limited. It is intended primarily to give selected officers an understanding of the constraints under which policy makers have to take decisions, thus enabling them to become familiar with the complexity and time required for decision making in the field of foreign affairs and defence. The object of this is to combat impatience amongst military officers towards politicians, hence (it is hoped) reducing the risk of a Latin American-type military coup.[17]

Although the IPJAC MOs have a limited impact, their role in the peace movement is not insignificant. They expose many young people to a more universal way of seeing the Arab–Israeli conflict – helping them to see an abstract enemy as a human being. In this way they help to stem the rising tide of particular forces so prevalent amongst young people. The IPJAC MOs may be seen as part of the 'reform' side of the peace movement. This is made evident by the fact that they most often aim to restore universal values, *within the Jewish state*, through their encouragement of tolerance, democracy and coexistence; they do not aim to radically restructure Israeli society. Rather, taking existing ideals, they aim to reform apparent defects in the social order. If their impact were to be measured solely according to this criterion, it is possible that they may be considered to have a fair impact on the attitudes of young people with whom most of them work.

THE ROLE OF RESEARCH AND POLICY INSTITUTES

An important 'sub-sphere' of the Israeli peace movement consists of MOs engaged in peace-related research and publication. In addition, such MOs organise symposia, train peace educators and facilitate Jewish–Arab dialogue. Perhaps the best example of such an MO is the Tel Aviv-based International Centre for Peace in the Middle East (ICPME). The Centre, which was started by staff and associates of the Israeli peace journal *New Outlook*, strives to 'serve as a focal point for all those, in Israel and abroad . . . actively involved in the quest for peace in the Middle East, regardless of nationality, ideology, religion or political affiliations.'[18] While aiming to act as a resource centre at the service of the peace movement as a whole, the ICPME in fact works most closely with the dovish political parties which it serves in a number of important ways.

Firstly, through its 'Knesset Members' Forum', it unites parliamentary doves from the different parties for discussion of issues closely related to the peace process. Secondly, it is able to take initiatives which the political parties are reluctant or unable to take. So, for example, when Willy Brandt visited Israel as a guest of the Labour Party in February 1985, he asked to meet prominent Palestinians from the West Bank. As it was impossible for Labour to arrange such a meeting (partly because the Palestinians would not have come to a Labour party event and partly because arranging such a meeting could be electorally disadvantageous), the Party asked the ICPME to make the arrangements.[19] The Centre, whose honorary president is the much-respected Haim Cohen, acts as neutral ground, not only for the various political parties (up to thirty MKs participate in the Forum), but also for Israeli politicians and Palestinian leaders from the West Bank. In March 1984, an Israeli–Palestinian dialogue was organised which was attended by forty Knesset Members who met with various Palestinian leaders. The dialogue with West Bank Palestinians has been continuous and, on a number of occasions, joint statements have been issued, stressing the need for a full solution of the Israeli–Palestinian conflict through mutual recognition, self-determination and coexistence. It is the belief of the ICPME that such a dialogue is in fact paving the way for 'real' negotiations with the Palestinians by creating an 'atmosphere of trust', by establishing the 'credibility' of dialogue and by helping to remove obstacles to the peace process by developing ideas for a solution. Put differently, the ICPME sees its role as 'breaking ground for the proper authorities to enter into direct negotiations (with the Palestinians) and come up with a working set-up'.[20]

A third important way in which the ICPME helps dovish parliamentarians is by undertaking policy-related research to provide them (as legislators) with the necessary tools to implement changes. So, for example, the Centre has undertaken research on the status and condition of the Arabs in Israel, focusing on such issues as the discrepancies in the amount of money received per capita by Jewish and Arab municipalities. The findings are then passed on to dovish Knesset Members who, as an established lobby within their parties and within the Knesset, act to push for legislation. Research published by the Centre, written by some of Israel's leading academics, has explored controversial subjects such as: 'The Military-Industrial Complex in Israel' by Dr Yoram Peri and Amnon Neubach and 'Peaceful Separation or Enforced Unity: Economic Consequences for Israel and the West Bank' by Dr Simcha Bahiri.

As an *international centre*, the ICPME plays the dual role of giving well-known Diaspora Jews a voice in the debate over the peace process and by providing them (through press briefs and newsletters) with news of Israel not often presented in the international media. Finally, through its Jewish–Arab Council for Peace Education, the Centre organises seminars for educators and community leaders concerned with Arab–Jewish relations. In 1984 a seminar was held on the theme of 'Evaluation and Research as Tools for Co-ordinators of Jewish–Arab Encounters'; it was attended by representatives from all of Israel's IPJAC MOs.

Another important research organisation is the Van Leer Jerusalem Foundation (VLJF). As an independent institute, it works on a wide range of social and policy issues concentrating, in particular, on the issue of pluralism in Israel. This includes the problems of Mizrachi–Ashkenazi relations, Israel–Diaspora relations and Jewish–Arab relations.

Unlike the ICPME, the VLJF does not work closely with the dovish political parties. Its main concern, in recent years, has been to study 'how Israeli schools should educate pupils in the twin issues of civic equality between Arabs and Jews in Israel and of relations between Israel and her neighbours in the Middle East.' Realising that, for more than thirty years, the Israeli education system almost totally refrained from tackling these crucial issues, the VLJF approached the Ministry of Education and Culture in 1982 with a proposal to examine what could be done to rectify the omissions of the past. With financial assistance from the Ford Foundation, the VLJF and the Ministry began co-operating in the production of a textbook for secondary schools on Jewish–Arab relations in Israel. Later a committee was established which proposed the outline of a comprehensive educational programme on Jewish–Arab coexistence. It was agreed that the VLJF would work as an equal partner with the Ministry to prepare textbooks and to train teachers for the new programme which would be implemented within three to five years. Recognising that 'kinder-gartens are at present breeding grounds for prejudice and negative stereotyping', the committee proposed that the programme should begin at this level by helping kindergarten teachers to dissipate negative stereotyping. In schools it recognised that 'a considerable asymmetry exists between what Arab pupils and Jewish pupils learn about each other's culture and history' (with Arab schools devoting substantial time to Hebrew, Jewish history and the arts, and Jewish schools 'less than the minimal' to the Arab equivalents). To rectify this, the committee undertook to expand the study of Arab language and culture in Jewish schools.

Going beyond schools, the committee proposed that a regular, bilingual series, 'for the whole family, on Jewish–Arab relations', be prepared for Israeli television. The committee hoped that the series would 'legitimise and humanise Arab–Jewish relations on the basis of equality and mutual respect', reinforcing at home what pupils would learn at school. Although the series was expected to be the most influential of all the programmes, it would also be the most expensive and the committee has yet to secure finances.[21]

It is yet too early to tell how successful the committee will be in implementing its suggestions. Judging from the opposition raised to the Ministry's directive encouraging IPJACs within the education system, it would seem that the implementation of most of the proposals is going to be an uphill battle. It should be pointed out, however, that the VLJF has a well-established record in the field of improving Jewish–Arab coexistence. Working with Neve Shalom, the institute has trained educators in IPJAC and has produced a guide book for practitioners. It has also established an evaluation team which attempts to assess the efficacy of IPJACs. In addition, the VLJF has produced a series of important studies revealing, in particular, emerging trends amongst Israeli youth. One such report revealed that about 50 per cent of Jewish high school students surveyed, held strong anti-democratic views with regard to non-Jews in general and to Arabs in particular.[22] The importance of such findings to IPJAC MOs and others in the peace movement should not be underestimated.

In the third sphere of Figure 2, I have included a list of 'Civil and Human Rights' Organisations'. Their work is based on the belief that peace cannot be achieved without justice. Organisations, such as the Israeli League for Human and Civil Rights, and individuals, such as civil rights lawyer Felicia Langer, have done a great deal, not only in defending human rights, but also in bringing the plight of Palestinians to public attention.

Their work has earned them the respect of many Palestinians, thus furthering the possibilities of Arab–Jewish coexistence in the future. In a sense, the 'justice MOs' best exemplify the desire to see universal values rigorously implemented, both within Israel proper and the occupied territories – regardless of national origin or political affiliation.

8 Dovish Parties and Protest Organisations

POLITICAL PARTIES AND THE PEACE MOVEMENT

The role of the dovish parties in the peace movement is, on the surface, fairly straightforward. They function within the electoral and parliamentary framework, representing the broad aims of the movement within Israel's national assembly, the Knesset. They attempt to gain enough political power, through the democratic process, to implement their vision of society. The relationship between the parliamentary sphere and the extra-parliamentary sphere is, however, highly complex below the surface.

The protest MOs are attracted by what influence the parties may have on governmental decision making. Yet, at the same time, they are repelled by the dangers inherent in any close association with one particular party which is bound to be a source of schism and conflict within the MO. Furthermore, in return for providing a voice inside the Knesset, the parties inevitably expect the protest MOs to provide electoral support and, to a certain extent, allegiance to party policies. Consequently, the relationship between the two spheres is ambiguous. Nevertheless, links do exist between the spheres which are clearly identifiable and of considerable importance.

As Figure 2 illustrates, different left-wing, dovish parties have links with different protest MOs. The two predominantly Arab parties, the DFPE and the PLP, have links with the anti- and non-Zionist protest MOs. This is most evident through the participation of party members in these protest MOs and vice versa. Not surprisingly, intense competition between the DFPE (predominantly communist) and the PLP (predominantly nationalist) has reduced the unity, and hence effectiveness of the MOs.

THE LABOUR PARTY

The place of Labour within the 'parliamentary sphere' of the peace movement is questioned by many peace activists who point out that it was under Labour that the settlement of the West Bank began. While this cannot be denied, it is also true that *officially* the party is willing to negotiate at least some territories for peace and that, at times, it has given its full support to Peace Now. Furthermore, it should be noted that the party itself is divided between hawks and doves; with this in mind it has been included in the first sphere of Figure 2.

There is abundant evidence of links between Peace Now and the Labour party. It is reported, for example, that Yossi Sarid, then a Labour Member of Knesset and a well-known dove, helped with the drafting of the officers' letter.[1] Soon after the formation of the MO, a number of prominent Labour party MKs supported Peace Now in a public letter. These included: Abba Eban, Yigal Allon, Yossi Sarid and the Labour Party Secretary-General, Uzi Baram.[2] Peace Now-organised events have frequently featured well-known members of the Labour party as speakers; notable examples include former Prime Minister Yitzhak Rabin and former Information Minister Aharon Yaniv.[3] Less than two months after Peace Now came into being, activists met with the then Labour party Chairman, Shimon Peres. Peres noted after the meeting that the 'party's position did not contradict Peace Now's'. He noted in particular that the party shared with Peace Now (a) an opposition to imposing Israeli rule over one and a half million Arabs, (b) a desire to preserve the democratic and Jewish nature of Israel and (c) a willingness for territorial compromise 'on all three fronts'.[4] A few days later, at a meeting of its executive, the Labour party openly declared that it 'supported' Peace Now, with the former Minister of Education, Aharon Yadin, declaring that Peace Now was a 'positive thing and Labour should not stay aloof from it'.[5] The single most dramatic instance of Labour lending its full backing to Peace Now was the demonstration which followed the Sabra and Shatilla massacres. Had it not done so, the demonstration would have been considerably smaller.

MAPAM

If Peace Now shares a close relationship with the Labour party, its relationship with the two Zionist parties to the left of Labour, Ratz and Mapam, may be described as intimate. Considering Mapam's history of backing peace endeavours (see Chapter 2), its support of Peace Now comes as no surprise. From the outset, the party – and in particular the affiliated Kibbutz Hartzi movement – provided massive support for Peace Now. This came not only in the form of Mapam members' active participation in Peace Now demonstrations, but also in the form of material resources (transport, finances) and the 'lending' of Kibbutz members to Peace Now to organise events. Mapam has never denied its support of Peace Now. Its political secretary, Victor Shemtov, boasted that Mapam activists have provided much of the organisational know-how behind Peace Now. One party member claimed that Peace Now would never even have lasted as long as it did had it not been for Mapam.[6] One journalist noted: 'There is a certain exhilaration about Mapam's involvement with thousands of politically unaffiliated young men and women.'[7]

In the 1981 and 1984 elections, Peace Now held long consultations with the dovish parties. Feeling that its aims were already represented, it decided not to enter the elections as a political party. While maintaining its extra-parliamentary role, Peace Now encouraged its supporters to vote for any of the parties which represented its aims.

RATZ

Despite the fact that Peace Now had supporters in all the dovish parties, it developed a rather special relationship with Ratz. In 1981, Ratz accepted a condition *imposed by Peace Now* that it would 'unconditionally join a coalition with the Labour Alignment if this enabled Labour Party Chairman Shimon Peres to form a government without the former foreign minister Moshe Dayan or the National Religious Party'.[8] Following the agreement, an 'unspecified number' of Peace Now activists joined Ratz. Peace Now activists, Dedi Zucker and Yuli Tamir, were placed as numbers four and five on the Ratz electoral list. Zucker summarised some of the demands that Peace Now insisted on having included in the Ratz electoral platform:

> We want negotiations (for peace) to be based on the national rights and rights of self-determination of all the peoples in the area, including the Palestinians. The Palestinians should be included in

the negotiations – specifically any group that accepts negotiations as the only way to settle the dispute. In keeping with the Geneva Conventions, changes in the law which have been made in the territories . . . should be cancelled. There should be no more Jewish settlement in the territories.[9]

The acceptance by Ratz of a Peace Now condition, and the introduction of particular Peace Now concerns into the party's electoral platform, represent the successful penetration of a social movement organisation into the political arena. In 1981 this did not amount to much because only Shulamit Aloni, the Ratz leader, was elected to the Knesset. But, in 1984, the well-known Peace Now activist, Mordechai Bar-On, became number two on the Ratz list – making the party a likely choice for Peace Now supporters. He was successfully elected to the Knesset giving the MO an unofficial voice within the political heart of the nation.

We have seen how the close association between the protest MOs of the peace movement and the different dovish political parties of the 'parliamentary sphere' of Figure 2 illustrates that the movement is not purely an extra-parliamentary movement. Not only do the extra-parliamentary groups penetrate the parliamentary parties, in a bid to gain influence over decision making, but vice versa: the political parties penetrate the 'extra-parliamentary' sphere of the protest groups in a bid to gain votes from a constituency sharing a similar world view.

PROTEST MOVEMENT ORGANISATIONS

OZ VE SHALOM

It has been argued throughout the preceding chapters that the formation of the Israeli peace movement can be seen as an active response in defence of universal values, which appeared to be threatened by various extremely particular trends – notably religious nationalism. As it stands, the argument is over-simplified. There are numerous religious Jews who uphold both the particular and universal aspects of Judaism. One remarkable individual who exemplifies this is Professor Yeshayahu Leibowitz, who is regarded by many activists in the peace movement as virtually a prophet. In 1967, just after the Six-Day War, Leibowitz, a religious man with an orthodox background, warned that unless the newly-occupied territories were returned, their occupation would give rise to oppression ('there is no such thing as a humane occupation') and ultra-nationalism which would undermine Israeli democracy. His outspoken opposition to the occupation and his incisive analysis of its consequences have earned Leibowitz the admiration of secular peace activists from a wide range of MOs. Another religious Jew who has fast earned the respect of the movement is Rabbi Jeremy Miligrom, an American-born Reform Rabbi, who has been involved in a number of MOs, including Reshet and Yesh Gvul.

Such individuals are not the only religious Jews to oppose the occupation. As mentioned in Chapter 2, a number of religious academics and members of the Mafdal (the National Religious Party) supported the post-1967 peace groups of the nascent peace movement. In 1975 they came together to form their own MO called Oz ve Shalom (Courage and Peace).

Many of the religious doves were reluctant to join Oz ve Shalom which, since its formation, had acquired the image of a left-leaning, liberal, academic group. Religious doves who had been to *hesder yeshivot* were particularly reluctant to join Oz ve Shalom. The invasion of Lebanon and the Sabra and Shatilla massacre led these young people to create a new religious MO which they hoped would not be burdened with the left-wing intellectual image of Oz ve Shalom. Netivot le Shalom (Pathways to Peace), as it was called, believed that its role would be to persuade *hesder yeshivot* comrades who were now members of Gush Emunim, to join the religious dovish camp. This, they felt, would be impossible if they became part of Oz ve Shalom because of that MO's image. Netivot le Shalom believed that it would at least be able to influence the religious political centre. However, within a very short time, the media had branded it as being a 'leftist religious' group. The new MO discovered, as others have, that the political centre in Israel is virtually non-existent: 'either one is for the occupation or against.'[10] Consequently the two religious groups joined forces and now share both offices and personnel. They have maintained their individual names and 'identities' (with Oz ve Shalom maintaining a more leftist profile) as this is considered useful when addressing different audiences. In the following presentation of the religious MOs, to simplify matters, reference will be made to 'Oz ve Shalom's ideology' – even though subtle differences between the two MOs on specific issues may thus be overlooked.

The existence of *religious Zionist* MOs would, at first sight, appear to undermine the concept of the peace movement as one defending universal values. It cannot be denied that Oz ve Shalom upholds particular Jewish values which, on the surface, appear to be similar to those of Gush Emunim, as discussed in Chapter 1. For example, both religious groups look to the teachings of Rabbi Abraham Kuk (senior) for inspiration; both believe that the Jews have 'an irrevocable right to Eretz Yisrael'[11] which they consider as sacred land promised to the Jews by God. At this point their ways part.

The essential difference between Oz ve Shalom and Gush Emunim is that, despite the former's commitment to values and ideals that are *particular* to Judaism, it continues to uphold *universal* values which are *rooted* in Judaism and Jewish tradition. This is most evident in its view of the way in which Palestinians should be treated. The religious MO strongly opposes Gush Emunim's religious ideology which 'ends up treating Arab Christians and Muslims in ways that resemble the persecution to which Jews were subjected for centuries'[12]; they equally oppose Kahane's 'final solution' for the Palestinian 'Question' – expulsion. Instead, Oz ve Shalom points out that 'the Jews have a revealed and revered tradition that teaches . . . that all human beings, not just Jews, are created in God's image and are worthy of being treated with dignity, respect and compassion.'[13]

Central to the dispute between Oz ve Shalom and Gush Emunim is the future of the 'promised land'. Although Oz ve Shalom believes that the Land of Israel belongs to the 'seed of Abraham', it also believes that 'the Palestinian Arab desire for national self-determination precludes the fulfilment of this historical and Biblical claim within the totality of the land.'[14] The religious MO consistently argues that, in addition to 'equity and compassion' for the Arabs, it is self-interest which demands that Israel seek a political and territorial compromise: 'The national soul of Israel is corrupted when it makes a military occupation imposed on us by a defensive war into a preferred, even normative condition.'[15] The election of Kahane, the activities of Jewish terrorists and the war in Lebanon are referred to as indications of the corruption resulting from the occupation. Withdrawal is essential to bring Jewish citizens back 'from the path of ethnocentrism and chauvinism' to enable Israel to fulfil its 'prophetic vocation' to be a moral 'light unto the nations'.

What really distinguishes Oz ve Shalom from any of the secular MOs is the nature of its discourse. It is the only MO within the peace movement which is able to confront Gush Emunim on its own ground, using the same terminology. Gush Emunim readily dismisses secular opponents of the occupation as being 'Hellenists' or not 'authentic' Jews. In the case of Oz ve Shalom, this is clearly impossible. They cannot be dismissed with the same ease; they wear the same knitted skull caps, grow equally long beards, don't break the Sabbath and quote from the same sacred texts. If anyone in the peace movement is in a position to persuade Gush Emunim members that the endeavour to settle the entire 'Land of Israel' endangers peace, it is the religious doves. For this reason, and because the debate focuses on 'the Jews' relationship to the Land of Israel' (a question at the heart of the dispute over the occupation) further investigation is called for.

As mentioned in Chapter 1, Gush Emunim's spiritual mentor, Rabbi Kuk senior, upheld the sacred task of settling the Land of Israel. Gush Emunim has consistently argued that the right of the Jews to the settlement of the Land is absolute. This claim is based, in part, on the writings of the Jewish sage, Rashi, who argued that the inclusion of Genesis in the Torah was intended to inform the Jews of God's division of the earth into nations and the lands which they possess, and the *absolute* right of the Jews to the Land of Israel.[16] Oz ve Shalom questions this interpretation, claiming that the right to the land is not absolute, but conditional on the ethical behaviour of the Jews. According to Uriel Simon, a founder of Oz ve Shalom:

> Following the act of creation, in the Book of Genesis, we are told of a whole series of expulsions from the land, as a result of sinning: Adam and Eve were expelled from the Garden of Eden; Cain became a wanderer after having killed Abel; and the children of Israel went down to Egypt because of the sins of their forefathers. . . The Master of the Universe intended the land of Israel for the people of Israel, but only in conjunction with the severe admonition that our real hold on the land is conditional on our behaviour.[17]

Simon goes on to point out that the Jews' 'religious right' to the land cannot be equated with a legal-political right that can be immediately effectuated in practice. The Torah, he argues, makes it clear that divine promise cannot be equated with actual ownership: upon Sarah's death, Abraham found himself without title to a grave-site in a land promised to him long before, enforcing him to buy the Cave of Machepelah. And indeed later, Abraham was forced to make a 'territorial compromise' in order to make peace between his shepherds and Lot's – a point much overlooked by Gush Emunim ideologues who point to Rabbi Zvi Kuk's teachings that 'not an inch' of the sacred Land of Israel should be given up.

Oz ve Shalom activists assert that Gush Emunim's view of the land itself as sacred is incorrect. This interpretation, they argue, has transcended the original *Halachic* meaning which held that the Land of Israel was holy because only there was it possible to observe 'the religious and ritual laws concerning agriculture, socio-economic customs and ways of life related to rural economy'.[18] Furthermore, claims to the sanctity of specific boundaries are rejected. Oz ve Shalom believes that the variety of boundaries for Eretz Yisrael that is to be found in the Scriptures, teach that 'it is impossible to attribute sanctity to phenomena that are essentially historical and subject to change.'[19]

Besides having fundamentally different perceptions of space (territory), Oz ve Shalom and Gush Emunim have equally differing perceptions of time. The controversy is over 'the appropriateness and implications of a messianic interpretation of history, applied to contemporary events'. For Gush Emunim, there is no doubt that Israel is living through the messianic period. For these religious Zionists, the signs are obvious: the return of the Jews from exile, the 'redemption' of the Land, the flowering of the desert and, since 1967, the acquisition and settlement of 'Judea and Samaria'. The belief that they are living through the period of Redemption, heralding the imminent coming of the Messiah, has tempted certain religious Zionists to 'accelerate the redemption' by carrying out acts which they believe can only speed the coming of the Messiah. It was with this in mind that the attempt was made to blow up the Muslim holy sites on Temple Mount.

Oz ve Shalom rejects Gush Emunim's interpretation of time as false. The religious doves interpret time 'in the spirit of Maimonides', restraining teachings about the messianic era. According to these teachings the period of Redemption will not bring about 'the rule of might over other nations, but (rather) the freedom to engage in the study of the Torah and its wisdom, thus enabling Israel to establish a just and moral society built on the Law'.[20]

Oz ve Shalom has shown special concern about the political implications of attempts to 'accelerate the redemption'. The literature of the MO condemns such attempts (associated with the extremist groups discussed in Chapter 1) as 'Sabbatianism'. The term refers to Sabbatai Zevi who was only one of various false messiahs in Jewish history. Oz ve Shalom attempts to make it clear that efforts to 'accelerate the redemption' have been 'condemned by Torah authorities throughout the ages'.[21]

For Oz ve Shalom, one of the most important Jewish values is *pikuakh nefesh* – saving lives. All other values are secondary to this. The preservation of the Sabbath, the settlement or redemption of the Land of Israel must all be regarded as secondary to the commandment to save lives. From this point of view, the attempt to blow up the Muslim holy sites was clearly a folly. Likewise, in Oz ve Shalom's view, the occupation and resettlement of the territories is wrong because it provokes Palestinian resistance, which leads to violence, oppression and the increased risk of war – all endangering life.[22] The war in Lebanon was a cause for great concern amongst the religious MOs because of the loss of life and because the war did not appear to be a defensive war, the likes of which are sanctioned by Jewish law. It led to considerable debate about the use of violence, the 'morality of warfare' and Jewish attitudes towards peace.

Oz ve Shalom's approach has been largely educational. Although it and Netivot le Shalom have organised 'prayer and protest' demonstrations (attended by 2000 to 3000 people at a time), and have participated in Peace Now demonstrations (when they have not been held on a Sabbath), the main thrust of the MOs' work has been to combat the *ideas* of Gush Emunim and Kahane. The religious MOs' main targets for this educational thrust have been the religious schools, youth movements and *yeshivot*. Netivot le Shalom has been particularly successful in entering these institutions, while Oz ve Shalom academics have focused on the universities, journals and newspapers to present their ideas. Considering the fact that Oz ve Shalom has a membership of only 600 to 700, it has been fairly successful in publicising its views over the last ten years. The essential question that remains to be answered is what impact these ideas have had.

Measuring the impact of ideas (as opposed to events or other factors) is a complex, if not impossible task. However, one safe indicator of the growing strength of a particular body of ideas is the growth in size and strength of the organisations which embody the ideas. Oz ve Shalom has seen a steady rise in its membership, requests for information and speakers as well as an increase in media attention, which would suggest that its ideas have had some impact amongst religious Zionists. However, the fact that the MO's most dramatic increase in membership activity and media attention came during the war in Lebanon, makes one question whether it was the *propagation of ideas or the reaction to the war* which was the more responsible for the MO's growth. The formation of Netivot le Shalom would suggest that it was primarily the war which gave rise to the surge of support for the ideas forwarded by the doves. Had it been Oz ve Shalom's success in spreading its ideas, surely there would have been no need to form a separate MO. The war shocked many religious Zionists who had attended *hesder yeshivot*. It moved them to accept and further key ideas that Oz ve Shalom had been propagating for seven years, despite their reluctance to join the MO itself because of its 'leftist academic' image. Thus Oz ve Shalom laid the ideological foundation upon which Netivot le Shalom built.

It is important to put the growth of the religious MOs into perspective. Despite the apparent decline in the growth of Gush Emunim, following the war in Lebanon and the trial of the Jewish terrorists, and the corresponding rise in support of Oz ve Shalom/ Netivot le Shalom, the latter remain incomparably smaller than the former. Gush Emunim continues to enjoy widespread support even though the number of new settlers is on the decline.[23] It now remains to be explained why this religious Zionist group is far more popular than the dovish religious MOs.

The first reason why Gush Emunim is more successful than Oz ve Shalom in the struggle to win the 'hearts and minds' of religious Zionists, lies in its different approach. As mentioned, Oz ve Shalom is primarily an *educational* organisation. A great deal of its members' time is spent in producing articles, lectures and press statements which refute, in a highly rational manner, the various arguments used by Gush Emunim to justify the settlement of the occupied territories. Gush Emunim, on the other hand, is primarily a *political* organisation, whose leaders 'are possessed by a sense of movement whose momentum must be maintained'.[24] Janet Aviad, sociologist and Peace Now treasurer, describes the difference between the two in this way:

> The members of Oz ve Shalom stress the necessity for clear, measured, rational thinking about ethical and religious matters, while statements and writings of leaders of Gush Emunim are characterised by enthusiasm, emotionalism, and less commitment to rationalism. Members of Oz ve Shalom stress the duties of criticism, analysis, moderation, and restraint. Gush Emunim is characterised by intolerance of criticism and a distinct inability to entertain alternative interpretations to any given situation. . . Gush Emunim has been a movement of action, an agency in the fulfilment of a messianic process. Oz ve Shalom was a response founded in order to clarify ideological and political problems arising from the praxis of Gush Emunim, through the written and spoken word.[25]

These basic differences were confirmed by Yehezkel Landau, information secretary of Oz ve Shalom. Pushed to describe exactly how Gush Emunim attempted to refute Oz ve Shalom's clear, rational arguments, he admitted that, in fact, the debate between the two was 'not logical, not rational, but emotional, subjective and meta-halachah.' To illustrate his point he described how he had had a three-hour conversation with a rabbi (who was a respected authority of the *Halachah*) about the Jewish terrorists. The rabbi was sympathetic towards them and Landau tried to get him to justify this on Halachic grounds. Finally, the rabbi admitted that he could not justify Jewish terrorism according to the Halachah and said:

> After the Holocaust, after everything we have suffered, it is time we rose up and showed our enemies a taste of their own medicine, and stop being the sissy, *galut* Jews we've been for the past 2,000 years. I think the Halachah should be suspended long enough to deal a decisive blow to our enemies and then we'll go back to halachic living.

Landau went on to explain that the rabbi had seen his brother shot by the Gestapo in Lithuania, and that had affected his life and relations with non-Jews ever since:

And this is the level at which the debate operates in this country – not at the logical, Talmudic–Halachic plane. . . . Religious arguments are being constructed selectively to justify a pseudo-messianic, mystical, militant, chauvinist world view that is against the clear teachings of the Hebrew prophets and rabbinic sages.[26]

In relating this extraordinary conversation and in insisting that the debate was not rational but essentially emotive, Landau revealed the chief reason for Oz ve Shalom's failure to win over more than a small minority of religious Zionists. Aviad confirms this:

First, the voice of rationality and moderation is always dim next to the voice of extremism and emotionalism. Second, the voice that introduces complications and ambiguities is always dim next to the voice of clarity and self-certainty. Third, a movement that engages in a critique of society in the name of transcendent values, and in a critique of the religious establishment according to the same criterion, is much less appealing than one which identifies the holy with an empirical order. Finally, a movement that speaks in the name of universal ethical values and the rights of the 'other' is much less comfortable than one that asserts the unique (particular) and superior rights of the nation.[27]

There are a number of other important reasons for Oz ve Shalom's lack of appeal to religious Zionists which Aviad does not raise. One of these is that the MO, with its rational approach, is simply not in keeping with the non-rational, anti-universal, spirit of the day (*Zeitgeist*).

It has been suggested that Israel's religious education system is largely responsible for the non-rational, particular trends which underlie the strength of Gush Emunim (and the weakness of Oz ve Shalom). Lawrence Kaplan, a specialist in Jewish intellectual history, asserts that the Jewish component of education in Israel's religious Zionist *yeshivot*, 'still follows in all essentials the education model and approach of the Eastern European *yeshivot* and their latter-day imitators, except that this education is overlaid with a coating of messianic, nationalist Zionism'.[28] Although Rabbi Kuk senior envisioned the establishment of new *yeshivot*, with curricula that would be fundamentally different from those of Eastern Europe, such a reform never took place. The result is that the Jewish component in Israel's religious Zionist schools and *yeshivot* has remained 'essentially fundamentalist, authoritarian, and *particularist in character*, having a narrow, if intense, range of concerns, and basically unconcerned with general *universal, social, ethical . . . and humanistic issues* [own emphasis].'[29] It is the combination of the traditional, particular approach of the Jewish Eastern European *yeshiva* and the modern, nationalistic Zionism of Israel that has created the right conditions for Gush Emunim. It is questionable whether Oz ve Shalom will be able to gain the support of any significant number of the religious Zionists who have found that the 'messianic-nationalist emotionalism' of Gush Emunim has 'injected new life and vitality into their own religious existence . . . [making] for a heady and exciting religious activism that stands in sharp contrast to the almost mechanical general routine of the religious community.'[30]

RADICAL ORGANISATIONS AND ZIONISM

Let us turn from the more particularistic MOs in the Israeli peace movement, to the more universalistic ones. These MOs come closest to the 'revolutionary' end of the reform-revolution continuum described in Chapter 2; they are the only ones making demands for 'core' changes in the Israeli social system and at the same time they tend to be more 'exclusive' than other MOs. Certainly they are more exclusive than Peace Now: they do not allow for the same variety of positions on issues such as the future of the occupied territories. They are less concerned about fitting in with the broader cultural values of Israeli society (such as Zionism); about securing external legitimacy, or about an ability to recruit new members. They tend to require greater active commitment from members and, not atypically, are subject to frequent schisms. Before entering into details, let us consider the general background of the radical MOs.

In the Israeli context, the term 'radical' may be used to describe all groups who do not accept the basic ideological tenets of political Zionism, pertaining to the establishment of a *Jewish* state in the Land of Israel, or who do accept them, 'but under circumstances of such extensive and comprehensive change as to be outside of, and unacceptable to, the broad consensus of Israeli society'.[31] There can be no doubt that the majority of activists in the peace movement's radical (universal) MOs have misgivings about Zionism. In interviews and publications, radical activists frequently refer to themselves as 'non' or 'anti-Zionists' – unfortunately, they rarely define these terms in a clear manner.

One of the reasons for this is that the term 'Zionism' is itself one of the most emotive, loaded and ambiguous terms used by both Israelis and Palestinians – of all political stripes. In Israel it is often used as a synonym not only for 'patriotism' but also for 'idealism' and even for 'altruism'. For example, helping the disabled may be referred to as 'an act of true Zionism'. However, for most Palestinian Arabs, far from being altruistic, Zionism is seen as oppressive and exploitive; the ideology in whose name they were deprived of their land and freedom – 'Evil Incarnate'.[32] In short, while most Israelis regard Zionism as being their liberation movement, the Palestinian Arabs see it, quite simply, as being an instrument of colonialism and imperialism.

The conflicting views of Zionism create considerable difficulties for radical Jewish Israelis who sympathise with the Palestinian view but, at the same time, are reluctant to reject the possibility of Zionism being a positive and necessary vehicle for Jewish national liberation. Not surprisingly, the confusion over 'Who is a Zionist?' (a question almost as complex as that of 'Who is a Jew?') often results in misunderstanding and conflict. Jewish radicals who define themselves as anti-Zionists, intending to mean they are opposed to the 'imperialist', 'expansionist' and 'racist' aspects of Zionism, are confronted by hostile Israelis who assume they are opposed to the 'national liberation' of Jews or the 'right of Israel to exist'. They are not seen simply as unpatriotic, but as traitors subverting the very existence of the state.

There are, in fact, a number of 'true' Jewish anti-Zionists who *do* believe that Israel should cease to exist altogether as a state. They propose a variety of alternatives based on their highly universal ideologies. These range from the position held by the anarchists, which envisions a stateless future for the region (to be called the 'Orient–Mediterranean Sea Coast'), to that held by the Revolutionary Communist League which advocates a unitary, socialist state, stripped of Zionist and Jewish elements (to be called Palestine). Such Jewish anti-Zionists are, however, a rare species – numbering no more than a few hundred at the most. Nevertheless, they have succeeded in attracting attention which has been totally disproportionate to their actual size. This has led to an overestimation of the size of Jewish anti-Zionist groups.

The case of Matzpen, probably Israel's best known anti-Zionist group, well illustrates the point. The Israeli authorities are said to have estimated that the group consisted of 'no more than a few thousand members'. In fact, one ex-Matzpen activist admitted that the group never had more than thirty or forty active members.[33] Matzpen's extraordinary ability to attract attention was due to a number of factors – which reflect the characteristics of an exclusive, revolutionary MO. Firstly, Matzpen members, realising that their anti-Zionist position was unlikely to gain wide acceptance in Israel, never attempted to form a political party. As they had little reason to attract the sympathy, let alone the votes, of a staunchly Zionist public, they did not hesitate 'to make as much noise as possible'.[34] Secondly, the unambiguously anti-Zionist position of the group could hardly be missed. Thirdly, the 'Establishment' attracted attention to the group by depicting it as 'the source of all evil not produced by the Rakah Communists'.[35] Finally, Matzpen, whose members had broken away from the traditional pro-Soviet line of the Communist party – adopting an internationalist Trotskyist platform – succeeded in gaining the sympathy of groups abroad. The New Left 'lionised' Matzpen giving it and its London-based wing, known as the Israeli Revolutionary Action Committee Abroad, considerable room for publicity – a fact much resented by Israel's Zionist majority.

Despite their success in attracting attention, the 'true' anti-Zionist groups are very much the exception – a small minority *even within the radical camp*. The majority of radicals, who are often depicted as 'anti-Zionists', are in fact 'non-Zionists'. They accept the existence of the State of Israel and, even though they are critical of certain characteristics and core values, they do not advocate replacing the present State with an alternative entity.

NON-ZIONIST POLITICAL PARTIES

Historically, the Israeli Communist Party (Maki) was the most significant non-Zionist force in Israel. Following the lead of the Soviet Union it never questioned Israel's right to exist, although it did question the idea of the Jews as a nation. For many years it was the only non-Zionist party in the Knesset voicing opposition to Israel's treatment of its Arab minority (then still under military rule) and Israel's links with the 'imperialist powers' (notably during the Suez crisis). United opposition to the above was, however, unable to prevent the party from being 'torn asunder' by the divergent currents of Jewish and Arab nationalism. The Jewish communists felt unable to accept the attitude of the predominantly Arab faction which, they argued, completely whitewashed the Arab national movement, and which presented Zionism 'as an imperialist Nazi monster'.[36] With the Arab faction remaining faithful to Moscow, the party split in 1965 along essentially national lines – shattering the communists' dream of a united Jewish–Arab revolutionary party.[37]

Rakah (the predominantly Arab faction) increased its vote amongst the Arab electorate, while Maki (the Jewish faction) lost overall support, getting no more than one seat in the following Knesset elections (1965 and 1969) – before ceasing altogether to exist. The party had attempted to form a common front with three small radical groups which had appeared on the Israeli political scene: Haolam Hazeh, Brit Hasmol and Siach. Negotiations failed and, in 1973, the remnants of Maki merged with a socialist peace group (Tehelet-Adom), to form a new party – Moked (Focus) – which gained a seat in the Knesset. Moked took a conciliatory view of Zionism, recognising it as a national liberation movement which had enabled the Jews to create an independent state where they could strive to create a socialist state based on productive Jewish labour. At the same time the party came out strongly in support of the Palestinians' equal right to self-determination, maintaining that Israel should withdraw totally from the territories captured in 1967 and negotiate peace with Palestinian representatives (including the PLO) and the Arab states.

In 1977 Moked's leader, Meir Pail, joined Arieh Eliav (Independent Socialists), Uri Avnery (Haolam Hazeh) and Sa'adia Marciano (Black Panthers), to form a new non-communist 'peace party' – Sheli (acronym for Shalom le Israel – 'Peace for Israel'). Sheli's platform, on the withdrawal from the territories and negotiations with the Palestinians, was similar to that of Moked's. In addition, the party aimed to close the social and economic gap between Israel's Jewish ethnic groups (hence the inclusion of the Black Panthers). The party won only two seats in the 1977 elections and, in 1980, it began to break up over a dispute concerning the rotation of its two seats between the four leaders mentioned above. In 1982 a final blow was dealt when members disagreed over whether or not to serve in Lebanon. A leading party member, Ran Cohen, decided to serve and was accused by some of the others of 'war crimes'.

In 1981, no non-communist party critical of Zionism and supportive of the Palestinians gained enough votes to enter Israel's tenth Knesset. However, in 1984, a new non-communist Jewish–Arab party – The Progressive List for Peace (PLP) – won two seats in the Knesset on a platform that was distinctly 'non-Zionist'. As noted in Chapter 4, the Jewish component of the PLP was made up largely of activists involved in an extra-parliamentary peace group founded in 1976 – the Israeli Council for Israeli–Palestinian Peace (ICIPP). Like Moked and Sheli, the PLP calls for a total withdrawal from the territories occupied in 1967 and for the establishment of a Palestinian state. But, unlike Moked and Sheli, the PLP is not a Jewish party with token Arabs – it defines itself as an *Israeli* party and divides its Knesset candidates equally between Arabs and Jews. The first principle in its manifesto calls for a written constitution which will ensure equal national and civil rights for the Jewish and Palestinian citizens of Israel. It is pointed out by PLP ideologues that:

> The Arab citizens of Israel, who are in theory equal citizens, have been living since 1948 under a system of discrimination which makes them, in practice, second-class citizens. To name only a few of the most harsh forms of discrimination: all jobs that are connected, even in the most remote way, to defence (which means a large part of the Israeli economy) are politically barred to Arabs; so is most of the government civil service; Arab municipalities receive far less financial support from the central government than do Jewish ones, and the same is true of schools and social services in the Arab sector; government plans for development and industrialisation almost completely ignore the Arab sector; government-owned lands are considered to be, not the common property of all Israeli citizens, but the property of the Jewish people, earmarked for Jewish settlement.[38]

The exclusion of Arab citizens from participation in key institutions of the state, and the state's adoption of national symbols particularistic to Judaism, are considered by the non-Zionists to be incompatible with universal ideals. The Jewish members of the PLP aim to 'struggle for a

different Israel – an Israel that is independent, humanistic, democratic, secular, pluralist, seeking peace and social justice; a state
belonging equally to all its citizens, women and men, Orientals and
Europeans, Jews and Arabs, secular and religious . . .'[39]

The desire to see *Israel become something other than a Jewish state* is
the essential factor that distinguishes radical non-Zionists from the
broader Zionist Left. It could be argued that, the greater degree of
commitment to universal values, the more likely is an Israeli Jew to
take a non-Zionist stance. Ironically, the anti-Zionist stance taken by
some Israelis stems from their extremely particular world view: the
ultra-orthodox, religious anti-Zionists refuse to recognise the State of
Israel because the state was not brought into existence by the Messiah
but by the work of secular Jews. In other words they reject the state
because it is *not particular enough* – it fails to meet 'requirements'
unique to religious Judaism.

THE BIRZEIT SOLIDARITY COMMITTEE

The extra-parliamentary, radical MOs are made up predominantly,
but not exclusively, of non-Zionists. In 1981, an event occurred which
was to bring together radical Zionists from Sheli, non-Zionists from
Rakah and Siach and anti-Zionists from Matzpen and the Revolutionary Communist League into a single, radical MO. In November of
that year the Likud government set up a 'civil administration' in the
West Bank, as a first step towards the creation of its version of
'autonomy', agreed upon in the Camp David accords. Within a week
the new administration showed its colours by summarily closing down
Birzeit University. The day after the closure, radicals from the above
groups, many of them faculty and students from the Hebrew
University, met at Birzeit and, in an act of protest and solidarity, broke
into the locked campus to symbolically reopen it. This event led them
to form a new radical MO – the Birzeit Solidarity Committee (BSC).

The new MO immediately distinguished itself from Peace Now in a
number of significant ways. To begin with, it was not an exclusively
Jewish organisation. Unlike Peace Now, the BSC organised demonstrations with Palestinian participation. Most of these were held on the
West Bank where, in the turbulent winter and spring of 1982,
Palestinians were confronting an attempt by the Likud to crush
resistance and nationalism: elected municipal officials sympathetic to

the PLO were sacked; universities were repeatedly closed and demonstrators were fired upon. At the same time, the government increased the number of Jewish settlements. The BSC confronted the authorities in a more determined way than did Peace Now. Numerous unauthorised demonstrations were held on the West Bank. On one occasion, 200 members of the BSC, who were holding an *authorised* demonstration in the main square of Ramallah, were confronted by Israeli soldiers who fired tear gas to disrupt the demonstration before arresting a number of activists. Such confrontations with the authorities may not have impressed the Israeli public, but they won the BSC considerable 'credibility' amongst Palestinians in the occupied territories.

The BSC, which devoted much of its time to supporting Palestinian students, detainees and refugees on the West Bank, accused Peace Now of opposing the occupation for the wrong reasons. Activists claimed that Peace Now did not oppose the occupation because it was oppressive and harmful to Palestinians, but rather because they were concerned about its harm to Israel's 'Jewish democracy' and the divisions it created amongst Israeli Jews.

The BSC also distinguished itself from Peace Now by taking a clear position on the future of the occupied territories. Criticising Peace Now's vague stance, the BSC called for a total withdrawal from the territories and for negotiations with the PLO leading to the establishment of an independent Palestinian state with East Jerusalem as its capital. In addition, the BSC demanded that all Jewish settlers beyond the 1967 line be evacuated and that their housing be given to the new Palestinian state, as Israel's contribution to resolving the refugee problem. Not surprisingly, Peace Now tried to dissociate itself from the radical stance of the BSC, prohibiting the participation of the MO as an organisation in its demonstrations: BSC activists were permitted to participate as individuals – which they did almost without exception.

Another distinctive feature of the BSC was its international perspective. The MO strongly condemned Israel's close links and dependence on the United States. It deplored, in particular, the system whereby the United States would provide to Israel 'aid' which would then be used to produce arms in Israeli factories for export to certain dictatorial regimes backed by the United States. The MO called for an end to Israel's links with all authoritarian regimes – notably South Africa – and condemned the provision of Israeli arms and military advisers to such regimes. A spokesman for the BSC argued that such links simply proved that Israel had taken a 'narrow' (that is, particularistic) view of Jewish history and the Holocaust.

> Israel, which was born as a place of refuge for people who suffered from racism and discrimination, should not become racist itself – the upholder of regimes that are neglecting human rights and in some cases, similarly to the Nazi regime in the '30s . . . We have not learned the lesson of the Holocaust, if we continue to collaborate with racist regimes like South Africa. It is proof that our approach to the Holocaust is very narrow . . . in the sense that we are dealing only with what happened to the Jews, not with the essence of the fascist system. If the fascist system had been doing to Blacks (what it did to Jews) we wouldn't have cared.

The spokesman went on to argue that Israel should withdraw from world affairs and 'go back to being a small Middle Eastern state . . . if it wants to be big, it must be big because of its qualities not its armouries.'[40]   On 5 June 1982, over 5000 members and supporters of the BSC joined in a demonstration to mark the fifteenth anniversary of the occupation of the territories captured in the 1967 war. With the impending invasion of Lebanon evident, the BSC demonstration was turned into the first of many against the war. In the weeks following the invasion, numerous *ad hoc* demonstrations were held by a variety of radical groups who opposed the war. These provoked much public hostility and were quickly dispersed by the police. A clear taboo was being broken by these demonstrations, for never before had Israelis protested against a war *while the fighting was still in progress*. The 1973 wave of protest had come in the wake of the war; protesting while troops were actually engaged in combat was unheard of and considered deplorable.

The BSC and other smaller radical groups immediately considered the war to be quite unlike any other that Israel had fought. In 1967 and 1973, when the threat to the state was evident, Israel had, they argued, fought defensive wars; in 1982 this was evidently not the case. The northern border had been almost quiet for eleven months and the Likud government's claim that the war was necessary to bring peace to Galilee was regarded with scepticism and suspicion. Radicals saw the war as an aggressive war designed to crush Palestinian centres of nationalism in Lebanon. Within two weeks, the BSC became a nucleus around which other radical groups gathered to form a new committee for co-ordinating protest against the war – the Committee Against the War in Lebanon (CAWL).

THE COMMITTEE AGAINST THE WAR IN LEBANON

On 13 June, the CAWL staged the first licensed demonstration against the war. The response was poor, with only about 300 turning out to demonstrate. There was still widespread reluctance to protest while Israeli troops were in battle; Peace Now made it plain that it would not demonstrate while many of its members were still fighting. However, as the war progressed, people's attitudes towards it rapidly changed. On 26 June, the CAWL staged its second licensed demonstration – this time an estimated 20,000 Israelis turned out, many of them being Peace Now activists and supporters. A distinct change in people's perception of the war and of the legitimacy of protest, had taken place. The success of CAWL's demonstration brought to an end the debate which had been raging within the ranks of Peace Now. With the taboo broken and a successful precedent set, Peace Now decided to call its own demonstration, only a week after that organised by the CAWL. The demonstration, attended by over 100,000 people, revealed exactly how widespread opposition to the war had become, confirming and magnifying what had already been revealed by the CAWL demonstration. There is no doubt that the CAWL demonstration acted as an important catalyst, prompting Peace Now to abandon its earlier reluctance to protest before the war was over. Indeed, many CAWL activists later pointed to this as the group's most important achievement.

It is of course possible that Peace Now would eventually have called for protest without being 'prompted' by the more radical CAWL, primarily because so many Israelis' perception of the war changed within the first two or three weeks after the invasion of Lebanon. There are a number of reasons for this which are worth noting. Firstly, soon after the invasion, it became apparent that the IDF, under the overall command of Defence Minister Sharon, was moving far beyond the original '40 km' limit declared at the outset. Early news of the extent of Israel's penetration into Lebanon spread, not through the media, but through soldiers returning home for 24 hours of 'rest and recuperation' leave. One mother, Naomi Ben-Tzur, described in detail the impact that her son's 24-hour visit had on her and her family and friends:

> When he came home for 24 hours, it was something really surrealistic. Family and friends came to see him . . . he just kept talking, usually he is quiet. My son was a tank driver. He told us he got the order to go forward as quickly as possible – not to stop. He drove for 40 hours non-stop! . . . They only stopped when they ran out of fuel – *long beyond the 40 km limit* . . . He told us they had started the war with the Syrians; that they could have avoided the Syrians, but they got the orders to fight them. We didn't know this. I was really shocked. We had been told on the radio that the Syrians started the fight with us. We didn't dream that we'd got the order to start the fighting. A cease-fire was agreed with the Syrians, then the soldiers got the order to attack – later they heard on the [Israeli] radio that the Syrians had broken the cease-fire! He told us the Israelis were now sitting on the Beirut–Damascus Highway. We didn't know that.[41]

Ben-Tzur, and many others like her, realised that the war was not being fought simply for the 'Peace of Galiliee', but for quite different objectives which were not being disclosed to the public. What, they asked, did the Beirut–Damascus Highway have to do with peace for Galilee? What was the point of going all the way to Beirut when the 'terrorist' bases, in the '40 km limit' (from where rockets had been fired on Israel's northern settlements), had been eliminated in the first days of the war? Why had Israel unnecessarily engaged the Syrians in battle? Why was Sharon so evidently misinforming the Israeli public about the war's objectives? The answers to these questions were not immediately evident. Nevertheless, for many moderates, the realisation that the army had penetrated beyond the declared limit was enough to change their perception of the war – and their willingness to protest against it.

The CAWL and other radical MOs played an important role in answering the questions posed by the war and in publicising and condemning Sharon's 'hidden agenda'. Throughout the war, they argued that the invasion was designed not to destroy PLO terrorism but to destroy a far more dangerous threat – the prospect of peace with the PLO. A peace which would ultimately have to result in negotiations and territorial concessions – an idea which Sharon, and other ardent supporters of Gush Emunim in the Likud, found abhorrent. The radicals pointed to the restraint the PLO had exhibited in the eleven months preceding the invasion, and to the increasing emphasis that the organisation had been placing on diplomacy rather than terrorism. It was this, they argued, that Sharon wished to sabotage. A PLO that carried out sporadic acts of terrorism, which brought only condemnation from the West, was hardly a threat to Israel. But a PLO that exhibited restraint and pursued a diplomatic path to peace was sure to win Western sympathy for its cause, with the threat of subsequent Western pressure to relinquish occupied territories as part of a peace agreement with the Palestinians.

Eighteen months after the invasion, Uri Avnery disclosed that before the invasion, the PLO had drafted a statement with the USA recognising Israel and had scheduled it for release in Paris on 14 June 1982. Avnery obtained his information from the late Dr Issam Sartawi, who had been instrumental in establishing the negotiations through the intermediary of the Tunisian Prime Minister Mohammed Mzali. Eight days before it was due to be released, Israel invaded Lebanon – effectively crushing the apparent PLO peace initiative. Sartawi told Avnery that he was sure Alexander Haig, then Secretary of State, had double-crossed the PLO by tipping off the Israelis.[42]

Radical activists in the peace movement insisted that, far from attempting to secure peace for Galilee, Sharon was intent on remoulding the politics of the entire area by fulfilling a 'grand design' that had its ideological roots in Ben-Gurion's day.[43] Indeed, on the eve of the 1948 war, Ben-Gurion had declared:

> The weak point in the Arab coalition is Lebanon, for the Moslem regime is artificial and easy to undermine. A Christian state should be established, with its border on the Litani river. We will make an alliance with it.[44]

This, radicals argued, was part of Sharon's 'hidden agenda'. Israel's actual support for the establishment of a Christian state can be traced back to 1951, when $3000 were secretly given to the Phalange election campaign.[45] After the 1975–6 civil war, Israel's determination to see a strong Christian government installed in Beirut evidently increased; between 1977 and 1982 Bashir Gemayel is said to have received $100 million – as well as military supplies and training – from the Likud government in Jerusalem.[46] During the war, objections mounted to Sharon's overt support for the Phalange which, radicals argued, bespoke of his intentions to reshape the balance of power in the region. Many radicals believed that Sharon's ultimate dream was to see a strong Phalangist government controlling the PLO in Lebanon, leaving Israel a free hand to crush Palestinian resistance in the occupied territories. In short, they believed that the invasion of Lebanon was simply a dramatic prelude to the annexation of the territories. For this reason the CAWL combined protest against the war with protest against the occupation.

Although the majority of Israelis had initially supported the invasion, by October 1982 only 40 per cent declared they were satisfied with the government's handling of the war. This percentage dropped to 25 per cent in June 1984 and, in September 1985, only 22 per cent agreed that: 'In the final analysis the Lebanese War was good for Israel.'[47] The rapid growth of the peace movement, in the first months of the war, corresponded to the growth of opposition to the war. It is impossible to determine the precise role the radical critique of the invasion had in developing this opposition. Although the radicals helped to legitimise protest, there was no indication that the many people who took to the streets accepted the radical critique of the war outlined above. Despite the fact that the war had a 'politicising' effect, in the sense that it drew people who had previously been uninvolved in politics into a protest movement, there is nothing to indicate that this led to a broader critique of Israeli society or a willingness to remain involved in protest. In fact, evidence suggests that the majority of those who had been uninvolved in politics withdrew from protest once the war was over. This can be illustrated by the case of Parents Against Silence (PAS), a 'non-political' single-issue MO, which emerged during the war and disbanded once the *official* withdrawal from Lebanon had taken place.

PARENTS AGAINST SILENCE

Parents Against Silence started in much the same way as Peace Now – with a letter. An Israeli mother, Shoshana Shmueli, out of concern for her son in Lebanon, wrote a letter to *Ha'aretz* demanding that the government withdraw Israeli soldiers from Lebanon. Her letter struck a chord that resonated in the hearts of hundreds of Israeli mothers. Hardly had the papers been distributed when she was inundated by calls from around the country. One of the calls was from Naomi Ben-Tzur who told Shmueli that a group of parents opposed to the war had already been formed in Jerusalem. Indeed, shortly after her son's visit, Ben-Tzur had called friends who had been equally disturbed by their sons' accounts of the war. A meeting was arranged to discuss whether parents had the right to protest while their sons' guns were still firing. As all the parents at the meeting had fought in previous wars, and had been 'educated as soldiers', they initially found the idea of protest extremely difficult to contemplate. According to Ben-Tzur, many inhibitions had to be overcome; loyalty to the IDF, previously held as sacred, was suddenly thrown painfully into question. The meeting lasted all night but, by dawn, the parents had decided that 'under such circumstances they had all the right in the world to protest.'[48]Three or four days later, fifty to sixty parents protested outside the Prime Minister's residence. So inexperienced were they, that they did not realise that police permission was required. The police, accepting their appeals to ignorance of the law, allowed the demonstration to continue. Supporters of the war were less conciliatory – they accused the parents 'of being traitors, of stabbing the nation in the back . . . of poisoning the wells and of supporting the PLO'.[49] Ben-Tzur's group of Jerusalem parents became one of a number of local groups, which had formed in response to Shmueli's letter, in the new national MO – Parents Against Silence.

The new MO drew together parents (primarily mothers) who had voted for different political parties – including Begin's Likud – but were not politically active. It was by far the most inclusive MO to emerge since the formation of Peace Now. The group succeeded in spanning one of two great divides in Israeli society: it had both religious and secular members. It failed, however, to bridge the socio-economic and ethnic divide, attracting virtually only middle-class Ashkenazim. The fact that it was not associated with any one political party worked greatly to its advantage when it came to gaining access to members of the Knesset and the government. The MO began to lobby all the political parties in the Knesset and, in June 1983, only weeks after Shmueli's letter, PAS met with Defence Minister Moshe Arens. The meeting bore no fruit and the MO decided to continue its struggle. Demonstrations continued but, more significantly, the group joined a twenty-four hour a day vigil outside Prime Minister Begin's residence, that was to last no less than three months.

The vigil is noteworthy as it became both a focus of solidarity and attack. Opponents of the war from Jerusalem would drop by, often with food and flasks of coffee, to express their sympathy. Others from out of town would make a point of going to the vigil while in the city, partly to express solidarity but also to feel that they were participating in 'the struggle'. The vigil also attracted activists from other MOs in the peace movement, turning it into a centre for the exchange of ideas as well as solidarity. Small gestures of solidarity took on greater meaning as the vigil was subjected to 'the insult and the fury' of supporters of the war. At first, attacks were petty and sporadic: 'people would come and spit on us and curse and throw stones.' On one particular occasion, a man appeared at the vigil holding up a white sheet covered with red paint. He approached a group of mothers from PAS and accused them of being responsible for the shedding of Jewish blood not only in Lebanon but also in the 1973 war. One of the mothers, who had lost her husband in the 1973 war, was deeply insulted and a furious exchange ensued. Such was the nature of much of the 'debate' between supporters and opponents of the war. After the Likud attempted to organise a counter-movement (called Parents Against Weakness), the attacks against the vigil became more organised and violent – forcing on occasion the intervention of the police. One mother was told by a counter-demonstrator that her son would be killed on return from Lebanon because she was a traitor. (It should be noted that no mother in PAS encouraged her son to refuse service in Lebanon – and no son did.) It was shortly after this death threat was made that a hand-grenade was thrown at the Peace Now demonstration and killed activist Emil Grunzweig. Never before had the chasm between doves and hawks in Israel been so deep.

Begin could not ignore the vigil (neither could his neighbours who complained of the noise!) and, on 17 June 1983, he met six representatives of PAS who presented him with a petition, signed by 10,000 Israelis, calling for the withdrawal of Israeli troops from Lebanon. Again PAS, as a politically unaffiliated, one-issue MO, gained access to the corridors of power which remained firmly closed to more radical groups with a broader critique of society. The meeting, which was carefully planned to have the greatest possible impact on Begin, well illustrates how a successful social movement organisation can reach and possibly influence the most powerful members of government. Such was its significance that Ben-Tzur's description should be quoted in full:

> I believe our meeting with Begin was a turning-point in his life. One has to remember that Begin was a king and he had a court . . . Nobody wanted to give him bad news. He didn't hear the bad news about the war; Sharon painted the news white. Later he said he didn't hear about events. He didn't know the truth about Lebanon and then comes a group of parents [mothers] who tell him everything. Looking back, I think it was the beginning of his decision to resign. He not only listened to us – he was 'ears only'. There was no limit of time. All his advisers were sitting there, not intervening in one sentence; nobody stopped us. We planned it very well. Each person in the group represented something [important to Begin]. For example, one mother was active in the underground before Israel was born. She could tell him: 'Look, I was a fighter like you were' – because we had been accused of not being patriots. I think the strongest impact was made on him by a woman who was a remnant of the Holocaust. She came from the same village he came from in Poland . . . she showed him the [concentration camp] number on her arm. She was married and she had children but she lost them in the Holocaust – she was the only survivor. She came to Israel, she married again and she had two sons. She told Begin: 'Listen, I didn't go through all this in my life to now lose my two sons in Beirut. You'll never convince me that if I lose a son it was necessary.' I think this had a tremendous impact on him, because for him the Holocaust is something [special] – then someone comes and tells him something like that! What I represented at the meeting was this: I was in Washington when the peace agreement with Egypt was signed. I was on the White House lawn and saw him taking his pen and signing his name. I told him that for me, as an Israeli citizen, this was the biggest day in my life; this was the starting of a new era. You realised that there is an alternative way; you don't have to shed your blood every couple of years – that peace is possible! Then, the same person who signed this agreement didn't let this peace with Egypt grow a little . . . and starts a new war – all the hopes for a peaceful future, all new horizons broken. So, I told him: 'We had so much hope in you and what did you do?' History was also

something important for him. He was very concerned about how he would enter history. We told him: 'Look, you had the opportunity to enter into history as a peace-maker – and now what? Another war! That's what you brought!' We also had a member from a village on the northern border, one that had suffered a lot from the terror activities. She said to him: 'You're not rescuing me by sending the army to Beirut. My son is in Lebanon and, if you asked me, I'd be ready to go back to the risks there were before the war. But I don't think the war is necessary. I feel that the soldiers who are losing their lives in Beirut shouldn't be doing it for me.'

Although Begin was apparently *visibly* moved by the meeting with the mothers, he made no concessions to them. They returned directly to the vigil, which was to continue until his resignation. It is of course impossible to assert that the vigil and the meeting were the main causes for his resignation. (The death of his wife is said to have been as responsible as anything else.) However, it is reasonable to see these events as contributory factors and to argue that PAS, the least radical of MOs, probably contributed more than any of the others to Begin's eventual withdrawal from Israeli politics.

Parents Against Silence continued demonstrating after the 1984 elections, even though many believed that the war was 'now in good hands'. When the withdrawal was officially over, the MO disbanded – despite the fact that a number of Israeli troops remained in southern Lebanon. Some members felt that this was an unfortunate decision, as the few mothers with sons still in Lebanon now had to face 'their' problem alone. In terms of social movement theory, the disbanding of PAS is a noteworthy exception. As noted by sociologists, successful social movement organisations tend to be disinclined to disband once an objective has been reached. Most often, they divert their energy to a new cause.[50] PAS probably disbanded so readily because its members lacked common political roots. The MO had no political 'tradition'. Once the single objective of withdrawal from Lebanon had been reached, nothing remained to bind the MO's diverse membership together. Although the political awareness of some of the mothers had been raised by the war and their participation in protest, most withdrew back to their private worlds once the war was over. That the disbanding of PAS was exceptional can be illustrated by the case of the next MO (examined below), which also formed in response to the war but did not disband once it was over – primarily because its political roots went much deeper.

YESH GVUL: THE LIMITS OF OBEDIENCE

Yesh Gvul (which means 'There's a Limit' and 'There's a Border') began as a one-issue MO formed by reserve soldiers who refused to serve in Lebanon. It first became known in September 1982, when reserve soldiers presented the Minister of Defence with a petition requesting that they not be sent to serve in Lebanon. The new MO drew in individual objectors from a range of backgrounds (including the Likud), although a majority of its active supporters were radicals from the CAWL, Rakah and other non-Zionist groups. Activists set aside potentially divisive political issues – such as the precise future of the occupied territories – to focus all their attention on opposing the war in Lebanon. What distinguished Yesh Gvul from all other MOs was its members' willingness to translate opposition to the war into a refusal to participate in it. In the course of the war, just over 140 soldiers – a majority of whom were Yesh Gvul members – endured imprisonment rather than serving in Lebanon.

By supporting a form of civil disobedience, Yesh Gvul was, in the eyes of most Zionists (including those in the peace movement), overstepping the accepted limits of 'legitimate protest'. Peace Now and PAS both strongly condemned Yesh Gvul's approach. Peace Now made strenuous efforts to dissociate itself from Yesh Gvul's 'disloyalty' to the state by prohibiting the MO from joining its demonstrations.

Yesh Gvul succeeded in attracting attention disproportionate to its size for a noteworthy reason. The MO brought into conflict two important Jewish values: loyalty to the State of Israel versus the right of a soldier to disobey orders which infringe upon his conscience. The significance of the latter value lies in Israel's own refusal to accept Nazi war criminals' claims that they were *not* responsible for their deeds because they were simply obeying orders. Israel maintained that individual German soldiers should have refused to obey state orders which violated their own consciences.[51] Never before, however, had this notion been 'tested' in an Israeli war. Past wars, with the possible exception of the 1956 Suez War, had not created the moral dilemmas created by the Lebanon war. For the first time, many soldiers found that they were being asked to fight in a war which they believed to be unnecessary and unjust; they found that they were being asked to carry out acts which went against their consciences. Yesh Gvul's response to this dilemma was unique; its members were the only ones who unambiguously placed loyalty to their conscience above loyalty to the state.

Some soldiers attempted to remain loyal to both. One such was a regular colonel by the name of Eli Geva. Geva refused to lead his troops into West Beirut, partly because he believed it would not be effective in terms of defeating the PLO, but also because, through his binoculars, he saw children playing in the streets. He asked to be relieved from his duties for reasons of conscience, but asked to remain with his troops as an ordinary soldier. Geva's case was widely publicised and eventually came to the attention of Begin, who met with him. Begin failed to persuade Geva to change his mind and, shortly afterwards, he was dismissed from the army, having been refused permission to continue as an ordinary soldier. Peace Now praised Geva's approach – he had acted in accordance with his conscience, but had not ultimately been disloyal to the state.[52] Peace Now also supported a short-lived, moderate MO (Soldiers Against Silence) composed of reservists who protested against the war but continued to serve in Lebanon. Many of the soldiers who did go to Lebanon still managed to signal their opposition to the war by returning, or refusing to receive, the 'Peace for Galilee Campaign Ribbon' issued by the IDF to all those in the army during the war. One Kibbutz (Sde Yoav) decided to instruct its members who had received the ribbon to return it.[53] By April 1983, thousands of reservists were reported to have signed a petition expressing their unwillingness to receive the ribbon.[54] Eli Geva, Soldiers Against Silence and the Lo La'ot (No to the Ribbon) soldiers, all walked a different tightrope attempting to balance conflicting loyalties and values. Hundreds of others are said to have escaped the moral dilemmas posed by the war by leaving the country for extended periods, changing address frequently, or feigning illness.[55]

I would argue that the ability of Yesh Gvul members to withstand the pressure on them, to 'serve their nation at a time of crisis', can be attributed to their strong commitment to universal values coupled with their radical critique of the particularistic aspects of Israeli society, which they believed were responsible for motivating the Likud government to take the nation to war. The universalistic 'framework of reference' was made most evident by one Yesh Gvul member – an Argentinian immigrant – who served one stint in Lebanon, and then refused to return after what he witnessed there. He maintained that he would not continue to serve in Lebanon because the (Israeli) repression he had seen 'reminded him of the treatment Argentinian soldiers dealt his mother, sister and himself'.[56]

Although Yesh Gvul faced stiff opposition from many quarters, it was not altogether alone in upholding the right of soldiers to place conscience above obedience to the state. Numerous well-known artists and poets supported the group, giving special performances of their work to help publicise the MO's position. One concert, held in support of Yesh Gvul, attracted 20,000 people, while demonstrations usually assembled between 1000 and 2000 supporters. In addition, the MO had the support of certain well-known academics – most notably Professor Y. Leibowitz.

Unlike PAS, once Israel officially withdrew from Lebanon, Yesh Gvul did not disband. Instead, a deliberate decision was taken by the MO to shift its attention from supporting soldiers who refused to serve in Lebanon to supporting soldiers who, for reasons of conscience, did not wish to serve in the occupied territories. Although this cause did not attract as much support as the refusal to serve in Lebanon, Yesh Gvul was able to publish, in 1986, a petition to the Prime Minister, signed by 350 reservists, which read:

19 Years of Occupation – THERE'S A LIMIT! . . . The War in Lebanon, the settlements and suppressive actions undertaken in the Occupied Territories indicate a lack of sensitivity for human life, the loss of values and the loss of a sense of reality. They close the option for peace with the Palestinian people and the rest of our neighbours; they isolate Israel among the nations and they prove that the Israeli government wants territories more than peace. The occupation has corrupted our values, and manifestations of extreme nationalism and racism have become acceptable in Israeli society. Jewish terrorist groups receive validation and racist theories have become legitimate. WE TOOK AN OATH TO DEFEND THE INTEGRITY AND SECURITY OF THE STATE OF ISRAEL AND WE ARE ABIDING BY THE OATH. WE THEREFORE REQUEST OF

YOU TO ALLOW US NOT TO TAKE PART IN THE PROCESS
OF SUPPRESSION AND OCCUPATION IN THE TERRIT-
ORIES.[57]

Shortly after the publication of the above declaration a number of
reserve soldiers were called and refused to serve in the occupied
territories. A year later the opposition was still going strong: in the
month of October 1987 alone, no less than fifty Israelis declared their
intention to refuse to serve in the occupied territories. In the same
month thirty-four high school students, soon to be drafted, wrote a
joint letter to the Defence Minister Yitzhak Rabin asking him to allow
them to serve inside the 'Green Line'. They expressed their concern
about the wave of injuries and killings 'on both sides' in the preceding
weeks which were 'additional proof of the necessity of bringing an end
to the occupation'.[58]

Yesh Gvul has continued to be active in other ways. On 25 October
1986 some 200 activists attached one-metre high, green plastic sheets
along part of the length of barbed wire fence which used to divide
Israel from the West Bank prior to 1967. Their objective was to draw
public attention to the pre-'67 'Green Line' which is fast disappearing
not only from official maps but also from public consciousness. Two
months later activists distributed pamphlets amongst the IDF soldiers
serving on the West Bank which stated:

> Since 1967, the IDF has become more of an occupation army than a
> defence force. Across the Green Line, soldiers are involved in acts of
> repression against the Palestinian population . . . The occupation
> not only harms the occupied population, but also dehumanises the
> occupier . . . The occupation does not defend the state, but is
> bringing on the next war. Remember you have the right to request a
> transfer to service inside the Green Line, within Israel. Remember,
> according to military law, you must refuse to obey orders that are
> clearly illegal.

Both the erecting of the plastic 'Green Line' and the distributing of
pamphlets attracted some media attention, but what really created a
storm and received extensive coverage was the publication by Yesh
Gvul of an anthology entitled *Gvul Hatziut* (The Limits of Obedience).
The book was not an account of Yesh Gvul's activities during the war

in Lebanon but rather a collection of writings examining the whole question of obedience to the state from the political, philosophical, legal, moral and military aspects. Nevertheless, most reviewers and critics chose to use the publication of the anthology as a springboard to discuss Yesh Gvul's stance during the war. Some of the hardest hitting criticisms came from the 'moderate' doves who had supported Peace Now's position and who had chosen to serve in Lebanon. One such person was Yossi Sarid (MK for Ratz) who claimed that refusal to serve in Lebanon had not shortened the war – which lasted three years – by 'as much as a single day'. He insisted that Yesh Gvul had had no impact on public opinion and argued that the MO's use of disobedience was not only ineffective but also dangerous. Writing in *Ha'aretz* he accused Yesh Gvul of providing Gush Emunim with 'a model for subversion' which could easily be used by the settler movement to 'formulate a perfect platform of secession and civil insurrection for the regional (settler) councils of Judea, Samaria and Gaza'. He criticised one writer in the anthology for suggesting that soldiers organise themselves into committees to coordinate their acts of disobedience and insubordination, pointing out that Gush Emunim could equally use such tactics if they believed an order to withdraw from the occupied territories was unjust. Supporters of Yesh Gvul hit back hard at Sarid and the other 'moderate' critics. They cited Brigadier-Colonel Dov Taron who, in December 1983, wrote: 'Draft resistance in the Lebanon war more than achieved its objective. The success of the resisters manifested itself in the government's realization that a war cannot simply be judged on the basis of its results, but must also be judged on the basis of the effects it has on the public's consciousness.'[59] Jerusalem journalist Haim Baram, an acute observer of Israeli society, accused Sarid of naïvety for suggesting that Gush Emunim needed the rational-humanistic arguments in Yesh Gvul's anthology to justify their stand over 'Judea and Samaria'. He pointed out that Gush Emunim's position is 'rooted in a form of irrationality that mixes messianism, fascism, a protofascistic attachment to the land, explicit racism, religious mythology and quasi-Khomeinistic impulses'. [sic] In an obvious reference to Sarid he went on to say: 'Whoever thinks that these people are in need of justification from Yesh Gvul is making a mistake and misleading others.'[60] Turning to the question of the efficacity of Yesh Gvul's draft resistance, Baram argued that the small group of resisters, along with the larger radical left of the peace movement, had 'served as a fuse which acted to ignite the dormant moderate doves . . . by establishing a new norm according to which one does not automatically fall into line the moment war is declared.'[61]

What is evident from the above account of Yesh Gvul's activities after the war is that the MO, unlike PAS, did not allow itself to disband or fade into obscurity overnight. To fully appreciate Yesh Gvul's decision not to disband and to shift its focus from Lebanon to the occupied territories, the MO's political roots must be examined.

Draft resistance in Israel (in one form or another) can be traced back to the establishment of the Israeli section of War Resisters International (WRI) in 1947. Early WRI draft resisters were pacifists; many of them were also Ihud (see Chapter 2). They tended to oppose military service for religious or philosophical reasons. They rarely related this opposition specifically to the Israeli context. Although Israeli law does not make direct provisions for conscientious objectors (COs), approximately sixty WRI pacifists (and probably many not related to WRI) have managed to obtain special exemption from the Minister of Defence. However, resisters who refused to serve for political, rather than philosophical reasons, were virtually unheard of until after 1967. Then, in the 1970s, the moral dilemmas posed by the occupation gave birth to a new breed of COs. They were not pacifists, opposed universally to military service, but 'limited objectors' opposed to service in the *Israeli army for specific political reasons of conscience.*

The first COs of this type became known to the Israeli public in 1971 when four young draftees sent a letter to Moshe Dayan, then Minister of Defence, stating that they were unwilling 'to serve in any army of occupation . . . [or] to particpate in the oppression of another nation'.[62] Because they waged a public campaign for exemption on political grounds, the four COs were treated severely, not only by the authorities but also by the media, the public and even their parents. Of the four, only one, Giora Neuman, maintained a public campaign. Under pressure, the others withdrew from public debate and were later granted exemption individually. Neuman continued his campaign and was imprisoned for consecutive periods of 35 days for a year. He was then court-martialled and finally granted what he had always requested – alternative service in a civilian hospital.[63]

Following Neuman's much publicised refusal to serve in any part of the IDF, a growing number of individual soldiers began objecting (on political grounds) not to military service as such, but to service beyond the pre-'67 'Green Line'. There are indications that, in the 1970s, a number of 'Green Line objectors' came to private agreements with their commanding officers, not to be sent into the occupied territories.[64] Then in 1978, a group of 27 high school students captured the nation's attention when they published a statement declaring their intention to refuse to serve beyond the Green Line. This was the first time that an organised group of 'limited objectors' collectively and publicly declared that there was a limit/border beyond which they were not prepared to go. Intense pressure was applied on the Group of 27 from all quarters. As with earlier objectors, those who stopped making their objection public were granted exemption mostly on 'psychiatric grounds' – while those who continued (notably Gadi El-Gazi and Guy Pilawski) faced long periods in prison.

Two things may be gleaned from the case of the Group of 27. Firstly, it became evident that the IDF was prepared to exempt soldiers not willing to serve beyond the Green Line, but only if negotiations were carried out in private. Public refusals, which brought into question the legitimacy and nature of Israeli rule in the occupied territories, were not to be tolerated. The second thing was that the only members of the group who were able to sustain the immense pressure on them to end the public campaign, were 'red-nappy babies' – radicals brought up in a 'radical tradition' by their parents. El-Gazi's parents were active Rakah members, while Pilawski's parents were members of Matzpen. These radicals became the core around which a protest group of limited objectors formed. The same was to be true when Yesh Gvul emerged in response to the Lebanon war; the essential difference being that the Group of 27 consisted of teenagers objecting to part of the regular service, while Yesh Gvul was a reserve soldiers' MO, organised by experienced political activists.

The immediate roots of Yesh Gvul can be traced back to the weeks preceding the war, when radicals from the BSC and other groups began drafting a list of reserve soldiers who would be prepared to refuse service in the occupied territories. They had approximately 200 people on the list when Israel invaded Lebanon. With the war presenting a more urgent threat, some of the activists, after much debate, decided to focus attention on refusing to serve in Lebanon. They soon discovered that this was a far more popular cause than refusal to cross the Green Line. Yesh Gvul's post-war decision to shift emphasis to the occupied territories, was in fact a return to a position held by radical activists who were influenced by the precedents mentioned above.

9 Non-Violence, Free Speech and Nuclear War

MUBARAK AWAD AND THE PALESTINIAN NON-VIOLENT STRUGGLE

In late 1983, as demonstrations against the Lebanon war were coming to an end, a well-built Palestinian started to attract attention as he toured the West Bank on his motorcycle, preaching the gospel of non-violence. Mubarak Awad was born to an orthodox Christian family of the Musrara quarter of Jerusalem. The family home was located in what became no man's land in 1948. Awad's father was caught in the cross-fire when the war broke out and, to this day, Awad does not know whether his father died from a bullet fired from the gun of an Arab or a Jew. On his father's death, Awad was taken to the orphanage founded by Katy Antonious, wife of the Palestinian historian George Antonious, where he spent his early, formative years. Katy Antonious had a strong influence on him, teaching him that: 'people are people and there is no reason to fear them or their rank.'[1]

Awad obviously took her teachings to heart; before the Six-Day War he was arrested by Jordanians for asking awkward questions about the budget of the Greek Orthodox Church and, shortly after the war, the Israelis charged him with incitement for trying to persuade the people of Bethlehem not to be afraid of the invading soldiers and not to flee from their homes. Awad spent six months in an Israeli prison and, in 1969, he left the country for the United States. He soon began studies in psychology at a Mennonite institution in Ohio. The Mennonites, the Quakers and other members of the 'peace churches' left their mark on the young Palestinian, as did his experience of the civil rights and anti-Vietnam movements. Awad returned after ten

179

years to the West Bank with a strong belief in the possibility of achieving justice and self-determination for the Palestinians through non-violent means.

Well-read and informed, with his shelves lined with the works of Gandhi, King and Gene Sharp, Awad began the difficult task of attempting to persuade Palestinians that non-violent means would bring them closer to the ends they desired than would the use of violence. He was faced with a number of immediate obstacles: firstly, he was a Christian, an undeniable disadvantage for any aspiring Palestinian leader; secondly, his ten years' absence, his US passport, US wife, US financial backing and his need to return to the USA every three months (to maintain his status as 'tourist' in Israel) created suspicion; thirdly his ideas were not readily grasped.

Non-violence is not new to Muslims. This has been made clear in recent years by the publication of two books on the subject. The one, by Iraqi writer Khalid Kishtainy, gives a detailed history of non-violence in the Middle East while the other, by Eknath Easwaran, tells the story of the Pakistani 'non-violent soldier of Islam', Badshah Khan, who mobilised a non-violent army of 100,000 men from amongst the Pathans of the Khyber Pass to confront the British. Still active at the age of ninety-six, Khan's life is said to have exploded three myths: 'that non-violence can be followed only by those who are gentle, that it cannot work against ruthless repression, and that it has no place in Islam.'[2] Despite these precedents it cannot be denied that, amongst Palestinians, the idea of non-violence has almost been synonymous with submission.

Awad's first attempt to persuade Palestinians of the viability of non-violent struggle against the occupation was hardly met with enthusiasm. Many Palestinians suspected him, amongst other things, of countering the PLO's strategy – which he strongly denied. To counter some of the opposition he faces, Awad presents his approach to non-violence as one based not on religious ideals but on 'self-interest'. He argues that it is more likely to succeed than the armed struggle which only provokes further repression from the Israelis and undermines international sympathy and support for the Palestinian cause. As his approach to non-violence is 'pragmatic' and 'political' rather than religious, Awad claims that Muslim and Christian Palestinians can participate equally. As for his position *vis-à-vis* the PLO, Awad argues that: 'If the PLO is "democratic", as it continually insists it is, then it must allow other voices.' In any case, Awad argues that he is not negating the PLO's use of violence but only pointing out its weaknesses. Fighting an uphill battle, Awad spent nearly three years writing, debating, arguing and holding seminars up and down the length of the West Bank in an energetic attempt to persuade Palestinians to adopt non-violence. All this may well have amounted to nil, and to Awad's disappearance into the backwaters of West Bank politics, had it not been for the Qattaneh olive trees.

Qattaneh is a tiny Palestinian village located in the hills north-west of Jerusalem. The village lies just over the 'Green Line' inside the West Bank. Its inhabitants are farmers whose livelihood has depended on their harvest of olives from trees nearby the village. On 11 January 1986, villagers were astonished when Israelis arrived in their village and started trimming the branches of their trees. Once trimmed, the trees were whitewashed with a chemical preservative and then wrenched from the earth by tractors, roots intact, before being lifted into trucks and driven away. According to a report in *Al-Fajr*:

> The villagers were aghast. They argued. They put themselves in front of the tractors, but they were ignored or dragged away. After five days of continuous destruction, they went for outside help. Forty to sixty years of work had been torn out of their land, their hands. Nearly 6000 olive and almond trees were lost.[3]

When Awad heard the story of the Qattaneh olive trees he acted promptly. Here was a flagrant violation of Palestinian rights which presented an opportunity for a non-violent response. The Israeli authorities claimed that the olive trees were newly planted on land belonging to Israel inside the pre-'67 'Green Line'; the Qattaneh farmers claimed that they had planted and harvested the land for as long as they could remember. To support their claim, the farmers produced Jordanian tax records for the land, as well as a 1956 mortgage document for olive tree planting which recorded dates of planting. With the farmers clearly within their rights, Awad began to mobilise support. Money was collected, contacts were called, supporters were summoned and, on 25 January, 150 Palestinians, Israelis and foreign residents invaded Qattaneh armed with spades, hoes and 500 young olive saplings.

Awad and his non-violent brigade (many of whom were members of the newly formed Israeli/West Bank Chapter of the International Fellowship of Reconciliation or of Awad's Palestinian Centre for the Study of Non-Violence [PCSN]) were met by an employee of the Israel Land Authority. He warned them that the authorities had decreed the area 'state land' and that if they attempted to replant the trees they would be arrested and sued. While Jonathan Kuttab, a lawyer and co-founder of the PCSN, pointed out to the official that the armistice maps of 1967 proved that the land was part of the West Bank or no man's land – not Israel – the volunteers spread out along the terrace planting the young saplings.

No sooner were the saplings planted than employees of the Land Authority began to uproot them. Not to be deterred, the non-violent volunteers simply replanted them. With the cameras of ITV (UK) rolling, a cat-and-mouse game ensued with young saplings being planted, uprooted and replanted many times. In the end, the Israeli authorities simply resorted to snapping the thin stems of the saplings. The volunteers responded by sitting around those which survived, protecting them with their bodies – a stalemate was the result. At last word came from the Israeli military governor based in Ramallah. He promised that, if the volunteers withdrew, the trees would remain in the land. Hopeful and exalted by the success of their non-violent action, Awad and his brigade withdrew. The next day thirty of the group returned to water the trees – not one remained.[4]

Israel/Palestine is a land of irony. Endless conflict between generations of Arabs, Jews and foreigners has, at times, produced situations so bizarre that, if they were not tragic, one could only smile. The case of the olive trees of Qattaneh is one. Once in the hands of the Israel Land Authority, the trees were made available to Jewish town councils for planting. Jerusalem, as it so happened, was in need of a few full-grown trees for a small memorial garden. The olive trees of Qattaneh were purchased from the Israel Land Authority and replanted near the new memorial honouring a brave American, much admired in Israel; one who had dedicated his life to civil rights – Martin Luther King Jr. Awad and others were horrified and protested against the use of the Qattaneh trees at the memorial honouring their non-violent mentor. They met with the Qattaneh farmers to discuss the matter and irony struck again. The farmers informed them that, if uprooted again, the trees would die. They said: 'We know Martin Luther King Jr was a great man. If someone asked us to give trees in his honour, we would do this. So let the trees remain.'[5] This message was passed on personally by Awad to Coretta Scott King, widow of the deceased civil rights leader, who communicated her thanks to the farmers of Qattaneh.[6]

Although Awad lost the battle for the olive trees of Qattaneh, he won something else – credibility. Many Palestinians who had previously been sceptical, reconsidered the use of non-violence in the light of what had happened at Qattaneh. They realised that, even if the farmers had lost their trees, Awad had succeeded in attracting considerable attention to their plight both within Israel/Palestine and abroad. International attention increased when a British documentary, broadcast by ITV, showed the attempts by Awad and his supporters to replant the saplings.[7] The film, 'Courage Along the Divide', which was screened privately many times in Israel and the West Bank, greatly boosted Awad's prestige amongst Palestinians.

Awad built on his 'success' at Qattaneh by carrying out further well-publicised, non-violent acts. Following numerous conflicts between Jewish settlers and residents in Hebron, the IDF took the decision to close off a row of Palestinian shops located in the central business district below a Jewish settlement called Dabboya. A fence was erected close to the shops, allowing only a narrow entrance which was guarded by Israeli soldiers. The soldiers purposefully searched all who wanted to enter the fenced-off shops – strongly deterring would-be shoppers. Fearing that this would eventually lead to the collapse of their business, the Palestinian shopkeepers appealed for help. Awad, supported by more and more Palestinians, some Israelis and a faithful contingent of Christian expatriates, responded by bringing as many 'solidarity shoppers' as possible to support the Palestinians' dying business. Again, although commercially speaking this may not have saved the shopkeepers, his response won him (and his non-violent approach) respect.

This was followed by further actions: a campaign to promote the purchase of only Palestinian products once a month; protest over the uprooting of olive trees in Medya (West Bank) and demonstrations calling for water to be supplied to the villagers of Al Obidieh (near Bethlehem). In November 1987 Awad and the PCSN organised a demonstration which was to involve 250 people and 250 animals – camels, sheep, goats and donkeys! The animals belonged to Palestinian farmers from the village of Kisan, south of Bethlehem, who had lost 80 per cent of their grazing land after Israeli authorities fenced it off and destroyed livestock shelters. Awad obtained a permit for the demonstration – which was to be held in Jerusalem – only to have it revoked the day before it was to occur. For good measure the police erected roadblocks at the entrances of the city.[8] Such demonstrations may not have resulted in justice for the aggrieved but they boosted Awad's call for a non-violent confrontation.

Although Awad has managed to overcome certain obstacles and has notched up a few successes, he is not about to become the Gandhi or the King of the Palestinians. What he represents is an interesting, rather than 'important' move amongst Palestinians towards non-violence. His struggle undermines the refrain of many Israelis in the peace movement that 'there is no other side', no 'Palestinian peace movement'. It is perhaps for this very reason that the Israeli authorities are keen to deport him. Awad holds a US passport and enters Israel on a tourist visa. When this expired in November 1987 the government refused to renew it while Awad refused to leave the country. With the threat of deportation hanging over his head, Awad found support flowing in from numerous circles. Hebrew University lecturer Eddy Kaufman told a press conference that many Jews believed in Awad's non-violent struggle and would 'join the battle to keep him in the country'.[9] The US Consulate reported that it was taking a 'special interest' in the case. Awad made publicised tours of a mosque, a church and a synagogue in a bid to get further support. He visited the Knesset, at the invitation of Yossi Sarid, where an attempt was made to have his case put on the Knesset agenda.

What is clear from the case of Awad and the PCSN is that many Palestinians do want peace and are prepared to work, non-violently, for it. But even these are not prepared to accept peace without justice; they will not accept a 'Pax Israelica' which would leave them without the self-determination they so desire. Awad and others are convinced that a non-violent approach is more likely to expose the injustices of the occupation and drive the Israelis to negotiations than is violence. Whether or not Awad will be able to mobilise enough Palestinians to make a real impact on the Israelis remains to be seen.

THE ALTERNATIVE INFORMATION CENTRE

On 16 February 1987 an event took place in West Jerusalem which alarmed many peace activists and Israeli leftists. Had it taken place in East Jerusalem – or elsewhere in the occupied territories – it would hardly have been noticed. On that day around twenty plainclothes policemen attached to the 'special branch minorities division' raided the premises of a licensed Israeli press and information office run by Israeli Jews: workers were arrested, printed matter was seized, computer hardware and software were confiscated and the office was closed for six months.

The Alternative Information Centre (AIC) had been opened in late 1984 by a 'collective' of radical peace activists to provide an alternative channel of information and analysis of events in Israel and the occupied territories. The centre was registered with the Ministry of the Interior and, in the summer of 1985, it was granted a license to publish *News From Within*, a fortnightly review directed at international readership interested in the Palestinian–Israeli conflict. From mid-1986, the AIC began to publish daily news sheets chronicling repression in the occupied territories. The centre, which was conveniently situated in West Jerusalem less than a minute's walk across the 'Green Line', was in close contact with numerous Palestinian, Israeli and foreign journalists who came to rely on its services to find out what was taking place in the occupied territories. Besides publishing and holding press conferences, members of the collective (most of whom were also active in radical MOs) actively participated in demonstrations against the government's policy in the occupied territories or in Israel proper.

In order to help finance its news and information services, the AIC collective offered typesetting and translation services. In addition to doing work for various MOs in the Israeli peace movement, the AIC had clients ranging from embassies to churches. Perhaps most important amongst its clients were the numerous Palestinian trade-unions, students', women's and cultural groups in the territories – an aspect of its work which was obviously of concern to the Israeli authorities.

The AIC was closed in accordance with an order enacted by the British mandatory government and appropriated by the Israelis in 1948. The 'Prevention of Terrorism Ordinance' was supposed to expire upon the termination of Israel's war-time state of emergency declared in 1948. Thirty-nine years later, with both the state of emergency and the Prevention of Terrorism Ordinance being still in force, the police have been able to shut down one press centre after the other. Until February 1987 such harassment of the press was confined to the occupied territories – with a strict form of 'self-censorship' existing in Israel proper. The use of the ordinance to close down a Jewish-run centre, in Israel proper, caused widespread concern in Israel and abroad. Messages of protest and of solidarity poured in, especially from liberal American Jews who saw the closure of the AIC as a serious erosion of freedom of speech in Israel. Within Israel hundreds of journalists, academics, libertarians, left-wing politicians and peace activists joined the Association for Civil Rights in Israel to protest against the closure. In a signed petition they noted: 'Administrative punishment without trial violates the basic democratic principle according to which a person is considered innocent until his guilt has been proven in court. If the police suspect the members of the information centre of breaking the law, it can put them on trial publicly, as is the custom in a democratic country.' The petitioners stressed that, as the centre's publications were submitted to censorship, this should have been enough to secure state security.

Within forty-eight hours of the closure, all the members of the AIC collective had been released from police custody except its director, Michael Warschawsky. He was subjected to two weeks of interrogation during which he was held in total isolation. He was denied reading or writing materials and only after repeated requests was he allowed to wash – once a week; he was denied the right to exercise in the courtyard, making it evident that the authorities were intent on making his detention as hard as possible. When finally indicted the judge accepted the prosecutor's request that he be denied bail.

Warschawsky's arrest and the closure of the AIC were justified by the police on the grounds that the AIC had been supporting a terrorist organisation. Amongst other things, the AIC was accused of providing typing services in 1986 to *Al Taqadum*, the newspaper of a Birzeit University student organisation. The prosecution alleged that the paper was in fact nothing less than the mouthpiece of the Popular Front for the Liberation of Palestine (PFLP). Similar allegations accused the AIC of typing leaflets for women's and workers' organisations, in the occupied territories, which the prosecution claimed were controlled by the PFLP. A final count concerned printed matter found in the AIC's archives which included leaflets, newspapers and journals published by a variety of Palestinian organisations – such as would be found in the files of any serious journalist or researcher dealing with the 'Palestinian question'.

Most of those who knew Warschawsky and the AIC found the charges of the state incredible – a poor attempt to cover up the more serious reasons for the closure of the centre. In a political 'post-mortem' of the affair, members of the collective and other analysts offered a number of reasons why the authorities had decided to 'kill' the centre. Firstly (and above all), they believed it was because the centre successfully offered journalists up-to-date information on the violation of human rights in the occupied territories. Secondly, the AIC's highlighting of the plight of Palestinian political prisoners brought international attention to focus on the conditions they faced in Israeli custody. One of the centre's publications which appeared to have particularly irked the security services, was a pamphlet on how Palestinian prisoners might respond should they be interrogated by the Shin Bet (Israel's secret service). Thirdly, the centre provided low-cost services which helped to sustain different radical organisations on both sides of the 'Green-Line'.[10] The final straw, which activists believe led to the centre's closure, was the collective's support of Mordechai Vanunu.

MORDECHAI VANUNU AND THE THREAT OF NUCLEAR WAR

Vanunu, one of a family of eleven from Morocco who emigrated to Israel in 1963, worked for nine years as a technician and operator at Israel's Nuclear Research Centre in the Negev, near Dimona. He volunteered, according to his brother Meir, to be among a group of workers laid-off from the facility in 1985, but not before taking many photographs of the plant. He left Israel in January 1986 and, after having travelled through Asia 'in search of peace and solitude' for some months, he met with a representative of the London newspaper *The Sunday Times*. Before the paper published the classified information on Israel's nuclear capabilities revealed by Vanunu, he suddenly disappeared from his London hotel and reappeared in police custody in Israel.

Exactly where, when and how Vanunu fell into the hands of the Israelis is not yet clear. Evidence suggests that he was lured out of London to Rome by a blonde Jewish-American from Florida named 'Cindy', employed as an Israeli agent. He was then apparently forcibly put onto a flight for Israel.[11]

As soon as he arrived in Israel under police custody, he was portrayed as an arch traitor who had sold off invaluable state secrets for a personal fortune. His father, a rabbi, was abused and driven from his synagogue as 'the father of the traitor'.[12] For the press, the Vanunu case offered everything: sensation, national security, censorship, treason, Israel's international relations, nuclear arms and the entire question of 'why he did it'. Concerning the latter, speculation was endless. For most, money was the prime motive: it was 'revealed' that Vanunu had speculated on the stock market and had incurred losses – this was held up as 'proof' of his 'abnormal' passion for money. Next, journalists discovered that Vanunu had converted to Christianity. As if *this* wasn't enough, it was revealed that he had once applied for membership in the Communist Party, that he was sexually impotent, had failed to find a girlfriend, failed his courses at university and was, essentially, a mentally ill, 'self-hating Jew'. Why else would a Jew betray Israel? To say the least, Mordechai Vanunu was not popular. He became, overnight, the man Israel loved to hate.

At best, activists in the different MOs of the peace movement remained silent – many actually joined in the lambasting and smearing of Vanunu. The issue of nuclear arms in Israel has never mobilised more than a few dozen activists. Most Israelis consider the possession of nuclear weapons to be a vital insurance policy against annihilation in the event of Arab (or Soviet) forces overcoming the IDF in a conventional war. The possibility of a nuclear explosion, set off by Israel and at the same time bringing about the total destruction of the Jewish state, is hardly debated. The only peace activists who were prepared to come out in support of Vanunu, and who were prepared to question Israel's 'secret' nuclear deterrence, were the non- and anti-Zionist radicals – many of whom were linked to the AIC.

Besides holding demonstrations against the way in which Vanunu had been returned to Israel and the way he was being treated upon arrival, the radical peace activists began to raise questions about Israel's nuclear policy. Working together with Vanunu's brothers, the activists attempted to present a more accurate picture of Vanunu's character and his reasons for 'spilling Israel's nuclear beans' to *The Sunday Times*. It was pointed out that Vanunu was an idealist who had been active in different peace groups and who had little interest in money. Had money been a motive, it was argued, he would have got far more for his revelations from a foreign government than he was supposed to get from the London newspaper. Far from being a fool, Vanunu was presented as an intelligent man of conscience who had succeeded in completing university 'even though most of his time was taken up with political activities for the underprivileged'.[13] Vanunu's brother explained that Mordechai had been strongly influenced by his reading about the implications of nuclear 'deterrence' and that his decision to act had been prompted by the Lebanon War which he opposed. East for Peace activist, Menny Barzilay, who knew Vanunu personally, rejected the press reports which portrayed Vanunu as unbalanced and argued that his revelations had, in fact, made Israel more secure. East for Peace carried out a poll amongst Mizrachim which revealed that a 'large number' of them believed that Vanunu was being persecuted because of his Moroccan origins. The MO gave Vanunu their full support.

The AIC collective dedicated a long article to the Vanunu case in *News From Within*. They rejected the slander suggesting that money, religion, impotence, personal failure or mental illness were behind his betrayal. Instead they argued the following:

> At some time during his Dimona years Vanunu realized that contrary to what ordinary folks normally suppose, nuclear research and development cannot safely be relegated to experts and professionals, because the entire system of professional expertise rests on the hermetic disconnection of the technical from the human. This was his discovery: shattering, profoundly insightful, perfectly true, albeit unoriginal, because Noam Chomsky, Daniel Ellsberg, George Kennan and Edward Thompson – to name a few . . . made the same discovery before Vanunu. But for Vanunu himself, this discovery had profound implications.[14]

Once Vanunu had rejected the separation of the technical and the human, he ceased to think in terms of 'targets' and began to think instead of thousands of civilians – human beings. Security ceased to be something Israeli and became more international. The AIC collective argued that, in revealing facts about Israel's nuclear capabilities, Vanunu was not being anti-Jewish or anti-Israeli but rather anti-nuclear. That instead of being derided as a traitor he deserved to be celebrated as a national hero who acted to protect not only Israel but possibly the entire Middle East from the threat of a nuclear holocaust.

In a letter from prison (published 20 November 1987), Vanunu dismissed the accusation that his act had been one of treason and espionage: 'Does it help the enemy to know that Israel has or doesn't have nuclear weapons? Can the enemy make use of such information? Can he, by dint of it, make his own nuclear weapons or take preventive action against nuclear weapons? What more can he do than worry and be weary of going to war?' Vanunu insisted that he was a man of conscience who did what he did 'after much thought and many doubts'. He upheld the right of citizens to know about their country's nuclear status: 'My belief is that in order to act against the nuclear danger we must, in the first stage, become aware of its existence and be conscious of the danger. To ignore it is a terrible danger which may harm the entire society and state in the future.'

Overseas, after some hesitation, Vanunu's case was adopted with enthusiasm: he was awarded the 'alternative' Nobel peace prize (worth $100,000) and nominated by more than forty British MPs for the real thing. Amnesty International supported him as a 'prisoner of conscience' while Britain's Campaign for Nuclear Disarmament (CND) picketed the Israeli embassy in his name. As if to underline the fact that he had not been motivated by money, Vanunu gave his prize money to be used for the establishment of a Washington-based lobby for a nuclear-free Middle East.[15] In December 1987, his case was presented to the Washington Press Club by his brother Meir and the Revd John McKnight (said to have been responsible for his conversion to Christianity). McKnight criticised Americans for remaining silent about Vanunu's kidnapping, his conditions of detention and about Israel's nuclear capabilities in general. He pointed out that:

> . . . it is ironic that while Israel is trying [the accused war criminal] Demjanjuk . . . because he followed the orders of his superiors and not his conscience, it is now accusing Vanunu of aggravated espionage for following his own conscience and not the orders of his superiors to keep secret the development of Israel's nuclear weapons.[16]

GIDEON SPIRO AND FREE SPEECH

One of the most vocal supporters of Vanunu in the Israeli peace movement was Gideon Spiro. Not only did he support Vanunu at press conferences, in newspaper articles and on the streets, but he loudly condemned the Israeli public and the peace movement for being apathetic and acquiescent when faced with the issue of Israeli nuclear arms. Before the Vanunu story, Spiro himself had been something of a 'first', in the same way that the closure of the AIC and the prosecution of Vanunu were 'firsts' in Israel, when he was prosecuted in 1986 under the 'Government Services Law'.

Born in Berlin in 1935, the young Spiro emigrated with his family to British-occupied Palestine in 1939. Although the family lived in Jerusalem, Spiro persuaded his parents to send him to school on a kibbutz. Along with many of his kibbutz peers, Spiro joined an élite paratrooper unit as part of his national service. In 1956 his troop was dropped behind enemy lines in the famous Mitla Pass battle in the Sinai. Spiro was decorated for bravery, gaining the respect of his superiors as well as his fellow paratroopers. As a reserve soldier Spiro participated in both the Six-Day War and the Yom Kippur War. He was drafted to serve in Lebanon but this time he refused to fight. Times had changed and so had Spiro.[17]

Over the years he had become increasingly critical of his government's policy over the Arab territories it now occupied and had become a leading activist in numerous MOs, namely: Yesh, an Arab–Jewish political group at Haifa University; Moked, the BSC, Yesh Gvul and the Committee Confronting the Iron Fist. Spiro worked full-time or part-time as a journalist, publishing hundreds of articles on the Israeli–Palestinian conflict, social and economic problems in Israel, Zionism and Israeli foreign policy.

From 1975 to 1986 he combined his journalism with a full-time position as manager of the Guest and Tourist Information Department of the Ministry of Culture and Education. The more critical Spiro became, the more he was felt to be a thorn in the flesh of the establishment. Through his work, Spiro was in a position to make his frequently unacceptable views known to a wide range of visitors in Israel – a fact that the Ministry was not willing to accept.

To remove that thorn, a law which had been in the statute books for thirty years – but which had never been used – was enacted. The

Government Services Law forbids a government employee 'to criticise the policy of their ministry, of other ministries, or of the government, in a press conference, in an interview with journalists, in a speech in a public place, in a broadcast, in a newspaper or in a book'. In early 1986 Spiro became the first civil servant in Israel to be tried under the law.

In the trial, the State of Israel produced nine letters written to different Israeli newspaper editors by the defendant, as evidence of his guilt. In one, written after the Sabra and Shatilla massacre, Spiro called on the Attorney-General to place the Minister of Defence, Ariel Sharon, and the Chief of Staff, Rafael Eitan, on trial following evidence linking them to the massacre. Pointing out that both men had acted as his commanding officers during the Sinai war, Spiro argued that he felt a personal responsibility to do all in his power to bring them to trial lest he be implicated by association as one who served under them. In an open letter to Eitan's successor, Major-General Moshe Levi, Spiro regretted that he was unable to congratulate him on his appointment as he had served as Deputy Chief of Staff during Israel's 'war of devastation in Lebanon . . . a war during which the Israeli army perpetrated war crimes against humanity'. In other letters Spiro argued that 'Jerusalem Day' was an artificial holiday with nothing to celebrate as long as the city's 'unity and liberation' was maintained by a heavy guard of the IDF and not by Israeli–Palestinian peace; he praised Yesh Gvul activists imprisoned during the Lebanon war; referring to meetings he had had with Arafat and other members of the PLO in Geneva, he argued that the PLO was moving to a political solution of the conflict; finally, he called for the release of Udi Adiv.[18] (see Chapter 4).

Despite the fact that, in the course of legal proceedings, government employees who had worked with Spiro testified that the accused had discharged all his duties faithfully and diligently, and had never given practical expression to his political opinions at his place of employment, Spiro was found guilty. The verdict against Gideon Spiro was immediate dismissal, cancellation of pension rights and the inability to hold any government position for five years. Commenting on the case, Avigor Feldman (Spiro's attorney and leading civil rights specialist) made the following points:

> Mr Spiro was tried for his political views, principally his call for peace, for recognition of the rights of the Palestinian people to

self-determination, and termination of the occupation which represses and denies civil rights . . . For these views he was condemned to forfeit his employment and abandoned to a very insecure economic future. This is a harsh sentence which will lead to the total gagging of government employees, and will prevent patriotic citizens who love peace and detest occupation and repression, from joining the government service . . . It is difficult to overrate the verdict's impact upon the democratic climate in the State of Israel. The government service is composed of a large group of citizens . . . All these persons are now barred from the free market of ideas and criticism and protest. The government service has become a closed totalitarian system imposing its views and policies upon its employees, intolerant towards their views and outlook, insofar as they clash with overall policy . . . The verdict projects a normative image of a government employee as political eunuch bound to serve his master, the Israeli government, and to refrain from criticism . . . even when its policy takes a massive toll of human life (as in) the Lebanon war, and offends the employee's conscience.[19]

The cases of the AIC, Vanunu and Spiro, all point to a new determination by the State to stem the tide of radical criticism of Israeli policy coming from Israeli Jews. To do this the State has had to dig deep to enact previously untested laws. These laws were not used in a more tolerant time when criticism was less severe and when, perhaps, the truth did not 'hurt' as much. Israeli radicals are not inclined to fabricate anti-government positions for the fun of it; their intention is rarely to hurt the State. Rather, they feel compelled by their consciences to proclaim their opposition to policies which they feel violate basic human rights and lead away from a peaceful resolution of the conflict which consumes the lives of both Israelis and Palestinians. They are, understandably, more and more alarmed by the State's response to their criticism which they see as a severe erosion of Israel's democratic character. Ever sensitive to moves towards totalitarianism, as Jews and as peace activists, they shudder at each step taken by the State which suggests the application of the 'norms' of occupation rule on both sides of the 'Green Line'.

10 Conclusions

It is difficult to present a conclusion to a subject that has yet to 'conclude'. The Israeli–Palestinian conflict in 1987 shows no hope of resolution and the peace movement continues to be active. Indeed, on 28 November, hundreds of Palestinian and Israeli peace activists gathered along the 'Green Line' near Jerusalem to mark the fortieth anniversary of the UN General Assembly resolution to partition Palestine. They held placards calling for an end to the occupation and the establishment of an independent Palestinian state. The demonstration was organised by a new MO called the Committee of Twenty Years of Occupation.

Looking back, it is clear that the level of activity of the peace movement dropped after the Lebanon war and the formation of a National Unity government. However, the election of Kahane to the Knesset led to a partial reactivation: new MOs emerged to confront Kahane in particular and racism in general; IPJACs were given governmental approval despite fierce opposition from many quarters and radical activists, particularly those involved in joint Palestinian–Israeli MOs, continued to struggle against the occupation while accusing others of retreating from the 'real issue'.

The general shift in focus, from confronting the occupation in the territories to confronting racism in Israel itself, illustrates an important point which I have stressed from time to time in the book. That is that the Israeli peace movement is primarily a 'reform' social movement, which *reacts* to 'negative trends' in Israeli society as they become apparent: as one threatening *particular* trend is replaced by another, so the movement responds – defending *universal* values which members continue to uphold.

It is unlikely that the peace movement will ever again demonstrate the degree of opposition that it did during the Lebanon war *as long as the Labour party forms any part of the national government*. The close association of many activists and supporters of the Israeli peace movement with the Labour party precludes the possibility of massive demonstrations which might embarrass Labour. However, were a Likud government to come to power and once again give top priority to the settling of the territories, or were it to launch another non-defensive war, it is possible that Israel might once again witness demonstrations such as the ones recorded in this book. Put simply, the protest activities of Peace Now (and consequently of the majority of the movement) are closely aligned to the future position of the Labour party in the Israeli government.

No matter which political party governs the State of Israel and the occupied territories, the majority of MOs in the Israeli peace movement will, one day, have to face the dilemma of how to reconcile universal values with an overriding Zionist desire to maintain Israel as a *Jewish* state. The only MOs confronted with this dilemma are the small anti-Zionist groups who represent no more than a small (albeit vocal) fraction of national opinion.

The tension created by this dilemma has been with the movement from the outset; it is revealed in Peace Now's constant advocacy of a 'sane Zionism' – a form of Zionism that will not betray the universal values upheld by the early socialist pioneers and which were embodied in the Declaration of Independence. Unquestionably the movement is united in the belief that Zionism cannot be 'sane', or even humane, as long as Israel continues to rule over almost one million Palestinians against their will. Different MOs repeatedly point to the same fact: *there is no such thing as a humane or enlightened occupation*; occupation begets resistance and resistance begets oppression which in turn begets further resistance – hence the movement's opposition to the occupation and its search for various alternatives.

The question that is rarely confronted by the Zionists in the peace movement, and that remains unanswered, is the following: if the occupation were to end, would it be possible to achieve peaceful Jewish–Arab coexistence within Israel proper? The conclusion I have reached is that, as long as Israel strives to maintain a national character that is distinctly Jewish, it is unlikely to achieve 'real' peace with its own substantial Palestinian minority. For this reason, the work of the IPJAC MOs cannot be easily dismissed as being irrelevant. Although their work may appear at times to be a finger in the dyke, its long-term significance may be greater than that of the protest MOs which tend to come and go with the ebb and flow of political events.

The questions of Jewish-Arab coexistence within the State of Israel and of the nature of the state in years to come are of course ones of pure speculation. The most immediate and politically explosive source of regional, and perhaps global conflict, remains the occupation and the unresolved 'Palestinian Question' that goes with it. A few Zionists in the peace movement claim to support the establishment of a Palestinian state, as a means to resolve this conflict, *precisely because they are Zionists*; in other words, *because* they believe in the right to self-determination for themselves as Jews, they also believe in it for the Palestinians who have lived in the land for untold generations. Indeed, it would seem that a growing number of Zionists are coming to the realisation that the Palestinians are as determined as they themselves were to achieve statehood in the land, not only of their ancestors, but of their birth.

There is little doubt that, as long as the occupation continues, the conflict in the region will continue to escalate. Western states seen to be supportive of Israel, as well as Jews everywhere, will continue to be targets of terrorism. The peace movement in Israel bears the enormous responsibility of encouraging its government to take the necessary steps to end the immediate source of this conflict – the occupation. It is certain that whatever steps are taken in that direction will require considerable determination and courage on behalf of the responsible government. Not so much because a tiny Palestinian state would be a threat to the military might of Israel but because *civil war* between those determined to make territorial compromises for peace and those unwilling to give up an inch of 'sacred' soil would be a real threat. For this reason, above all others, it is essential that the peace movement demonstrate the strength of that side of Israeli society opposed to the occupation and encourage its growth; no democratic government will act without knowing that it has the support of the majority of the electorate.

Although, at times, it would seem that the two sides are fairly equally balanced, the peace movement has been unable to tip the scales in favour of territorial compromise. This may be partly due to the divisions within the movement or to the widespread perception amongst Israelis that there is no 'other side' to talk to – no *acceptable* Palestinian leadership with whom to negotiate a settlement. The ICIPP has been unable to persuade Israelis of Arafat's growing moderation and his willingness to negotiate a settlement based on Palestinian self-determination in the occupied territories. The 'anti-contacts' law prohibiting meetings and dialogue with the PLO only confirmed the anathema that most Israelis feel for their enemy. It is to be regretted that so few Israelis are prepared to talk to their real enemy – the PLO. Instead the government attempts to name 'moderate' Palestinians with whom it is prepared to negotiate – as if it is possible to choose the leaders of one's enemy. No war has ever been brought to a conclusion through one side selecting individuals from the other to negotiate with. The PLO remains, for the vast majority of Palestinians, their 'only legitimate representative'; no Israeli-selected Palestinians will ever have the credibility needed to reach a negotiated settlement. It is unfortunate that the Israeli government chose not to deal with Sartawi and the other members of the PLO who initiated dialogue with peace activists. The invasion of Lebanon played straight into the hands of the Palestinian rejectionists by demonstrating Israeli intransigence and 'proving' that Arafat's diplomatic thrust would meet with little success. The position of the moderates within the PLO was thus weakened, further reducing the possibility of a strong non-rejectionist, 'other side' emerging within the Palestinian camp.

Many in the Israeli peace movement hope that one day Arafat will embark on the dramatic and courageous path chosen by Sadat and imagine that the movement will respond by pressurising the Israeli government to make compromises. Such a gesture would evidently have to be totally unambiguous as previous messages and signals sent by Arafat to the Israelis have been met with scepticism. It is unlikely that Arafat would be prepared to take such a unilateral step while Israel remains determined to hold on to the occupied territories and unwilling to negotiate with the PLO. Furthermore, with the Israeli peace movement shifting its focus to the diffuse task of combating racism and promoting democracy, it seems unlikely that it will, in the foreseeable future, be able to mobilise to force the government to fulfil what for the Palestinians are the essential preconditions for peace – an end to the occupation and negotiations with the PLO.

Notes

CHAPTER 1

1. See Barry McLaughlin (ed.), *Studies in Social Movements* (New York: The Free Press, 1969) and J. A. Banks, *The Sociology of Social Movements* (London: Macmillan Press, 1972).
2. Charles Tilly, *From Mobilization to Revolution* (London: Addison-Wesley, 1978).
3. Check the glossary for Hebrew and other foreign terms as well as the names of groups, organisations and political parties.
4. S.N. Eisenstadt, *The Transformation of Israeli Society: An Essay in Interpretation* (London: Weidenfeld and Nicolson, 1985) p. 45.
5. Reported in an interview with Adam Keller of the Israeli Council for Israeli-Palestinian Peace, Tel Aviv, 1985.
6. R. J. Isaac, *Israel Divided: Ideological Politics in the Jewish State* (Baltimore: John Hopkins University Press, 1976) p. 5.
7. Gwyn Rowley, 'The Land of Israel: A Reconstructionist Approach', in David Newman (ed.), *The Impact of Gush Emunim: Politics and Settlement in the West Bank* (London: Croom Helm, 1985) p. 125.
8. Ibid., p. 127.
9. Isaac, op. cit., p. 61.
10. Ibid., p. 54.
11. Ibid.
12. Lilly Weissbrod, 'Gush Emunim Ideology – From Religious Doctrine to Political Action', *Middle Eastern Studies*, vol. 18, no. 3, July 1982.
13. Ibid.
14. Euhud Sprinzak, 'The Iceberg of Political Extremism', in Newman (ed.), op. cit., p. 33.
15. *The Jerusalem Post*, 12 February, 1985.
16. Kurt Kanowitz, 'The Role of the Army in Israeli Politics', *New Outlook*, August-September 1984, p. 11.
17. Ofira Seliktar, *New Zionism and the Foreign Policy System of Israel* (London: Croom Helm, 1986) p. 206.
18. The *Jerusalem Post*, 11 July, 1985.
19. Sprinzak, op. cit., p. 36.
20. For an in-depth study of this process see: Lilly Weissbrod, 'Delegitimation and Legitimation as a Continuous Process: A Case Study of Israel', *Middle East Journal*, vol. 35, no. 4, 1981, pp. 527–43.

21. The term Mizrachim is used in its untranslated form to avoid the connotations inherent in the English translation 'Orientals'. It refers to Jews who are not Ashkenazim; namely those from Afro-Asian (Muslim) countries who may or may not be descendents of the Sephardic Jews of Spain and Portugal.

22. Eisenstadt (1985), op. cit., p. 152.

23. S. Aronson and N. Yanai, 'Critical Aspects of the Elections and their Implications', in D. Caspi *et al.* (eds), *The Roots of Begin's Success* (London: Croom Helm, 1984) p. 28.

24. Weissbrod, op. cit., p. 529.

25. Amos Oz, *In the Land of Israel* (London: The Hogarth Press, 1983) p. 133.

26. Ibid., p. 134.

27. David Schnall, 'Gush Emunim: An Impact Assessment', in Newman (ed.), op. cit., p. 22.

28. This disquiet was expressed by many peace activists I interviewed between 1985 and 1987. It was a constant theme expressed at meetings and made explicit in movement pamphlets. It was also stressed by academics and journalists who identify with the peace movement even though they may not participate actively.

29. *The Jerusalem Post*, 26 July, 1985.

30. *The Jerusalem Post*, 21 August, 1985.

31. *The Times*, 19 July, 1984.

32. *The Jerusalem Post*, 30 August, 1985.

33. Ora Namir interviewed by Mark Segal, *The Jerusalem Post*, 23 September, 1985.

34. Eti Ronel, 'The Battle Over Temple Mount', *New Outlook*, vol. 27, no. 2, February 1984, pp. 11–14.

35. W. Laqueur, *A History of Zionism* (London: Weidenfeld and Nicolson, 1972) p. 303.

36. On the growth of Revisionism see L. Brenner, *The Iron Wall: Zionist Revisionism from Jabotinsky to Shamir* (London: Zed Books, 1984).

37. M. J. Aronoff, 'Political Polarization: Contradictory Interpretations of Israeli Reality', in S. Heydemann (ed.), *The Begin Era: Issues in Contemporary Israel* (London: Westview Press, 1984) p. 54.

38. Ibid., p. 55.

39. Quoted in Brenner, op. cit., p. 147.

40. Aronoff, op. cit., p. 57.

41. Brenner, op. cit., p. 147.

42. On the role of Dash in ending Labour's rule see H. R. Penniman (ed.)., *Israel at the Polls: The Knesset Elections of 1977* (Washington: AEIPRP, 1979).

CHAPTER 2

1. For more on social movement theory see MacLaughlin, op. cit., Banks, op. cit. and Tilly, op. cit.

2. Laqueur, op. cit., p. 414.
3. Yitzhak Epstein, 'A Hidden Question' (Address to the Seventh Zionist Congress), *New Outlook*, vol.28, no.12, 1984, p. 27.
4. Ibid.
5. I. F. Stone, 'The Other Zionism: Accomodating Jew and Arab in Palestine', *Harper's*, September 1978, p. 65.
6. A. Goren (ed.), *Dissenter in Zion: From the Writings of Judah L. Magnes* (Cambridge, Mass.: Harvard University Press, 1982) *passim*.
7. Aharon Cohen, 'In Memory of a Pathfinder', *New Outlook*, vol.10, no.3, 1967, p. 48.
8. Details of the bi-national proposals are contained in: Judah Magnes and Martin Buber, *Arab-Jewish Unity: Testimony before the Anglo-American Inquiry Commission for the Ihud (Union) Association* (London: Victor Gollancz, 1947).
9. Ibid., p. 47.
10. Laqueur, op. cit., p. 253.
11. Ibid.
12. Stone, op. cit., p. 70.
13. M. Ghilan, *How Israel Lost its Soul* (Harmondsworth: Penguin, 1974) p. 81.
14. Isaac, op. cit., p. 97.
15. Ibid., p. 78.
16. Ibid., p. 88.
17. Eisenstadt (1985), op. cit., p. 387.
18. Ibid., p. 389.
19. Yosef Goell, 'The Case of the Democratic Movement for Change: Interview with Dr Israel Katz', *The Jerusalem Post*, 30 June, 1987.
20. Arnold Lewis, 'The Peace Ritual and Israeli Images of Social Order', *Journal of Conflict Resolution*, vol.23, no.4, December 1979, p. 688.
21. Ibid.
22. Peter Heller, 'Anwar Sadat's Visit to Jerusalem: Its Significance for the Peace Process', *Journal of South Asian and Middle Eastern Studies*, vol.VII, no. 4, Summer 1984, pp. 12–18.
23. Lewis, op.cit.,p.693.
24. Ibid., p. 696.
25. Ibid.
26. Quoted in Phillip Gallon, 'Anatomy of a Movement', *The Jerusalem Post*, 14 April, 1978.
27. This particular translation of the now famous letter is by Lewis, op. cit., p. 698.

CHAPTER 3

1. This description of the founding of Peace Now was given by a founding member, Yuli Tamir, at the Jewish Colloquium, Oxford, 10 February, 1986.

2.	Interview with Jay Hurwitz (Peace Now), July 1985.
3.	*The Jerusalem Post*, 23 August, 1978.
4.	Ibid., 17 April, 1978.
5.	Ibid., 27 July, 1979.
6.	Ibid.
7.	Ibid., 14 June, 1979.
8.	Ibid., 11 June, 1979.
9.	Ibid., 6 January, 1980.
10.	Seliktar, op. cit., p. 236.
11.	Peace Now Pamphlet (English), 1985.
12.	*The Jerusalem Post*, 15 April, 1986.

CHAPTER 4

1.	Interview with Reuven Amiel, Committee for Upper and Lower Nazareth Co-operation, 1985.
2.	Reuven Hammer, 'Pandora's Box', *The Jerusalem Post*, 8 August, 1984.
3.	The following account of anti-racist protest and legislation is compiled from interviews with activists from Citizens Against Racism (notably Mike Levine) and from newspaper reports.
4.	*The Jerusalem Post*, 7 August, 1986.
5.	Ibid.
6.	Interview with Haim Baram, journalist, 1987.
7.	*Israel–Palestine*, no.53–54, December 1976.
8.	Ibid.
9.	Ibid.
10.	For Avnery's own account see Uri Avnery, *My Friend, the Enemy* (London: Zed Books, 1986).
11.	Ibid., p. 120.
12.	Ibid., p. 72.
13.	Ibid.
14.	Ibid., pp. 3–14.
15.	*News from Within*, vol. II, no. 36, 6 October, 1986.
16.	Ibid.
17.	Ibid.

CHAPTER 5

1.	Daniel Gavron, 'Smashing the Stereotype', *The Jerusalem Post Magazine*, 8 July, 1983.
2.	Interview with Shlomo Elbaz, East for Peace, July 1985.
3.	Chaim Raphael, *The Road to Babylon: The Story of the Sephardi and Oriental Jews* (London: Weidenfeld and Nicolson, 1985) p. 250.
4.	Major differences between Ashkenazi and Mizrachi immigrants are

noted by A. Shama and M. Iris, *Immigration Without Integration* (Cambridge (Mass.): Schenkman, 1977).

5. A. N. Chouraqui, *Between East and West: A History of the Jews of North Africa* (Philadelphia: The Jewish Publication Society of America, 1968) p. 290.

6. Shama and Iris, op. cit., p. 82.

7. Ibid.

8. Ibid.

9. Rivkah Bar Josef, 'The Moroccans: Background to the Problem', in S.N. Eisenstadt, *et al.* (eds), *Integration and Development in Israel* (Jerusalem: Israel Universities Press, 1970) p. 424.

10. Bat Ye'Or, *The Dhimmi: Jews and Christians Under Islam* (Toronto and London: Associated University Press, 1985) passim.

11. H. J. Cohen, *The Jews of the Middle East, 1860–1972* (Jerusalem: Israel Universities Press, 1973) p. 4.

12. Doris Bensimon-Donath, *Evolution du Judaïsme Marocain sous le Protectorat Français 1912–1956* (Paris: Mouton & Co., 1968).

13. H. J. Cohen, op. cit., p. 16.

14. Bat Ye'Or, op. cit., p. 80.

15. Cohen, op. cit., p. 10.

16. Ibid., p. 4.

17. For a full account of this see Raphael, op. cit.

18. Chouraqui, op. cit., p. 156.

19. Marion Woolfson, *Prophets in Babylon: Jews in the Arab World* (London: Faber and Faber, 1980) p. 80.

20. Martin Gilbert, *The Arab–Israeli Conflict: Its History in Maps* (London: Weidenfeld and Nicolson, 1979) p. 50.

21. S. N. Eisenstadt, 'The Process of Absorption of New Immigrants in Israel', in Eisenstadt *et al.*, op. cit., pp. 354–8.

22. Chouraqui, op. cit., pp. 304–5.

23. L. J. Davis and M. Decter, *Myths and Facts 1982: A Concise Record of the Arab–Israeli Conflict* (Washington: Near East Report, 1982) p. 122.

24. H.J. Cohen, op. cit., p. 16.

25. Roumani, op. cit., p. 25.

26. Bensimon-Donath, op. cit., p. 112.

27. Ibid., p. 182.

28. Ibid.

29. See in particular D. Caspi, *et al.*, op. cit.; D. Peretz and S. Smooha, 'Israel's Tenth Knesset Elections – Ethnic Upsurgence and Decline in Ideology', *Middle East International*, vol.35, no.4, 1981; and Yael Yishai, 'Israel's Right-Wing Jewish Proletariat', *The Jewish Journal of Sociology* vol. XXIV, no. 2, 1982.

30. Israel Shahak, 'The Oriental Jews in Israeli Politics', *Middle East International*, 15 June, 1984, p. 15.

31. Peres and Shemer, op. cit., p. 105.

32. Ibid., p. 94.

33. Quoted in *News from Within*, 22 July, 1986.
34. P.S. Cohen, 'Ethnicity, Class and Political Alignment in Israel', *The Jewish Journal of Sociology*, vol.25, no. 2, 1983, p. 120.
35. Statistical Abstract Israel, quoted in Yishai, op. cit., p. 20.
36. Amos Oz, *In the Land of Israel*, p. 36.
37. A Gonen, 'A Geographical Analysis of the Elections in Jewish Urban Communities', in Caspi *et al.*, op. cit., p. 81.
38. P. S. Cohen, op. cit., p. 129.
39. Ibid., p. 127.
40. Erik Cohen, 'Ethnicity and Legitimation in Contemporary Israel', *The Jerusalem Quarterly*, no. 28, 1983, p. 113.
41. Ibid., p. 116.
42. Ibid.
43. *The Jerusalem Post*, 10 March, 1972.
44. For a full account see Mony Elkaim, *Panthères Noires d'Israël* (Paris: François Maspero, 1972).
45. *The Jerusalem Post*, 16 June, 1972.
46. Ibid., 25 September, 1975.
47. Ibid., 2 March, 1977.
48. Ibid., 15 August, 1979.
49. Ibid., 9 June, 1980.
50. *In Jerusalem*, 13 September, 1985.
51. Interview with Sa'adia Marciano, ex-Black Panthers, July 1985.
52. Interview with Jacques Pinto, East for Peace, August 1985.
53. Elbaz, op. cit.
54. Ibid.
55. Quoted in Amnon Rubinstein, *The Zionist Dream Revisited* (New York: Schocken Books, 1984) p. 51.
56. Ibid., p.52.
57. Ibid., p. 56.
58. Michael Bar-Zohar, *Ben-Gurion* (London: Weidenfeld and Nicolson, 1978) p. 77.
59. Isaac, op. cit., p. 52.
60. Ghilan, op. cit., p. 102.
61. Ibid., p. 113.

CHAPTER 6

1. *News from Within*, 22 July, 1986.
2. *Al Fajr*, 25 July, 1986.
3. *Al Awdah English Weekly*, 24 August, 1986.
4. Interview with Adam Keller, PLP, 1987.
5. Ibid.
6. Ibid.

7.   *The Times*, 8 November, 1986.
8.   On the life of Eliachar see Phillip Gillon, *Israelis and Palestinians, Co-Existence Or . . . : The Credo of Elie Eliachar* (London: Rex Collings, 1978) and Elie Eliachar, *Living with Jews* (London: Weidenfeld and Nicolson, 1983).
9.   Nissim Rejiwan, 'The Orientalization of Israel: An Exposé of a Myth', *New Outlook*, January/February, 1987.

CHAPTER 7

1.   The account of Neve Shalom is based on interviews with founder, Bruno Hussar, and with other members of the community, notably Anne Le Meignen and Wellesley Aron. Written sources included the *Neve Shalom Newsletter* and its French equivalent *Lettre de la Colline*.
2.   Joel Greenberg, 'Government Ministries back new institute for Jewish–Arab Co-Existence', *Press Bulletin*, State of Israel Government Press Office, 19 April, 1983.
3.   I am grateful to Jan Demarest and Samir Abu-Shakrah for insights into the different approaches of MOs and the radical protest MOs' critique of IPJACs. (Interview September 1985) For a critique of one particular IPJAC (from a radical perspective), see J. Demarest and S. Abu-Shakrah, 'Response to "Buberian Learning Groups: Existentialist Philosophy as an Ariane Thread for Education for Peace"', *Teachers' College Record*, Winter, 1983–4.
4.   Rahel Rosenweig, 'Partnership', *New Outlook*, June/July, 1977, pp. 31–4.
5.   Rahel Rosenweig, 'Turning Enemies and Adversaries into Partners', unpublished mimeograph distributed by Shutafut.
6.   Tsiyona Peled and David Bar-Gal, *Intervention Activities in Arab–Jewish Relations: Conceptualization, Classification and Evaluation* (Jerusalem: Israeli Institute of Applied Social Research, 1983) p. 80.
7.   Demarest and Abu-Shakrah, op. cit., p. 8.
8.   S. Smooha, 'Issues in Arab–Jewish Relations in Israel' in A. Hareven (ed.), *Every Sixth Israeli: Relations Between the Jewish Majority and Arab Minority in Israel* (Jerusalem: The Van Leer Jerusalem Foundation, 1983) p. 108.
9.   Eli Rekhess, 'The Politicization of Israel's Arabs', in Hareven, op. cit., p. 138.
10.   Rafi Israeli, 'Arabs in Israel: The Surge of a New Identity', in Hareven, op. cit., p. 175.
11.   Demarest and Abu-Shakrah, op. cit., p. 9.
12.   Ibid.
13.   Peled and Bar-Gal, op. cit., p. 80.
14.   *The Jerusalem Post*, 8 August, 1985.
15.   Peled and Bar-Gal, op. cit., p. 83.

16. *The Jerusalem Post*, 20 September, 1985.
17. Eytan Gilboa, 'Educating Israeli Officers in the Process of Peace Making in the Middle East Conflict', *Journal of Peace Research*, vol.XVI, no. 2, 1979, pp. 155–62.
18. Interview with David Shaham, Executive Director ICPME, September 1985.
19. Ibid.
20. Ibid.
21. 'The Comprehensive Education Project on Relations Between Arabs and Jews and Between Israel and Her Neighbours: A Project Directed by the VLJF for the Israeli Ministry of Education and Culture' (Jerusalem: VLJF, July 1984) p. 1.
22. Mina Tzemach and Ruth Tzin, 'Attitudes of Adolescents with Regard to Democratic Values' (Jerusalem: VLJF, 1984) p. 4.

CHAPTER 8

1. *The Jerusalem Post*, 21 April, 1978.
2. Ibid.
3. Ibid., 25 July, 1979.
4. Ibid., 25 May, 1978.
5. Ibid., 12 May, 1978.
6. Interview with Jay Hurwitz, Mapam, 1985.
7. *The Jerusalem Post*, 12 May, 1978.
8. Ibid., 25 March, 1981.
9. Ibid.
10. Interview with Yehezkel Landau, Oz ve Shalom, 1985.
11. Oz ve Shalom, *English Bulletin*, no. 1, p. 2.
12. Oz ve Shalom Publications, *Religious Zionism: Challenges and Choices*, Jerusalem, (no date), p. 2.
13. Ibid.
14. *English Bulletin*, op cit.
15. Ibid.
16. Uriel Simon, 'Religion, Morality and Politics', in *Religious Zionism*, op. cit., p. 2.
17. Ibid.
18. Uriel Tal, 'Historical and Metahistorical Self-Views' in *Religious Zionism*, ibid., p. 10.
19. Ibid.
20. Ibid.
21. Shimon Glick, 'A Dangerous Idolatry', in Oz ve Shalom, *English Bulletin*, no. 6, 1985, p. 19.
22. Larry Cohler, 'Israeli Religious Peace Group: Sanctity of Life More Important than Territories', *Long Island Jewish World*, 8 February, 1985.
23. *The Jerusalem Post*, 7 December, 1985.

24. Janet Aviad, 'Religious Zionism Today', in *Religious Zionism*, op. cit., p. 28.
25. Ibid., pp. 29–30.
26. Landau, Interview, op. cit.
27. Aviad, op. cit., p. 31.
28. Lawrence Kaplan, 'Education and Ideology in Religious Zionism Today', in *Religious Zionism*, op. cit., p. 37.
29. Ibid.
30. Ibid., p. 34.
31. David J. Schnall, *Radical Dissent in Contemporary Israeli Politics: Cracks in the Wall* (New York: Praeger Special Studies, 1979) p. 6.
32. *The Other Israel*, no. 10, August, 1984, p. 9.
33. Interview with Reuven Lasman, ex-Matzpen, 1985.
34. Ibid.
35. Ghilan, op. cit., p. 9.
36. Dunia Habib Nahas, *The Israeli Communist Party* (London: Croom Helm, 1976) p. 64.
37. For a detailed account see Alain Greilsammer, *Les Communistes Israéliens* (Paris: Presse de la Fondation Nationale des Sciences Politiques, 1978).
38. PLP Manifesto, printed in *The Other Israel*, no. 9., June–July 1984, p. 2.
39. Ibid.
40. Interview with Gideon Spiro, BSC, 1987.
41. Interview with Naomi Ben-Tzur, PAS, 1985.
42. *International Herald Tribune*, 22 February, 1984.
43. See for example *The Other Israel*, no. 14, April, 1985.
44. Quoted in Bar-Zohar, op. cit., p. 166.
45. Cheryl Rubenberg, 'The Israeli Invasion of Lebanon: Objectives and Consequences', *Journal of South Asian and Middle Eastern Studies*, vol. VIII, no. 2, 1984, p. 5.
46. Ibid.
47. *The Jerusalem Post*, 13 September, 1985.
48. Ben-Tzur, interview, op. cit.
49. Ibid.
50. Demerath and Marwell, op. cit., p. 244.
51. On this see Hannah Arendt, *Eichmann in Jerusalem: A Report on the Banality of Evil* (London: Faber and Faber, 1963).
52. *The Jerusalem Post*, 26 June, 1982. For a detailed account of Geva's case, see J. Timmerman, *The Long War: Israel in Lebanon* (New York: Vintage Books, 1982) pp. 138–44.
53. *The Jerusalem Post*, 12 April, 1983.
54. Ibid., 13 April, 1983.
55. Interview with Thoma Schick, War Resisters International, 1985.
56. *The Jerusalem Post*, 5 October, 1982.
57. *Ha'aretz*, 6 June, 1986. Reprinted (in English) in *The Other Israel*, no. 22, May–June 1986, p. 5.

58.   *Al Fajr*, 25 October, 1987.
59.   Quoted by Michael Lowry in *Al Fajr*, 14 January, 1986.
60.   Haim Baram, *Ha'aretz*, 7 February, 1986, quoted in ibid.
61.   Ibid.
62.   Quoted in Davis *et al.*, op. cit., p. 112.
63.   Interview with Giora Neuman, Matzpen, PLP, August 1985.
64.   Thoma Schick, 'The Price of Conscience in Israel', *Al Fajr* (weekly), April 9–15, 1982, p. 12.

CHAPTER 9

1   David Richardson, 'Confrontation Quest', *The Jerusalem Post*, 25 November, 1983.
2.   *PCSN Newsletter*, vol. 1, no. 2, 1986.
3.   *Al Fajr*, 31 January, 1986.
4.   Interview with Yvette Nahal, IFOR, 1987.
5.   *PCSN Newsletter*, op. cit.
6.   Ibid.
7.   'Courage Along the Divide', produced and directed by Victor Schonfeld, SPI, CTV Co-production, broadcast on ITV (UK), 9 September, 1986.
8.   *Al Fajr*, 29 November, 1987.
9.   Ibid., 22 November, 1987.
10.   See *News From Within*, 24 February, 1987.
11.   *Al Fajr*, 6 December, 1987.
12.   *The Guardian*, 10 November, 1987.
13.   *The Jerusalem Post*, 20 February, 1987.
14.   *News From Within*, 23 November, 1987.
15.   *The Guardian*, 10 November, 1987.
16.   *Al Fajr*, 6 December, 1987.
17.   Spiro, interview, op. cit.
18.   Letters furnished by Spiro to the author.
19.   Press release of A. Feldman, February 1987.

Bibliography

Abu-Shakrah, J. 'A Critical Look at Israeli Dialogue and Education for Peace with Palestinians Inside the Green Line'. Paper presented to the Arab Studies Society, Jerusalem, 16 August, 1984 (unpublished).

Amad, A. (ed.), *Israeli League for Civil and Human Rights: The Shahak Papers* (Beirut: Palestine Research Centre, 1973).

Arendt, H., *Eichmann in Jerusalem: A Report on the Banality of Evil* (London: Faber and Faber, 1963).

Avnery, U., *Israel Without Zionists: A Plea for Peace in the Middle East* (New York: Macmillan, 1968).

——, *My Friend, the Enemy* (London: Zed Books Ltd., 1986).

Ayalon, H., Ben-Rafel, E. and Sharot, S., 'Variations in Ethnic Identification among Israeli Jews', *Ethnic and Racial Studies*, vol. 8 (July 1985).

Bahiri, S., *Peaceful Separation or Enforced Unity: Economic Consequences for Israel and the West Bank/Gaza Area* (Jerusalem: I.C.P.M.E. Publications, 1984).

Banks, J.A., *The Sociology of Social Movements* (London: Macmillan, 1972).

Bar-Zohar, M., *Ben-Gurion* (London: Weidenfeld and Nicolson, 1978).

Bensimon-Bonath, D., *Evolution du Judaïsme Marocain sous le Protectorat Français 1912–1956* (Paris: Mouton, 1968).

——, *Immigrants d'Afrique du Nord en Israël: Evolution et Adaptation* (Paris: Editions Anthropos, 1970).

Berger, P.L. and Luckmann, T., *The Social Construction of Reality: A Treatise in the Sociology of Knowledge* (New York: Anchor Books, 1967).

Blatt, M., Davis, U. and Kleinbaum, P. (eds), *Dissent and Ideology in Israel: Resistance to the Draft 1948–1973* (London: Ithaca Press, 1975).

Brenner, L., The Iron Wall: Zionist Revisionism from Jabotinsky to Shamir (London: Zed Books Ltd., 1984).

Buber, M., Magnes, J. and Simon, E., *Towards Union in Palestine: Essays on Zionism and Jewish-Arab Cooperation* (Jerusalem: Ihud (Union) Assoc., 1947).

Buber, M., *Israel and Palestine: The History of an Idea* (London: Horovitz Publishing, 1952).

Caspi, D., Duskin, A. and Gutmann, E., *The Roots of Begin's Success: The 1981 Israeli Elections* (London: Croom Helm, 1984).

Chouraqui, A., *Between East and West: A History of the Jews of North Africa* (Philadelphia: The Jewish Publication Society of America, 1968).

Cohen, E., 'Ethnicity and Legitimation in Contemporary Israel', *The*

Jerusalem Quarterly, no. 28 (1983).
Cohen, H.J., *The Jews of the Middle East, 1860–1972* (Jerusalem: Israel Universities Press, 1973).
Cohen, P.S., *Modern Social Theory* (London: Heinemann, 1968).
——, *Jewish Radicals and Radical Jews* (London: Academic Press, 1980).
——, 'Ethnicity, Class and Political Alignment in Israel', *The Jewish Journal of Sociology*, vol. 25, no. 2, (1983).
Comay, M., *Zionism, Israel and the Palestinian Arabs* (Jerusalem: Keter Books, 1983).
Davis, L.J. and Decter, M., *Myths and Facts 1982: A Concise Record of the Arab-Israeli Conflict* (Washington: Near East Report, 1982).
Davis, U. and Mezvinsky, N., *Documents from Israel 1967–1973: Readings for a Critique of Zionism* (London: Ithaca Press, 1975).
Demarest, J. and Abu-Shakrah, S., 'Response to "Buberian Learning Groups: Existentialist Philosophy as an Ariane Thread for Education for Peace"' *Teachers' College Record*, Winter, 1983–84.
Demerath, N. and Marwell, G., *Sociology: Perspectives and Applications* (New York: Harper and Row, 1976).
Deshen, S., 'Two Trends in Israeli Orthodoxy', *Judaism*, vol. 27 (Fall, 1978), no. 4.
Eisenstadt, S.N., *The Absorption of Immigrants* (London: Routledge and Kegan Paul, 1954).
——, *The Transformation of Israeli Society: An Essay in Interpretation* (London: Weidenfeld and Nicolson, 1985).
——, Bar-Yosef, R. and Adler, C. (eds), *Integration and Development in Israel* (Jerusalem: Israel Universities Press, 1970).
Eliachar, E., *Living with Jews* (London: Weidenfeld and Nicolson, 1983).
Elkaim, M., *Panthères Noires d'Israël* (Paris: François Maspero, 1972).
Epstein, Y., 'A Hidden Question: Address to the 7th Zionist Congress', *New Outlook*, vol. 28 (1984), no. 12.
Etzioni-Halevy, E., 'Protest Politics in Israeli Democracy', *Political Science Quarterly*, vol. 90 (Fall 1975), no. 3.
Frankel, W., *Israel Observed: An Anatomy of the State* (New York: Thames and Hudson, 1980).
Garaudy, R., *The Case of Israel: A Study of Political Zionism* (Paris: Spag-Papyrus, 1983).
Ghilan, M., *How Israel Lost its Soul* (Harmondsworth: Penguin, 1974).
Gilbert, M., *Exile and Return: The Emergence of Jewish Statehood* (London: Weidenfeld and Nicolson, 1978).
——, *The Arab-Israeli Conflict: Its History in Maps* (London: Weidenfeld and Nicolson: 1979).
Gilboa, E., 'Educating Israeli Officers in the Process of Peace Making in the Middle East Conflict', *Journal of Peace Research*, vol. XVI (1979), no. 2.
Gillon, P., *Israelis and Palestinians Co-Existence or . . . : The Credo of Elie Eliachar* (London: Rex Collings, 1978).
Goren, A. (ed), *Dissenter in Zion: From the Writings of Judah L. Magnes*

(Cambridge (Mass.): Harvard University Press, 1982).

Greilsammer, A., *Les Communistes Israëliens* (Paris: Presse de la Fondation Nationale des Sciences Politiques, 1978).

Habib Nahas, D., *The Israeli Communist Party* (London: Croom Helm, 1976).

Hareven, A. (ed), *Every Sixth Israeli: Relations Between the Jewish Majority and the Arab Minority in Israel* (Jerusalem: The Van Leer Jerusalem Foundation, 1983).

Heller, P., 'Anwar al-Sadat's Visit to Jerusalem: Its Significance for the Peace Process', *Journal of South Asian and Middle Eastern Studies*, vol. 7, (1984), no. 4.

Heydemann, S. (ed.), *The Begin Era: Issues in Contemporary Israel* (London: Westview Press, 1984).

Isaac, R. J., *Israel Divided: Ideological Politics in the Jewish State* (Baltimore: John Hopkins University Press, 1976).

Kanowitz, K., 'The Role of the Army in Israeli Politics', *New Outlook*, August–September, 1984.

——, 'Making Conflict a Routine: Cumulative Effects of the Arab-Jewish Conflict Upon Israeli Society', *The Journal of Strategic Studies*, vol. 6 (1983), no. 3.

Landau, Y. (ed.), *Violence and the Value of Life in Jewish Tradition* (Jerusalem: Oz ve Shalom Publications, 1984).

Laqueur, W., *A History of Zionism* (London: Weidenfeld and Nicolson, 1972).

Lehman-Wilzeig, S., 'Public Protest Against Central and Local Government in Israel, 1950–1979', *The Jewish Journal of Sociology*, vol. 24 (1982), no. 2.

——, 'The Israeli Protestor', *The Jerusalem Quarterly*, no. 26 (Winter 1983).

Lewis, A., 'The Peace Ritual and Israeli Images of Social Order', *Journal of Conflict Resolution*, vol. 23 (1979), no. 4.

Magnes, J. and Buber, M., *Arab-Jewish Unity: Testimony before the Anglo-American Inquiry Commission for the Ihud (Union) Association* (London: Victor Gollancz, 1947).

McLaughlin, B. (ed.), *Studies in Social Movements* (New York: The Free Press, 1967).

Milson, M., 'How to Make Peace with the Palestinians', *Commentary*, May, 1981.

Newman, D. (ed.), *The Impact of Gush Emunim: Politics and Settlement in the West Bank* (London: Croom Helm, 1985).

Oz, A., *In the Land of Israel* (London: The Hogarth Press, 1983).

Peled, T. and Bat-Gal, D., *Intervention Activities in Arab-Jewish Relations: Conceptualization, Classification and Evaluation* (Jerusalem: Israeli Institute of Applied Social Research, 1983).

Penniman, H.R. (ed.), *Israel at the Polls: The Knesset Elections of 1977* (Washington: AEIPPR, 1979).

Peretz, D., *The Government and Politics of Israel* (Boulder: Westview Press, 1983).

—— and Smooha, S., 'Israel's Tenth Knesset Elections: Ethnic Upsurgence and Decline of Ideology', *Middle East Journal*, vol. 35 (1981) no. 4.

Peretz, K., 'Kahane: Symptom of a Deeper Malaise', *Middle East International*, no. 232, 24 July, 1984.

Raphael, C., *The Road from Babylon: The Story of the Sephardi and Oriental Jews* (London: Weidenfeld and Nicolson, 1985).

Ronel, Eti, 'The Battle Over Temple Mount', *New Outlook*, vol. 27 (1984) no. 2.

Rosenweig, R., 'Partnership', *New Outlook*, June/July 1977.

Roumani, M., *The Case of the Jews from Arab Countries: A Neglected Issue* (Jerusalem: W.O.J.A.C., 1973).

Rubenberg, C., 'The Israeli Invasion of Lebanon: Objectives and Consequences', *Journal of South Asian and Middle Eastern Studies*, vol. VIII (1984) no. 2.

Rubinstein, A., *The Zionist Dream Revisited* (New York: Schocken Books, 1984).

Rutherford, E., *Palestinians and Israelis on Peace*, Department of General Studies, Derby Lonsdale College, 1978.

Schnall, D., 'Gush Emunim: Messianic Dissent and Israeli Politics', *Judaism*, vol. 26 (Spring, 1977) no. 2.

——, *Radical Dissent in Contemporary Israeli Politics: Cracks in the Wall* (New York: Praeger Publishers, 1979).

Seliktar, O., *New Zionism and the Foreign Policy System of Israel* (London: Croom Helm, 1986).

Sella, A. and Yishai, Y., *Israel the Peaceful Belligerent, 1967–1979* (London: St. Antony's/Macmillan, 1986).

Shahak, I., 'The Oriental Jews in Israeli Politics', *Middle East International*, 15 June, 1984.

Shama, A. and Iris, M., *Immigration Without Integration* (Cambridge (Mass.): Schenkman, 1977).

Smooha, S., *Israel: Pluralism and Conflict* (London: Routledge and Kegan Paul, 1978).

Smooha, S. and Hofmann, J., 'Some Problems of Arab-Jewish Co-Existence in Israel', *Middle East Review*, vol. 9, no. 2, 1967–1977.

Stock, E., *From Conflict to Understanding: Relations Between Jews and Arabs in Israel Since 1948* (New York: Institute of Human Relations Press, 1968).

Stone, I., 'The Other Zionism: Accommodating Jew and Arab in Palestine', *Harper's*, September 1978.

Stone, R., *Social Change in Israel: Attitudes and Events 1967–1979* (New York: Praeger, 1968).

Tilly, C., *From Mobilization to Revolution* (London: Addison-Wesley, 1978).

Timmerman, J., *The Long War: Israel in Lebanon* (New York: Vintage Books, 1982).

Tsiyona, P. and Bar-Gal, D., *Intervention Activities in Arab-Jewish Relations: Conceptualization, Classification and Evaluation* (Jerusalem: Israel Institute of Applied Social Research, 1983).

Weiler, J., *Israel and the Creation of a Palestinian State: A European Perspective* (London: Croom Helm, 1985).

Weingrod, A., *Group Relations in a New Society* (London: Institute of Race Relations, 1965).

Weissbrod, L., 'Delegitimation and Legitimation as a Continuous Process: A Case Study of Israel', *The Middle East Journal*, vol. 35 (August 1981) no. 3.

——, 'Gush Emunim Ideology: From Religious Doctrine to Political Action', *Middle Eastern Studies*, vol. 18 (July 1982) no. 3.

Wolfsfeld, G., 'Collective Political Action and Media Strategy: The Case of Yamit', *Journal of Conflict Resolution*, vol. 28 (September 1984) no. 3.

Woolfson, M., *Prophets in Babylon: Jews in the Arab World* (London: Faber and Faber, 1980).

Ye'Or, B., *Oriental Jewry and the Dhimmi Image in Contemporary Arab Nationalism* (Geneva: Editions de l'Avenir, 1979).

——, *The Dhimmi: Jews and Christians under Islam* (Toronto and London: Associated University Press, 1985).

Yermiya, D., *My War Diary: Israel in Lebanon* (London: Pluto Press, 1983).

Yishai, Y., 'Israel's Right-Wing Jewish Proletariat', *The Jewish Journal of Sociology*, vol. 24 (1982) no. 2.

——, 'Dissent in Israel: Opinions on the Lebanon War', *Middle East Review*, Winter 1983/4.

Interviews

The following interviews were conducted in Israel between June 1985 and February 1987. An open-ended format was used to allow for flexibility and the in-depth exploration of issues that were of particular interest to the interviewee. In most cases, the interview was recorded on tape. When this was not possible, notes were taken during or immediately after the interview.

In some cases, repeated interviews were carried out over a period of weeks with key informants who were generous with their time and patient with my ignorance and persistent questioning. Their exceptional contributions to my understanding, not only of the Israeli peace movement but also of broader issues arising from the Arab-Israeli conflict, are acknowledged below with an asterisk (*).

Note: The place-name following the name of the MO is where the interview was conducted.

Abu-Shakrah, Jan and Samir. (Educators) Ex-Education for Peace Project, Jerusalem.

Agawi, Khalil. (Co-founder), Re'ut, Tel Aviv.

Aharoni, Ada (Dr). (Co-founder) Gesher, Haifa.

Amiel, Reuven. (Founder) Committee for Nazareth-Upper Nazareth Co-operation, Upper Nazareth.

Aron, Wellesley. (Veteran Member) Neve Shalom, Neve Shalom.

Balzam, Shlomo. (Activist) Netivot le Shalom, Jerusalem.

Banvelgi, Robert. (Activist) Yesh Gvul/Rakah, Jerusalem.

Ben-Dov, Zvi. (Activist) Citizens Against Racism, Haifa.

Ben-Tzur, Naomi. (Activist) Parents Against Silence, Jerusalem. (*)

Ber, Shmuel. (Treasurer) Shutafut, Haifa.

Bergen, Kathy. (Projects Manager) Mennonite Central Committee, East Jerusalem. (*)

Chertok, Chaim. (Founder) Mashmia Shalom, Yerucham.

Danino, Etty. (Activist) East for Peace, Tel Aviv.

Eady, Elias. (Secretary and Educator) Neve Shalom, Neve Shalom.

Elbaz, Shlomo (Professor). (Co-founder) East for Peace, Jerusalem.

Emmanuel, Hadara and Joseph. Israeli Interfaith Association, Jerusalem.

Golan, Debbie. (Activist) Oz ve Shalom, Jerusalem.

Gvirtz, Amos. (Co-founder) Jewish-Arab Action Committee for Jaffa Arabs and Israeli section of International Fellowship of Reconciliation (IFOR), Jaffa. (*)

Hanna, Chanaka. (Activist) Parents Against Silence, Jerusalem.

Hurvitz, Jay. (Activist) Peace Now, Kibbutz Galon.

Hussar, Bruno (Fr.) (Founder) Neve Shalom, Neve Shalom and Jerusalem. (*)

Jabbour, Elias. (Founder) The House of Hope, Shefaram.

Keller, Adam. (Editor and Activist) Israeli Council for Israeli-Palestinian Peace, Tel Aviv.

Lasman, Reuven. Ex-Matzpen/AIC Collective, Jerusalem. (*)

Leibowitz, Wendy. (Ex-activist) Interns for Peace, Haifa. (*)

Leibowitz, Yeshua (Professor). (Philosopher) Supporter of Yesh Gvul and Radical MOs.

Le Meignen, Anne. (Member) Neve Shalom, Neve Shalom.

Levine, Mike. (Co-founder) Citizens Against Racism, Jerusalem. (*)

Marciano, Sa'adia. (Co-founder) Black Panthers, Jerusalem.

Miligrom, Jeremy (Rabbi). (Activist) Reshet/Yesh Gvul, Jerusalem.

Nahal, Yvette. (Activist) IFOR, Jerusalem. (*)

Na'or, Dapha. (Activist) Parents Against Silence, Jerusalem.

Pandas, Daniel. (Activist) East for Peace, Jerusalem.

Pinto, Jacques. (Activist) East for Peace and Yesh Gvul, Jerusalem.

Revkin, Sari. (Coordinator) Shatil, Jerusalem.

Satel, Abed. (Activist) Jewish-Arab Action Committee for Jaffa Arabs, Jaffa and Acre. (*)

Shaham, David. (Executive Director) ICMPE, Tel Aviv.

Shaqr, Nahle. (Activist) Jewish-Arab Action Committee for Jaffa Arabs, Jaffa.

Shick, Thoma. (Coordinator) War Resisters International, Tel Aviv. (*)

Spiro, Gideon. (Activist) BSC/CAWL/Yesh Gvul/CCIF, Jerusalem. (*)

Wolfsfeld, Gadi. (Researcher), Jerusalem.

Zilberstein, Stella. (Activist) Shutafut, Haifa.

Glossary

Aliya (Ascent). Term designating immigration to Israel. Emigration from Israel is termed Yeridah (Descent).

Ashkenazi (pl. Ashkenazim). German or other European Jew.

Beit Hagefen (House of Vines). Jewish-Arab community and youth centre in Haifa. Established in 1963, sponsored partly by Ministry of Education and Culture.

Betar. Revisionist youth movement.

Birzeit Solidarity Committee. Founded in 1981 after the temporary closure of Birzeit University. Strongly opposed to the occupation, in favour of a Palestinian state in the occupied territories. Members mostly non-Zionists.

Black Panthers. Mizrachi protest movement, most active in early seventies, primarily in poor Jerusalem neighbourhoods.

Brit Hasmol (Federation of the Left). Extra-parliamentary group made up largely of ex-members of Mapam. Active in the late sixties.

Brit Shalom (Covenant of Peace). First peace group in madatory Palestine. Founded in 1925 by intellectuals. Advocated a bi-national solution for Palestine. Supported by Buber.

Bund. Eastern European non-Zionist socialist organisation.

Citizens Against Racism. Group founded in 1984 (after the election of Meir Kahane to the Knesset). Branches in Jerusalem, Tel Aviv and Haifa – independent of each other.

Committee Against the War in Lebanon. Later formation of the Birzeit Solidarity Committee. Umbrella organisation of radicals opposed to the war in Lebanon.

Committee Confronting the Iron Fist. West Bank Palestinian group with limited Jewish participation. Opposed to repression in the occupied territories. Supportive of Palestinian prisoners. First active in 1985.

Dash (Democratic Movement for Change). Political party founded by Yigal Yadin in 1977. Won 15 seats in the Knesset but failed to maintain unity, dissolved before next elections.

Democratic Front for Peace and Equality. Political party established by Rakah in 1977. Predominantly Arab.

Dhimmi. Term designating the status of Jewish and Christian minorities (as 'peoples of the book') under Islam.

Dove. In the Israeli context, a person opposed to the continued occupation and settlement of the territories captured in 1967 and in favour of a territorial compromise and Jewish–Arab coexistence.

East for Peace. Peace group formed in 1983 by Mizrachi intellectuals.

Edot ha'Mizrach (Communities of the East). Term used to refer to immigrant groups from North African and Middle Eastern countries.

Eretz Yisrael. The Land of Israel.

Fatah. A major faction of the PLO, loyal to Yasser Arafat.

Fellahin. Arab tenant farmers.

Galut. Yiddish term used to refer to the Diaspora.

Givat Haviva. Educational Institute of the Kibbutz Hartzi movement.

Group of 27. A group of high school students who refused to do military service in the occupied territories in 1978.

Gush Emunim (The Block of the Faithful). Religious-nationalist movement engaged in settling the occupied territories.

Haganah (Defence). Pre-state military organisation established in 1920 which later became the Israeli Defence Force.

Halachah. An accepted decision in rabbinic law. Also refers to parts of the Talmud concerned with legal matters.

Haolam Hazeh (This World). Name of a left-wing newspaper owned and edited by peace activist Uri Avnery. Also name of Avnery's political party (now defunct) which gained entry to the Knesset in 1965 and 1969.

Hashomer Hatzair (The Young Guards). Left-wing Zionist group which supported bi-nationalism. Later became part of Mapam.

Haskalah (Enlightenment). Movement for spreading modern European culture among Jews c. 1750–1880.

Hassidism. Religious revivalist movement of popular mysticism.

Hawk. In the Israeli context, one who supports the annexation of the occupied territories and is not prepared to make any territorial compromise for peace. One who supports an aggressive policy *vis-à-vis* the Arabs.

Herut (Freedom). Right-wing Revisionist party established in 1948 by the disbanded Irgun under the leadership of M. Begin.

Hesder yeshivah (pl.*yeshivot*). Institution combining Talmudic studies and army service.

Histradut. Israel's massive trade union which also runs the health service and is itself an industrial giant.

Hutzpah. Dare and/or cheek.

Ihud (Union). Peace group founded in 1942 by Judah Magnes, Martin Buber and others to revive the activities of Brit Shalom and to advocate bi-nationalism.

Institute for Education and for Coexistence between Jews and Arabs. Government-backed institute founded in 1983 by Gorshon Baskin to gain state support for IPJACs.

International Centre for Peace in the Middle East. Centre established by *New Outlook* magazine. Publishes press briefs and conducts research on the Arab–Israeli conflict; organises seminars for educators and community workers seeking to improve coexistence; facilitates meetings between Jews and Arabs and holds regular forums for dovish Members of Knesset of different parties.

Irgun (Irgun Tzevai Leumi – National Military Organisation). Founded in 1931. Formally affiliated to Ze'ev Jabotinsky's Revisionist Party; opposed the Haganah's policy of 'restraint' toward the British. Open conflict broke out between the two military organisations from 1944 to 1948.

Israeli Council for Israeli–Palestinian Peace. Founded in 1976 to establish dialogue with the PLO. Advocates the establishment of a Palestinian state in the occupied territories. Affiliated to the Progressive List for Peace.

Israeli Interfaith Association. Established in 1958 to sponsor educational and social activities aimed at promoting interfaith understanding in Israel.

Kach (Thus). Party of Rabbi Meir Kahane, outspoken advocate of the expulsion of Arabs from the entire 'Land of Israel'. Kahane established the Jewish Defence League in New York before moving to Israel.

Kashrut. Jewish religious dietary laws.

Kibbutz Hartzi Federation. Kibbutz movement affiliated to Mapam.

Land of Israel Movement. Movement established in the wake of the Six-Day War. Advocated the retention of the occupied territories. Opposed to exchanging 'land for peace'.

League for Arab-Jewish Rapprochement. Successor of Brit Shalom, established in 1939.

Mafdal. The National Religious Party.

Maki (Miflagah Komunistit Israelit – The Israeli Communist Party). Original name of ICP, maintained by Jewish faction when the party split along Jewish–Arab lines in 1965.

Mapam (Mifleget ha-Poalim ha-Me'uhedet – The United Workers' Party). Established in 1948; incorporated Hashomer Hatzair. Left-wing Zionists who once favoured bi-nationalism. Supportive of Peace Now and other MOs.

Matzpen (Compass). The Israeli Socialist Organisation named after its publication *Matzpen*. Established in 1962 by communists opposed to Maki's pro-Moscow line. Anti-Zionists with support from the New Left abroad.

Mazzot. Unleavened bread used during Passover.

Mizrachi (pl. Mizrachim). Term, usually translated as 'Orientals' or 'Easterners', used to refer to the Jews of North Africa and the Middle East. They may or may not be descendents of the one-time Sephardic Jews of Spain and Portugal; as opposed to Ashkenazim.

Moked (Focus). Political party formed in part by the remnants of Maki. Gained a Knesset seat in 1973.

Moshav (pl. Moshavim). Co-operative agricultural settlement in which members own their homes.

Movement for Peace and Security. A short-lived 'movement' backed by Begin's Likud to demonstrate support for Likud policy.

Movement Organisation. Any relatively independent group involved in the peace movement.

Netivot le Shalom (Pathways to Peace). Religious peace group founded in 1982. Works closely with Oz ve Shalom.

Neve Shalom (Oasis of Peace). Jewish–Arab co-operative settlement established near Latrun. Operates a 'School for Peace' and runs highly professional IPJACs.

New Outlook. English language publication based in Tel Aviv dedicated to peace in the Middle East. Not very well known in Israel – even within the peace movement.

New Zionist Organisation. Established in 1935 by Jabotinsky as a revisionist alternative to the WZO.

Nitzanei Shalom (Interns for Peace). Established in 1976 by an American reform rabbi. Until recently, it placed mostly American Jews in Arab villages where they carried out development projects and organised IPJACs.

Other Zionism Group. Name of a small Jerusalem 'intellectual circle' which was instrumental in writing the officers' letter and founding Peace Now.

Oz ve Shalom (Courage and Peace). Religious doves opposed to the occupation of the territories captured in 1967. Founded in 1975 by academics and members of the Mafdal.

Palmach (Pelugot Mahatz – Storm Troops). Elite unit established in 1941 by the leadership of the Haganah. Officers were primarily left-wing kibbutz members. Disbanded in 1948.

Parents Against Silence. Peace group formed by parents opposed to the war in Lebanon. Disbanded voluntarily after the withdrawal of Israel from Lebanon.

Parents Against Weakness. Short-lived 'movement' created by the Likud to demonstrate support for the war and to discredit PAS.

Pax Christi. International Catholic peace organisation.

Peace Now. Originally a small, obscure Tel Aviv peace group that gave its name to the mass movement which first formed in 1978. The largest ('hub') MO in the peace movement.

Pioneers of the East. A Mizrachi intellectual group established in 1917. Part of its programme was to encourage the teaching of Hebrew amongst Arabs and Arabic amongst Jews.

Progressive List for Peace. A non-Zionist, non-communist Jewish–Arab party established in 1984. Two seats in the Knesset.

Rakah (Reshimah Komunistit Hadashah – The New Communist List). Name adopted by the Arab faction when the Israeli Communist Party split in 1965. Now dominant part of DFPE.

Ratz (Citizens' Rights Movement). A political party founded by Shulamit Aloni in 1973. Strongly opposed to religious coercion; links with Peace Now. Three Knesset members.

Reshet (Network). Name of umbrella organisation formed in an attempt to link the activities of MOs engaged in IPJACs.

Revisionists. Political party of Zionists advocating a Jewish state on both sides of the Jordan. Founded in 1925 by Zeev Jabotinsky, the party was absorbed by Menachim Begin's Herut after the establishment of the State of Israel.

Sephardi (pl. Sephardim). Jews descended from the one-time Jews of Spain and Portugal. Sometimes used to refer to all Jews who are not Ashkenazim.

Sheli (Shalom le Israel – Peace for Israel). Political party made of different non-communist radicals in favour of withdrawal from the territories. Won two seats in the Knesset in 1977. Split over rotation agreement.

Shinui (Change). A liberal Zionist party founded by Amnon Rubenstein which briefly joined Yigal Yadin's Dash in the 1977 elections.

Shutafut (Partnership). Haifa-based MO which works closely with Neve Shalom. Runs professional IPJACs.

Siach (Smol Israeli Hadash – The Israeli New Left). Established in 1969 by dissident splinters from Mapam and Rakah. Made up primarily of non-Zionists, although its ex-Mapam members (based mostly in Tel Aviv) are explicitly Zionists.

Soldiers Against Silence. A short-lived group of reserve soldiers who protested against the war in Lebanon but continued to serve there. They held joint demonstrations with PAS.

Talmud (Teaching). Compendium of discussion on Jewish oral law (Mishnah) by generations of religious scholars and jurists.

Terror Against Terror. Jewish terrorists arrested and tried for attacks on Arab civilians.

Tnuat Ha Herut. See Herut.

Ulpan Akiva. Language teaching institute in Netanya which combines Hebrew and Arabic lessons with an IPJAC.

Van Leer Jerusalem Foundation. Jerusalem-based research institute which focuses on problems related to the Arab–Israeli conflict. Works closely with IPJAC organisations.

Yesh Gvul (There's a Limit/Border). Group of reserve soldiers who faced imprisonment rather than serve in Lebanon. Later some refused service in the occupied territories.

Yeshivah (pl. *yeshivot*). Jewish theological institution.

Yishuv. The pre-state Jewish community in Palestine.

Zeitgeist. German term meaning 'the spirit of the time/era'.

Index